QUEER CAMBRIDGE

Queer Cambridge recounts the untold story of a gay community living, for many decades, at the very heart of the British Establishment. Making effective use of chiefly forgotten archival sources – including personal diaries and letters – the author reveals a network that was in equal parts tolerant and acerbic, and within which the queer fellows of King's College, University of Cambridge, explored bold new forms of camaraderie and relationship. Goldhill examines too the huge influence that these individuals had on British culture, in its arts, politics, music, theatre and self-understanding. During difficult decades when homosexuality was unlawful, gay academics – who included celebrated literary and scientific figures like E. M. Forster, M. R. James, Rupert Brooke and Alan Turing – lived, loved and grew old together, bringing new generations into their midst. Their remarkable stories add up not just to an alternative history of male homosexuality in Britain, but to an alternative history of Cambridge itself.

SIMON GOLDHILL, FBA, is Professor of Greek Literature and Culture at the University of Cambridge and a fellow of King's College, Cambridge. One of the world's best-known authors on ancient Greek literature and culture and their reception in the modern West, he has written more than twenty books which have been translated into twelve languages and won three international prizes. He has lectured and broadcast around the world on both radio and television.

'*Queer Cambridge* succeeds on a number of fronts. It is a fascinating analysis of a remarkably coherent group identity and its transmission across generations. It is a revelatory work of institutional history, delivering rich insight both into one institution in particular and into how institutions in general work to create and solidify identity and values. And it is a book that says new and unusual things about the place of same-sex desire at the heart of the Victorian and Edwardian English cultural establishment. I agree with pretty much every word of *Queer Cambridge*, and learned something new and surprising on every page.

– Darryl Jones, Professor of Modern British Literature
and Culture, Trinity College Dublin

'Unique in its examination of a multi-generational queer community, *Queer Cambridge* expertly maps the interpersonal relationships between a wide range of individuals and displays the range of behaviours present within this community. Goldhill demonstrates how same-sex desire long preceded the development of the modern category of "the homosexual" and fleshes out influential individuals such as Lytton Strachey and John Maynard Keynes in ways not achieved elsewhere.'

– Charles Upchurch, Professor of British History, Florida
State University

'In this exciting, authoritative, gossipy, giddy book, sleuthing homosexualist Simon Goldhill charts the sprawling topography of same-sex desire contained in little more than a few square yards. An indispensable microhistory of Cambridge and the networks of queer men that thrived within the walls of its most famous college – from flamboyant Oscar Browning to the devastating Rupert Brooke, tortured Arthur Benson to the flirtatious Dadie Rylands – *Queer Cambridge* shows how vital a sense of place is to queer intimacy, community and identity, and how indispensable its study is to any history of sexuality.'

– Diarmuid Hester, Research Associate in English,
Emmanuel College and author of *Nothing Ever Just
Disappears: Seven Hidden Histories*

'This powerful, moving and hugely enjoyable slice of homosexual history, meticulously researched and written with sympathy, wit and elegance, recreates a queer college community and its evolution from the nineteenth century to the present. In a story shaded with nuance, Goldhill presents a judicious assessment of the evidence: letters, diaries, college records, anecdotes, legends, paintings, photographs, biographies, confessions. He opens up this closed college world of secrets like an oyster, filled with pearls and brine.'

– Patricia Duncker, author of *Hallucinating Foucault*

'There are few more interesting writers on sex and relationships than Simon Goldhill. Through a fascinating picture of the transformations of a community of gay men from the nineteenth century to today, *Queer Cambridge* offers provocative reflections on how we write queer history and how we think about identity and belonging. It is also a love letter to a college and university that he knows so well.'

– Helen Morales, Argyropoulos Professor of Hellenic Studies, University of California, Santa Barbara

QUEER CAMBRIDGE

AN ALTERNATIVE HISTORY

SIMON GOLDHILL
University of Cambridge

Shaftesbury Road, Cambridge CB2 8EA, United Kingdom

One Liberty Plaza, 20th Floor, New York, NY 10006, USA

477 Williamstown Road, Port Melbourne, VIC 3207, Australia

314–321, 3rd Floor, Plot 3, Splendor Forum, Jasola District Centre,
New Delhi – 110025, India

103 Penang Road, #05–06/07, Visioncrest Commercial, Singapore 238467

Cambridge University Press is part of Cambridge University Press &
Assessment, a department of the University of Cambridge.

We share the University's mission to contribute to society through the pursuit
of education, learning and research at the highest international levels
of excellence.

www.cambridge.org
Information on this title: www.cambridge.org/9781009528061

DOI: 10.1017/9781009528078

© Simon Goldhill 2025

First published 2025

Printed in the United Kingdom by TJ Books Limited, Padstow, Cornwall

A catalogue record for this publication is available from the British Library

*A Cataloging-in-Publication data record for this book is available from the Library
of Congress*

ISBN 978-1-009-52806-1 Hardback

CONTENTS

Colour plates can be found between pages 150 and 151.

PLATES

FIGURES

ACKNOWLEDGEMENTS

It is a pleasure to thank first those who were interviewed for this book: Professor Sir Geoffrey Lloyd, Dr Tess Adkins, Professor Iain Fenlon and especially John Dunn and James Trevithick. Second, I would like to thank the archivist team at King's College, who went beyond the call of duty in helping me, especially Tom Davies and Patricia McGuire. Third, and with long-lasting gratitude and pleasure, I thank the friends who read and commented on drafts of this book as it developed: Helen Morales, Catherine Conybeare, Daniel Orrells, Mario Telò and Darryl Jones.

A Brief Introduction to a Large Topic

~

This is a book about a staircase and the men who lived on it. In traditional Cambridge and Oxford colleges, the central, oldest buildings, where people live and teach, are constructed around staircases (rather than hallways or corridors). Each staircase has an entranceway with rooms located either side of the staircase, up a series of floors. These staircases are usually labelled in alphabetical order, starting with 'A Staircase' (not to be confused with 'a staircase') and each room on the staircase has a number: so my room in my college is E5 – the fifth room on E Staircase, on the top floor, overlooking the River Cam. People often feel very attached to these staircases, because of the intimacy of living so closely together with a few friends (or enemies). Most staircases have only a few rooms, rarely more than twelve, often only six or eight. In the imagination – and in reality – the staircase becomes a place where emotional memories are laid down, life choices made, friendships for life formed. This book started when I realised that three very significant figures in the history of King's College, Cambridge, each of whom was what we would now call gay, had lived in the same room, H1, a year apart. I thought it would make a stimulating short piece for the college blog: 'A room with a view' … But as I started reading, I discovered not only that there were other men, whom I had not known about, who lived on H staircase, and on G staircase, the next staircase along, who were also men who desired males, but also that there was a flourishing community over several generations who happily took up residence in these rooms and elsewhere in college. A picture gradually emerged of a unique world of male desire, which was very different from the histories of homosexuality that I had read. This book sets out to paint the picture of this community, this queer place.

I have called the book *Queer Cambridge* because it is set in Cambridge, significantly and integrally so. 'H Staircase' (my working title) wasn't likely to be as instantaneously informative as a publisher would desire, nor would 'Queer King's' (though that has a certain ring). In an age when global history has a premium, my story has an even more intimate narrative than my title suggests. (I hope no reader is too disappointed by their favourite queer icon – or their relatives – not being included: this is not an encyclopaedia.) What is at stake, however, is far larger and embracing: how are we to tell the story of what has been defined as a transgressive desire in society? What – how *queer* – is a queer community? Can one particular place open a revelatory portal onto the broad histories that define modernity's transitions?

But before we enter this world in all its riveting detail, I want to explain a little further why this book has been written and how it fits into what has become the burgeoning field of gay history. A very brief introduction …

There are trajectories in the history of homosexuality that are by now well established, at least in academic circles, at least in the West. The first concerns the very word 'homosexuality'. It was first used in English in the translation of Richard Krafft-Ebing's *Psychopathia*

Sexualis, a foundational work of German sexology, in 1892, no earlier. That's why David Halperin provocatively called his book of 1990 *One Hundred Years of Homosexuality*. (The very first usage of the word actually seems to have been by Karl-Maria Kerbeny in the late 1860s, but it is Krafft-Ebing who started its popularity: 1892 is the date that counts.) Homosexuality as a term won out gradually over other scientific coinages, insults and self-identifications: Urning, Uranian, Invert, Sodomite and so forth, which now look as distinctly old-fashioned in contemporary English as 'phlogiston', if they are understood at all. There was, for example, a group of poets who – with self-conscious and provocative explicitness – called themselves the 'Uranians', linked as they were by their love of youths; but 'homosexuality' was not really a common term in English until the 1920s, and even then it still had the aura of a rather faddish technical term, especially to older speakers, who were not quite sure if they did indeed have something called a 'sexuality'.[1]

This changing language constitutes a fascinating example of what is meant by a 'fugitive discourse'.[2] As male desire for other males flits in and out of view in a society that denigrated it and, indeed, made it illegal as well as despicable, the words to refer to it shift in usage, always on the run, and construct both a vocabulary of insult, on the streets, in the courts or newspapers, and also a language of self-identification and recognition, a private shared way of talking that excluded those not in the know. Much as the n-word has been reclaimed in recent times *by* black usage *for* black usage, so the word 'bugger' became a familiar term of recognition and

3

endearment among men in the first quarter of the twentieth century (whatever the sexual activities in mind) – and now, likewise, 'queer' has been shifted from insult to a term of pride, especially, belatedly, by literary critics. ('Bugger' now has become so blanched in England that anyone might say 'oh, bugger' when she spills her coffee, or do 'bugger all' on a wet Sunday: even 'bugger off!' is at the gentle end of cursing.) The language of desire, like the language of race, is politicised, medicalised, legalised – and also works to escape all these institutionalised frameworks, never fully successfully, in humour, concealment, challenge and refusal. The old and grumpy regularly moan about not knowing the right word to use these days.

The *scientific* language of sexology, however, marks a new direction for understanding male desire. Desire is now a sign and symptom of a *pathology*. You could *be* a 'homosexual'. Homosexuality became an identity. Even if you never had sex, you could be a homosexual. With this identity came an internalised shame encouraged by religious institutions, legal restrictions and social humiliation. And thus came, too, the strategies to respond to such shame, from in-your-face outrageousness to desperate suicide, from anguished denial to quietly enacted fulfilment – and many other ways of dealing with what was now life as a homosexual: a condition. When we say homosexuality, we raise not just questions of who is being referred to, but also how desire relates to identity. Can who you *fancy* really define who you *are*?

One consequence of this pathologisation for us is a pressing historical question: how, then, should we think about male desire for males *before* this pathology became the embedded normative way of thinking, before it

4

seemed natural to define people as homosexuals? Of course, there are plenty of examples of men desiring males from any period of history, which historians have been quick to collect, and indeed there has been focused, loving attention on societies like that of ancient Athens when such desire was an expected and normal part of erotic experience; and there has been a similar attention, at a more localised level, on more recent groups or institutions where men who desired men gathered in private, or in public concealment, such as molly houses in the eighteenth century – male brothels and drinking houses – which find modern echoes in the gay bars and saunas of the twentieth century and beyond. For some historians – Michel Foucault would be an icon of such thinking – this means that there were no homosexuals before the turn into the twentieth century; previously there were only men who committed sex acts with men. There was no possibility of self-recognition as a homosexual in the sense of an identity. Erotic object choice did not define who you were. For others – and here James Davidson has been more influential in taking the question to the heart of Greek love than the medievalist John Boswell has proved to be – there are signs that there were men who were recognised in the past as desiring men exclusively or obsessively, who could be contrasted with women-mad lovers.[3] A type, across time and culture. Was homosexuality always there, waiting, like Australia, for a Western authority to come and give it a name? Or was homosexuality not experienced as a condition, or as an identity, because nobody had the full-scale medical, legal and social language to identify it as such? A hundred (plus) years of homosexuality, named and shamed? Or multiple centuries, under different names? In response to such polarised and polarising claims, medieval and early modern scholars in particular have tried to find a third way, sometimes dubbed 'queer unhistoricism', which in its most persuasive form attempts to move away from the insistence that choice of sexual partner as determining identity is the best or only way to discuss the evidence of the past, and seeks other routes to explore desire's expressivity: 'we are doing battle here, *per amore*, with history'.[4] The *homo-* in homosexual poses a question that is constantly at work in such discussions, though not always made explicit: how much am I the same as the person I desire? How different are the men who desire men from each other? And – the repeated turn to Greece adds – how similar and different are the moderns from the ancients?

When it comes to male desire for males, arguments about its acceptability have often turned on what is taken to be 'natural' or 'unnatural'. It matters greatly therefore to show the long continuity of such desires, a constant and inevitable presence in society. Consequently, arguments about the recent invention of homosexuality have often been confused with a polemic about whether male desire for males exists across time and different cultures, always already there – natural even when stigmatised. If there were no homosexuals before the nineteenth century, what does that mean for people who now think of their identity in such terms? This is a case where self-interest (in all senses) is all too likely to confuse historical argument.

This book runs from roughly the 1880s forward to the 1960s (and to today, of course). There were undoubtedly men who desired men before this in Cambridge, even on occasion a brief and small 'thriving subculture of sodomy' (which Byron, for example, discovered in the first decade of the 1800s).[5] But there is a point to starting where I do. This story begins with men who certainly did not have an agreed language of recognition or identity, but who lived through the invention of homosexuality as a vocabulary and a form of understanding; and it ends with gay liberation's legal moment in Britain in 1967. The first chapter indeed is about the discovery of (their) homosexuality and the struggle these men experienced, as the science of sex and the public language of comprehension changed across their lifetimes. The fluidity of how these men expressed themselves and the variety of their deeply engaged behaviour across this earlier era makes for an especially complex and fascinating social picture. The anxiety about how to name people as sexualised beings and what they get up to – nowadays focused usually on the ever expanding list of letters that began with LBGQ, and, most heatedly, on the issue of trans – is not merely a modern worry, though it is often presented as a sign of the times. Or, rather, it is *precisely* a worry through which modernity understands or fails to understand itself *as* modern – a dynamic, ironically enough, that was already part of an intense debate about self-recognition in the early years of the last century. (Modernity is always forgetting the modernities of previous generations.) How desire can be imagined depends on the narratives available – and their capacity for change – and on the institutional framework for expressing such desire. The men I will be discussing all inhabited the same place – physical space and conceptual arena – and their different responses to their own time and erotic urges provide a particularly rich portrait of an era of fundamental transformation.

In short, the shifting, transformative self-understanding of male desire for males across the last 150 years provides the grounding for his book. At one point, I thought I would subtitle the book 'An Alternative History of Homosexuality', but that would have given the wrong signals, because *every* word in such a phrase just raises an awkward question. Is *homosexuality* ever an adequate term? What assumptions and difficulties does it bring? Can it get beyond the ideology of its own formation in nineteenth-century sexology? Can homosexuality have a *history*? If so, is it a history that starts at the end of the nineteenth century or does it go back to David and Jonathan in the Bible (or earlier, if you like)? Is there only one history or are there multiple narratives? Is it a story of Western repression and discovery? A universal category? The subtitle ended up – consequently – as 'an alternative history'... At least 'alternative' will do, I think, provided that it is clear that it is a history of an alternative – an alternative to many histories of gay life as well as to the formal history of the university – and that I don't mean an exclusionary alternative, but rather one of the multiple narratives that can be written. It is *a* history. But my wager is that it is a history that is telling, and worth telling – because it will tell us something alternative to the familiar accounts.

When David Halperin called his book *One Hundred Years of Homosexuality* he was knowingly echoing Gabriel García Márquez's marvellous novel, *One Hundred Years of Solitude*. This echo is not just a casual gesture of arty sophistication. The history of homosexuality – as I will continue to call it, with all due demurrals, for convenience's sake – has most often been written as a history of fragmentation, loneliness, solitary searches for other solitary men, a world of the city street. There are many exceptions, some of which play a major role in this book; examples where men not only had long-term relationships with men, but also on rarer occasions did so in public. Edward Carpenter (1844–1929) was a guru who lived in Derbyshire for thirty years with George Merrill. A visit to Edward Carpenter was part of a liberal education for many writers and artists.[6] George Merrill, who placed his hand on E. M. Forster's buttock, transforming Forster's sensibility (Forster tells us), was instrumental in Forster turning to write *Maurice*, his novel of gay love that was published only posthumously. Forster himself, much more quietly, had a long-term relationship with a married policeman. Howard Sturgis, also a novelist, though a rather mawkish one, lived for decades with William Haynes-Smith, who was known to everyone in their immediate social circle as 'The Babe', a name E. F. Benson took for the title of one of his best-selling university novels of young men about Cambridge, *The Babe, B.A.* – an insider joke. Yet the majority of stories of gay life concentrate on the city as an alienating environment, made threatening by violent and invasive policing, and made discomforting by social stigma and repression. The life of John Addington Symonds has become paradigmatic, partly because he has left such a full set of personal reminiscences. (The focus on his erotic life, mind you, has rather overshadowed the rich complexity of his intellectual world, his own sense of being a 'stifled anachronism', investigated recently and most obsessively – his word – by Shane Butler.) Symonds vividly describes his internalised shame, his transformative reading of ancient Greek texts that offered a different view of the world, his gradual growth of physicality and his serial pickups of soldiers for sex. It was Symonds too who translated Krafft-Ebing and thus introduced the word 'homosexuality' into English. His publication of *A Problem in Greek Ethics* – in only ten copies to start with – is also a fine example of how reading books on Greek love and on sexology formed a crucial part of many men's self-understanding and self-recognition. 'He has read Havelock Ellis' – the famous theorist of sexology and homosexuality in particular – could be a coded wink between men well into the twentieth century (the quotation is from a letter in the 1940s, open to censorship, of course, about a potential friendship with a young soldier during the Second World War).[7] As Symonds – and many others – found out, some working-class men were content enough to earn some much needed extra money by providing sexual services for middle- and upper-class men. The working-class men, it appears, did not see themselves, nor were seen, as being homosexual for having sex with men: it was a financial arrangement of convenience. ('Homosex' without the homosexuality …)[8] The middle- and upper-class men avoided the social anxiety of a relationship in their own social circle, and, in many cases, followed their own desires for a particular sort of manliness. With guardsmen on the Strand in London such arrangements were almost as regularised as with the female prostitutes on Piccadilly. Oscar Wilde called such hookups 'feasting with panthers' (as we will see), and it was the cross-class intimacy almost as much as the same-sex activity that seems to have dismayed the court in his trial.[9] For many young men, however, their desires made them solitary, frightened and confused. In London and other expanding, industrialised cities, where loneliness was all too easily a way of life, the urban experience was definitional of homosexual activity. The German sexologist Magnus Hirschfeld, looking on as a foreigner, contrasted European and British sex. While the European men enjoyed mutual masturbation, the English, he declared, resorted to silent anonymous groping in parks and alleyways, a misery enforced by the 'conspiration [sic = conspiracy] of silence about homosexuality in England'.[10]

Against this picture of fragmentation, anxiety and disdain, other more actively and positively communal scenes also flair into vision. Berlin before the Second World War allowed a brief, remarkable licence for queer life, both for men and for women, until the Nazis violently destroyed it as a matter of policy. There were celebrated bars and clubs in Paris in the same period, which were also eventually closed. British men and women, especially from the more elite classes, visited both cities to escape not just from the restrictions of British social expectation but also from the chance of being exposed in their own communities. Every major city in Europe and in the Americas has a discrete and fascinating story of its own queer past, its nostalgias, pains, celebrations and self-serving memories.[11] Working with such accounts, modern sociologists and historians of sexuality have been fascinated about when, where and whether a queer community can be recognised, both in the past and in the present – when, that is, you can recognise something beyond some friendships, or beyond particular styles of behaviour: an acknowledged group, existing over time with its own urban space(s).[12] In the self-styling of both academic and more personal, anecdotal narratives, the 1960s, with its legal and social changes, marks a crucial turning point. While 'friendship networks are the avenues through which gay social worlds are constructed', from the 1960s onwards, what were first called gay ghettos and then, more happily, gayberhoods, became a regular feature of the self-recognition of city living. To begin with, these were seen as 'a spatial response to a historically specific form of oppression', places where queer people could dress, live their lives and express affection publicly without fear of violence or unpleasantness: the Castro in San Francisco, Boyztown in Chicago (East Lakeview); Old Compton Street in London, the seaside town of Brighton.[13] It became possible to 'construct a gay city in the midst of (and often invisible to) the normative city'. Gayberhoods were 'inseparable from the development of the gay community as a social movement': part of the sexual politics of the city.[14] Gradually – more quickly in some cities – it was intently recognised that the queer population – by which was meant largely white, middle-class, employed, single men without children – had considerable disposable income. Gayberhoods were also sites of gentrification, and thus deeply attractive to developers. And they were cool destinations for tourism, especially for queers from elsewhere. (There is no city living that is not deeply infected by capitalism's structures of power.) With a few exceptions – the most celebrated being the Castro in San Francisco – the boundaries and focus of gayberhoods also shift (like the fugitive language of queer discourse). How much such spaces constitute a community is constantly questioned by those living in them. 'More a concentration … than a community', commented one queer woman of the once renowned Park Slope district of Brooklyn: 'several networks of people', with different values and aims, soon on the move to elsewhere in the city. Any district's demography could change, and change rapidly. 'There goes the gayberhood' has become the catchphrase for the mix of feelings about such change – nostalgia, surprise, anger, along with a recognition that different styles of living become attractive at different points in a person's life-cycle (queer or not): the older are happier to get away from the wilder side of the gayberhoods. Is the move away from the ghetto a desirable triumph of assimilation, or a sell-out into imitative bourgeois comfort? Queers are not alone among minority groups in asking this question.[15]

For all these narratives of the coming of modernity – and there are many variations and many different cities analysed in such terms – the past is another country. Modernity sees itself as progress, with its hard-won turning points, and for many people this has been simply true, and simply positive – reasonably enough, for all that there are still counterforces of hostility, often violent, against such acceptance of queer men and women in society (there is no city living without conflict, either). But my story slows down as it reaches the rupture of the 1960s. When I say I am offering an alternative history it must be clear that I am not redrafting the history of male desire for males from David and Jonathan to Ian McKellen. When I state that this alternative history is about the unique role of a particular community, it would be ridiculous to be taken to mean that there are no other claims to be a community, certainly in the present, and even and most saliently in the past. Rather, this book offers a picture of one community profoundly surprising in its longevity, its singular place, its influence beyond itself, and its existence within an era of severe legal and social restriction on the practice and expression of desire. As such, it offers precisely an alternative picture of the other country of the past, an alternative picture of what a queer community could mean, then, even then. And it is a story with consequences for how we think about the here and now of belonging.

It has been important, politically and historically, to describe the effects of the legal restrictions and the severe policing of nineteenth- and twentieth-century Britain, which lasted even beyond the time of the legalisation of (some) sex between (some) men in 1967. The evidence for the difficult solitude, and patterns of intermittent sex with men who were not likely to be met again, has been well catalogued within the history of homosexuality.[16] 'My real life', wrote the American writer Frederic Prokosch, 'has transpired in darkness, secrecy, fleeting contacts and incommunicable delights ... My real life has been subversive, anarchic, vicious, lonely and capricious.'[17] This sharp reality has been turned by some activist critics into a positive spin: for them, this style of life can challenge the assumption that long-term monogamous relationships need to be the bedrock of social propriety and stability (an activism that strives to reclaim old pain into new moral insistence and even hope).[18] The brief encounters of solitude form one necessary framework for the history of homosexuality. But this book is about something else: it is about a community of men, many of whom came to Cambridge as eighteen-year-old youths and stayed their whole lives; many started at Cambridge, stayed a few years, and then left to make their careers elsewhere in Britain or internationally but came back to Cambridge regularly. They maintained their relationships across time and space, a bond forged as undergraduates or young academics. The college, true to its monastic origins, was a community of single men.

There are many outstanding, full and carefully researched biographies of some of the luminaries of this world – Maynard Keynes, E. M. Forster, Lytton Strachey, Rupert Brooke – which do not need rehearsing in all their detail. So too the Bloomsbury Group, as it has come to be known, has fascinated generations of subsequent scholars, not least for their outspoken attitudes towards conventional behaviour and attitudes. This book aims to do something slightly different (though for sure it has drawn on this work gratefully). First, I am interested in what difference a *place* makes. In contrast to arguments about the universal nature of male desire or the broad evolution of human sexuality – both, it must be said, thoroughly nineteenth-century obsessions as well as modernity's shibboleths – this book starts by looking at one staircase in one college in one university: the men who lived on H staircase in King's College, Cambridge. Now, I could make a claim that the University of Cambridge was at the centre of the educational system and class structure of the largest empire the world had ever known, and thus of an importance far beyond my evidently – supremely – parochial focus. But actually, although this (self-)importance is partly justifiable, and although such self-promoting grandiosity certainly is a regular element of the self-representation of the characters in this story, never slow to see themselves as acting on the broadest of world stages, I am more fascinated precisely by the small scale itself. The few dozens of men I will be discussing revelled in the minutiae of their lives, fixated on the narcissism of small differences between their rooms, other colleges, the cuts of jib through which they presented themselves to the world – while, in many cases, making major international contributions to economics, the novel, poetry, world politics, art, music ... I want to see what difference it made that they did all live in this small place, talking, drinking and living together, in their odd domesticity. The college was *not* the streets of London, *not* the ports or resorts of Europe, and certainly *not* simply a public arena. It was a closed community that fascinated the outside world (and was fascinated by itself), and that had a continuing influence on the public life of the country. How does such an institutional framework change the possible narratives of homosexual history?

But I am also fascinated by how this community itself as a community contrasts with the solitude of the city streets with its pickups. This community was forged through relationships, friendships, affairs that stretched over many years, and were maintained through the contretemps and shared memories of a contentious familial group of men. There are two immediate, crucial consequences of this. First, as the discourse of homosexuality was being invented, disseminated and explored, this transformative process of self-definition was taking place at the same time within this group of men who were making their own social world through repeated stories, retrospective anecdotes and prospective planning. The community's own transformation was shaped by and contributed to the shaping of public comprehension and narratives of male desire – and struggled to reject, work with and fit into such a new shaping of possibility. With all the self-reflection of an Escher picture, they were drawing the map on which they would locate themselves. What a homosexual history might look like was a constant subject of conversation over many years between men who became the heroes of this history of homosexuality. This is a history of homosexuality through people who spent hours talking about (the history of) homosexuality. Secondly, each of the men in this story grew up and changed across these years, unless they died young and became fixed images of floppy-haired youthfulness. The young men who came from school to university, to be met and educated by older dons, became those older dons in turn, or returned to college as friends from outside. Although many a biography takes a person from birth through to death, for sure, such monocular narratives rarely capture the sense of change within a community, the way in which as you grow older you grow into your mentor's shoes while observing the young Turks coming up, and experience such transitions together with friends. The community is formed in *intergenerational* passing on – of stories, possessions, values – and in working out how tradition is both to be exercised and to be recalibrated over time, as you respond to external pressures, the logic of internal change, and institutional development. A community like a college depends on the performance of tradition, but each performance is a form of re-creation: there is no tradition without the enactment, but every enactment also opens the possibility of changing the script or allowing the script to alter over time. Nobody quite takes the place of his mentor. In the period covered by this book there were the seismic shocks of two world wars, the

Great Depression and the move from an elite education system towards a more democratically open institution, marked by an extraordinary change in size and intellectual ambition. How the college was changing was a subject of the same fascinated, constant conversation as how homosexual experience was changing.

Sara Ahmed coined the phrase 'giddy places' as she searched to articulate the relation between space and what she calls queer phenomenology.[19] A college can feel like a 'giddy place', where each year there is an influx of young people whose lives are in a transitional and potentially transformational state. The memory of college life, as repeatedly articulated through memoirs and biographies, is paradigmatically a memory of self-discovery, of coming to be the person – the hero – of a later story. The time of student life, like all rites of passage, allows for – demands even – bad behaviour, a period of licence, a certain giddiness. Yet a college, especially a college founded in the fifteenth century, also projects an institutional groundedness, an awareness of its own long history, the permanence of a home. Unlike the shifting attractions of a molly house or gay bar or club, the University of Cambridge has centuries of giddiness in its records, and, most pertinently, is peopled by the academics who have chosen to make a home in it. A home without a family, or without a family in its established sense: for most of the decades of this history, many fellows lived in college, and even when they had houses (and even wives and children in them), spent many evenings dining in college, as well as working there. A wonderfully eccentric example is Nathaniel Wedd, a great friend of many of the leading figures in this book, especially E. M. Forster (see Figure 1).

FIGURE I Nathaniel Wedd in full Edwardian splendour – boater, cane and all.

In the 1920s, when he was in his fifties, he had been married to a female classicist from Newnham College, Rachel Evelyn White, for over a decade. He continued to live in college; his wife visited him for breakfast each morning in his rooms; he went to High Table for dinner on his own each night; she dined – better food, he grumbled – at a restaurant on King's Parade opposite the college gates, and retired to her rooms for the night, also on King's Parade, not a hundred metres from her husband's rooms. 'There were no children' is the dry comment of the fellow who records this bizarre set-up – and who insists, looking back in continuing bafflement forty years later, that Wedd was 'not a homosexual'. 'A fellow may not live with his wife in college' is still the rule (though now it is wife or husband), and Wedd's was one way, I suppose, to negotiate the regulations.[20] And for most students, college marks a decisive break – expressed in multiple forms of intensity and effectiveness – with a child's experience of family life. The continuity of the architecture of the college, visually dominated by the Gibbs Building, the chapel and the lawns they frame, and the continuity of the fellows as a real and imagined community, is what people who came back to visit college, in the imagination or in person, came back to. A continuing other place, a place of continuing potential otherness, recalled as the place of choices made and future stories begun: where once ... where another route was then still open.

This focus on a *single location*, on a *community of men* in this location, and on the *transformation* of this community over time – both as an institution and as a set of individuals – provide the three pillars of this book. In this way, the story offers a different and complementary picture of homosexual experience from the standard narratives.

It must be immediately emphasised that this is not an idealised or idealising narrative. It does not set out to imagine a homosexual society, a brotherhood, an elite cohort of lovers or any of the other familiar fantasies that have so often arisen from the oppressions and disappointments of the present. Almost all the characters we will meet come from what would today be recognised as an elite, although most would then have distinguished themselves as middle class rather than aristocratic. Several went to the same highly privileged private schools before university (a few to the same prep schools too), and most had the support and benefits of a wealthy upbringing in an imperial society confident in its entitlements. Many reflect the attitudes and assumptions of such a background. Some behave not so much flamboyantly as nastily – selfish, cruel, malicious, rapacious. All are white. All are men: King's College did not admit women until 1972. There were only two women's colleges in Cambridge, and women could not be awarded degrees like the men until after the Second World War. Although there are women who appear in these stories and appear as strong, emotionally and intellectually engaged actors (think Virginia Woolf or Lydia Lopokova), the focus of the book follows the expectations of the times it describes, and the consequent sources of evidence, that all too often marginalise women even and especially in the domesticity of college. Queer heroines, like Jane Harrison, have their stories elsewhere.[21]

The archive for this history is huge – far more than any one scholar could hope to control. I have made liberal use of others' work, and spent a good deal of time in the archives myself. There are thousands and thousands of letters, millions of words of diaries and journals, biographies and autobiographies. Desire is always veiled, and illegal desire hidden, even when in plain sight: these papers rarely reveal a simple narrative, or tell all the details a historian might want, especially when the texts are published. When the texts are painfully explicit, it is almost always a sign of deep trauma or passionate need to break free of conventional repression, itself a sign of internal anguish. Consequently, a history of homosexuality has to move sinuously between recognising the importance and function of the veils and trying delicately to see behind them. There is always too much and too little said in any story of desire. The archives here reflect that dynamic at a grand scale.

The period this book covers, as I have already indicated, is one of political and social turmoil – not just the two World Wars and the devastating consequences of economic deprivation, but also the febrile political discussions – and revolutions – that arise in response to the violence of empire, industrialisation and the competition between nation states. As was recognised at the time, the aftermath of the First World War constituted a social change of extreme proportions. The young men and women of the 1920s were desperate to articulate how different they were from their Victorian parents and grandparents – a dynamic repeated in the 1960s and 1970s. The localised history I trace is set against these national and international tectonic changes. I make little attempt to tell this history of transformations at such a grand scale: that would be a quite different project which many have already chronicled with real insight and incisiveness. Yet especially in the second chapter of the book, we will see that many of the figures of this history contributed significantly to these narratives of world history, and some did so from a perspective explicitly informed by their experience as gay men, as 'homosexuals'. The relation between the local and the wider national and political culture is a constant thread of the book. Each of the book's leading figures self-consciously set out to make a difference to national and even international culture, and did so with varying instrumental force.

The college is an educational institution, and there are few topics more heated in current discussion in academia and in the public imagination of schools and universities than the proper place of sexuality in such institutions. The questions have become public debates of increasing virulence, extremism and obfuscation, matched by attempts at regulation which, like all attempts to regulate desire in society, become increasingly clumsy and inoperable the more comprehensive and watertight they seek to be. (Against this desperate drive towards certainty, Katherine Angel, more sensibly, though, inevitably, more provocatively, writes: '[W]e need to articulate an ethics of sex that does not try frantically to keep desire's uncertainty at bay. A sexual ethics that is worth its name has to allow for obscurity, for opacity and for not-knowing.')[22] Universities, certainly since the nineteenth century – examples back to antiquity are evident too, but less directly relevant – have been places where conventions and rules of sexuality have been put under particular stress: universities are places of challenge and experimentation (and have a lot of young people sequestered together, away from direct parental control). There has always been a worry about what young people get up to at university. This book tells many stories of sexualised relationships between teachers and pupils, colleagues in the workplace, students together, elite men and vulnerable or needy working-class men and youths. It would be trite if true to say that it is pointless to apply our contemporary moralising to all these examples from the past: it is much harder to escape the limitations of our own assumptions than the ease of such an assurance would suggest. More saliently, it is integral to such relationships that they were constantly the subject of moral consternation at the time. But mainly because they were between men; only occasionally because they involved students and dons. Indeed, one of the issues that has to be faced in this history of homosexuality is the regular pattern of young men who willingly and intently became the objects of desire of older men in these institutional contexts, and then – in the community – became in turn over time the older men looking back towards a new generation of young men who were turning to them. This pattern is much harder to evidence with women, either in heterosexual or lesbian relationships. In the diaries and letters I have read, this experience of (male) transition is wondered about, used to reflect on aging – both maturing into manhood and becoming old – joked about, taken very seriously as a scene of love – but very rarely, if ever, moralised as a dangerously corrupt power relation, at least until quite recently. The community of men in King's was constantly talking about its relationships and what they meant and how to evaluate them – it was E. M. Forster, after all, who made 'only connect' the watchword of his personal politics – but the terms in which this anxiety was expressed were quite different from today's insistence on power and disparity. A history of homosexuality has to discuss how relationships between men are differently conceptualised, and all the more so in an educational institution, especially in the past.

One motivation for writing this book was reading an influential and inspirational study of the history and historiography of homosexuality, Heather Love's *Feeling Backward: Loss and the Politics of Queer History* (2007). In it – among its many detailed investigative analyses – she generalises that 'The longing for community across time is a crucial feature of queer historical experience, one produced by historical isolation of individual queers, as well as by the damaged quality of the historical archive.'[23] What I hope to show in this book is that there were places where a longing for community became realised in a group of single men living together over time, working together and recognising each other as men who desired men – who could be called homosexual and then gay and then queer. These were not isolated individuals, though we will certainly come across stories of loneliness and despair as there are bound to be in any such history. Rather, thanks to the intimacy of teaching, the sociality of college and the scope of empire, there was an international network that looked back to King's, which remained a special haven for them. Many of these men became figures who made significant contributions on the international stage. All archives are 'damaged', but the archive of homosexual experience is huge if carefully self-edited by the discretions of propriety, shame and legality. Heather Love sees in queer history 'nothing but wounded attachments'.[24] I am tempted to say that 'nothing but wounded attachments' sums up human interaction pretty well (which would give no priority to queer experience). And of course acknowledging the oppression and denigration which many queer people did and continue to experience is an absolutely necessary starting point for any history of homosexuality. But in this history we will also see love, friendship and care stretching over decades. Perhaps no relationship can escape its wounds, but there is also something at least beyond wounds that brings humans back together in hope and desire.

There are four chapters that follow, each with a central motivating question. Chapter 1, 'The Discovery of Homosexuality', focuses on the earlier years of this history and a group of men who found it very difficult to find themselves on the map of desire, to see where they stood in the normative world of Victorian erotics. They could not speak the vice that dare not say its name – though they talked about it non-stop. How to be 'homosexual' before homosexuality? Or rather – and much more complicatedly – how did living through the shifts that the pathologisation of desire effected, change a sense of identity for these men who desired men – their self-understanding? Chapter 2, 'The Politics of Homosexuality', looks at a group of men who committed themselves to political change, and who did so fully in the knowledge that their own forms of desire gave them a different perspective on social norms and the possibilities of freedom from convention. Some aimed to change the world institutionally – through the foundation of the League of Nations, say; some through changing the physical environment of cities; others through transforming economic or political understanding; others still by working for government. The intensity of discussion in college transferred to an intense and committed contribution to the political life of the nation (and beyond). They wanted to create a world in which they would be happier to live. Chapter 3, 'The Art of Homosexuality', brings on stage a group of actors, musicians and artists, who set out to change the imagination of the community. Performance became an expression of queer identity because concealment and revelation, acting an other's role, were endemic strategies in the negotiation of conventional society by queer men. If the 'stylistics of living' can be a route into understanding the bio-politics of experience, here was a group of men who flaunted a stylistics of living to change the politics of the personal – to change how life could and should be pictured.[25] How is the art and the artist's life interlinked? The final chapter, Chapter 4, 'The Burial of Homosexuality', concentrates on the post-Second World

War period, when policing became even more fierce in Britain, and the return to a paraded social normality after the war created an even more hostile atmosphere for homosexual life, as it did for women in the public sphere. It is not by chance that this is the era when the Cambridge spies became notorious: concealment, playing a role, lying became a compelling necessity for gay men. Several of the fellows who appear in this chapter married. Yet in 1967, homosexual sex between men above the age of twenty-one in private was legalised, and although this immediately resulted in even more aggressive stances by public authorities, gradually, though scarcely at the same time across all communities and regions, things became a little easier for gay men, at least for some gay men, as pride marches, fighting back, legal developments and a changing public acceptance transformed the possibility of gay experience – as, differently, frighteningly, murderously, the AIDS epidemic had a profound effect on the lives – and deaths – of so many people, especially in major international cities. By the mid-1970s King's had a flourishing, flamboyant and open gay scene, which survived beyond the AIDS epidemic and the slow development of adequate medical treatments. Homosexuality, however, became a word less and less used, politically and socially. What had become a key term in the changing status of men who desired men was sidelined, buried. The book ends, somewhat mournfully, with one of the old dons of today looking back across these years, a reflection on change and loss, cued by the search for an alternative history of homosexuality – and his own failed hopes for an alternative history for himself.

As an undergraduate, I had spent many an evening in this don's rooms on H staircase, with friends, talking and drinking. We have often reminisced together since, as the friends of those days continued to add new stories to our memories. I had been educated in an all-boys school, a day-school, where no boy to my knowledge then was openly – or for that matter secretly – homosexual (gay was not quite yet the term of art for us), and where, in accord with the public culture of the era, homosexuality was the prompt to insult or humour (the two responses connected by their obvious aggression and disavowal). 'To my knowledge' is not just a sign of the insecure ignorance of adolescence, but because the obvious aggression and disavowal made it so difficult for anyone to express anything but an insistently, performatively, masculine public face. It was consequently an eye-opening experience for me aged eighteen to enter a place where flaming queens screeched welcomes in the bar, where men talked avidly of sexual experiences with men, and women with women; where serious, more intense conversations about the politics of sexuality and the enactments of gender were commonplace; where feminist theory and gay liberation were part and parcel of engagement with the world. What was being acted out was a range of possibilities, but in an accepting and explorative way not yet experienced by me in my growing up, and not yet expected in the public media or indeed in the life of most of British society. The presence of public (and private but known) displays of differing forms of affection and desire came hand in hand with a certain social and intellectual porosity or fluidity or openness – the conditions for a genuine shared generosity (with enough argument to make it all feel critical and pressing). As we will see, this open-mindedness was – at its best – self-consciously part of King's self-representation: a moment in a long history of a (self-)critical acceptance of difference. Potential breeds potential: seeing otherness becomes a way of exploring otherness within yourself. Which can be a painful and dismaying experience too: there was also a lot of anguish and confusion, including for those who were excluded from such openness, or who wished not to be exposed to it. Acknowledgement of otherness and active acceptance of difference certainly do not remove hierarchies, fears, anxieties or even cruelties.

Cambridge has a particular image in modern society, not just as one of the oldest and greatest universities in the world, but also as an enclave of upper-class white guys, who, thanks to films, books and folk-memory, appear as beautiful young men running around a courtyard or drinking in oak-lined rooms, taught by elderly men in gowns, who politic furiously. It is the back-drop for narratives about spies and athletes, murder stories and choirs. There are decent historical reasons for some of this image. For many of the decades of the story I am writing, the university was almost entirely male, largely drawn from the upper reaches of British society, and largely white; and, for most of the period, many of the undergraduates enjoyed a very unpressured academic time (except at exam season), which was much taken up with sports, socialising, and gentle reading under trees. There are consequently many stories – from Thomas Hardy's *Jude the Obscure* onwards, an Oxford version – of *not fitting in* and of policing the boundaries of belonging. Especially as the university opened up from the 1950s onwards, the sense of potential alienation has been carefully nourished in anticipation as much as in practice. There are no doubt some people for whom Cambridge is still an entitlement (they are the frightening ones). But for most this is simply not true. It's rather that most people come up to Cambridge already prepared for social anxiety. How to fit in, what normal might be, how to behave, are the questions of adolescence, for sure, but bringing together a large group of young people from very different backgrounds in a place that has so many inherited expectations of snobbishness, intellectual brilliance, and simply being very different from home, is a recipe for a performative giddiness. Other people's apparent confidence, other people's stated discomforts, your own uncertainties combine to make the narrative of being an undergraduate a story of precarious belonging, especially in the opening months of being at Cambridge. Living up to Cambridge, living through Cambridge, living in Cambridge … Many students try out new forms of living and thinking (some resist any such transformation), many reimagine their sense of self, and many of them act it out, quietly or loudly. For me, arriving from North London, a Jew from a left-wing background, studying the counter-cultural choice of ancient Greek, besotted with theatre and poetry, the still dominatingly Christian Cambridge provided a confusing and thrilling potential for finding another way of making a life, another, transformative sense of self. The feeling that the moorings of a previous family life were shifting, along with the expectations of the social community I had inhabited, was both unsettling and frantic – and not wholly easy to look back at, now. But the feeling of surprise and change has never left me, however much I have become part of the establishment here. It is still the case that the people who seem to think themselves simply at home, entitled to be in Cambridge, appear most off-putting to me.

It is also clear to me that I was drawn to others who felt this sense of unsettled and anxious excitement as intently as me. Queerness – it is essential to recognise for this book – is not the same thing as homosexuality, or so I take it to mean in at least some current usage. In the past, 'queer' has often been used to denote gay men especially, both lovingly and aggressively. In the usual way of fugitive language, which because of its changeability always has a certain untimeliness in it, queer is still sometimes used in this way: as a marker of those who define their identity through same-sex desire. (It is not possible, of course, to calibrate all its usages across all communities; and there is yet an effective and affective politics of reclaiming such a term ...) But 'queerness' is also used in a more productive critical mode, which is important for how this book has taken shape. Homosexuality, as we have already said, is a pathology and a type that aims to define an identity. Between medical science, psychology, insult and stereotype, it offers both the lure of self-definition and the danger of denigration and dismissiveness, both towards oneself and towards others. Queerness, however, in this critical mode aims to capture something else. Queerness strives to name what can't quite be pinned down, the sense that *how* normal you are, or *how* perverse, *how* much you fit in or don't belong, remains a question – certainly to yourself and perhaps to others too. It makes sense to ask *how queer* in a way that it is far less coherent to ask 'how homosexual'. (We will meet homosexuals who do not have sex with anyone, and others who have sex with women. It is not challenged that they *are* homosexuals, by themselves or by their friends.) There are times when queerness is still used these days, perhaps too easily, as a marker of a paraded identity – a claim to stand out rather than not to fit in. But one reason why I was happy to sit in the don's rooms talking personally is that it was a space where fitting in remained an exploratory question rather than a social demand – where identity was not so much a badge to be thrust at others, but a process to be tested. Against the privileged entitlements that Cambridge offered and the hostile conservatism of a wider society's expectations, perhaps it is no surprise that gays, lefty Jews (and other miscreants of racialised thinking), theatricals of all types, artists (and so on) found allies in each other. In *Queer Cambridge* I write about the men I have chosen to portray not so much because they are homosexuals, simply, but rather because they are queer. And that made H staircase for me – to a degree, uncertainly but pointedly, with different consequences, and different anxieties – a *shared space*.[26]

I wrote a few pages back that 'this is not an idealised or idealising narrative. It does not set out to imagine a homosexual society, a brotherhood, an elite cohort of lovers or any of the other familiar fantasies that have so often arisen from the oppressions and disappointments of the present.' That remains true. But I can't deny that I do think that there is an immense value in this promise of a porous, multiform, open-minded, (radically) open community. On the one hand, I know that my own values, understanding and sensibilities have been transformed by my experiences and friendships within such a community over many years (and still ongoing). How to live, Socrates' old enquiry, remains still the most pressing question.

An unexamined life isn't worth living (or so Socrates, who died for the idea, claimed), and the fissures of the self – for me at least – could not have been recognised without these encounters with differing ways of living, or, to be more precise, without the nourished expectation that such encounters with difference should require self-examination (rather than prurience or dismissiveness). Part of this book's motivation stems from the recognition that my own self-understanding has been shaped by the messy richness of these engagements with imagining other ways of finding not just pleasure but also flourishing or well-being or attentiveness. This experience has deeply affected how I care to live my life. On the other hand, so many imaginings of idealised communities – utopias – portray a society that does not change, made up of people who know their place, and where conflict, difference and transformation are absent. Plato's *Republic* is one such idealisation, which shows both the lure and the dangers of such totalitarian and authoritarian longing for stability, never fully undone by the ironic voice of Socratic persuasion. In this sense, the changing and messy community of King's College is certainly not *ideal*. But it is still possible to value deeply the way it handles some of its messiness with generosity and receptiveness to its differing perspectives. In today's political and social world, after the isolation of the COVID-19 pandemic, with the violence and hostility of political polarisation, and increasing social and economic division and divisiveness, vividly and horrifically expressed in racist and other forms of violence within cities, and in military aggression between countries, it is indeed compelling to relearn why such receptiveness and generosity might open doors to a more fulfilling social negotiation of difference and conflict in the public sphere. What's more, universities across the world are faced by forces, internal and external, that are setting their face against such messy freedoms and generous critical acceptance of differing perspectives. This alternative history of homosexuality also aims to offer a microcosm of a much larger agenda about how we might want to inhabit our social space together.

The chapters that follow trace a broadly thematic rather than a biographical line. For what I hope are obvious reasons, I have decided not to concentrate on figures who are still alive, and to put something of a halt on the story when homosexuality becomes legal – though a look over that particular fence will also close the book. Together, these snapshots of lives – and they can here be no more than snapshots – provide a remarkable collage of a community in formation – and an alternative history of homosexuality.

I hope by the end it will have become clear why I think it needed writing.

I

The Discovery of Homosexuality

~

H staircase is not a metaphor, nor an allegory, nor a
symbol. It is next to G staircase, which is next to
F staircase, in the Gibbs Building in King's College,
Cambridge. The Gibbs Building (see Plate 1) is a fine
eighteenth-century classical edifice designed by Gibbs,
which has three floors, each with two rather grand sets of
residential rooms either side of the staircase, although now
most of these sets are used as offices. It stands at the centre
of the college. Yet it also turns out that H staircase, alongside G staircase, not to mention A staircase across the
court, was the centre of a very active and socially influential
culture of men who desired men – over a series of generations spanning more than a century (see Figure 2).

Most rooms in the building, like H1, are actually three
rooms: two smaller inner rooms and a much larger outer
room. The inner rooms were used as bedrooms or studies,
the outer room for teaching, socialising, hanging out.
Either the rooms were shared with one person in each of
the bedrooms, the usual set-up for students; or a fellow
might have the full set of rooms for himself. Across the
courtyard is the dining hall, the senior combination room
(the private social space for fellows) and the library. There
are other meeting rooms and accommodation there and
down towards the river. The college is an enclosed space
with gates that can be locked at night, and it has a strong
sense of community. It talks of itself as a community, it is

FIGURE 2 H Staircase, the entrance, with the window of H1 on the left and H2 on the right.

recognised from outside as a community, with shared ideas of what it means to be part of the community. Students are admitted to a college and have a strong sense of affiliation to it from the start. The standard first question to ask a Cambridge student is 'What college are you at?'

This story of H staircase, however, offers us a surprisingly different understanding of the topography and temporality of male desire for males in the nineteenth and twentieth centuries. It provides a remarkable and telling map of how these male desires were expressed and expressible, from the celibate to the predatory, as the language of desire transformed towards the pathologised 'homosexuality' that still runs through contemporary language; of how knowledge, memories of the past, expectations and hopes were passed on between men and groups of men over time; of how these men experienced their desires and the possibilities they evoked, not only as they themselves changed over a long period – Dadie Rylands, the literary scholar and theatre director, lived in the college for nigh on eighty years – but also as the wider British society changed, and, with it, the scale and role of the college as an educational institution. In this community, men grew and aged from undergraduates into fellows and professors and, for some, lived in retirement in their same rooms, as life fellows of the college. Undergraduates and fellows also left to take up major roles in British society – the arts, politics, the army, finance – but returned regularly to college, and to friendships maintained over large distances and many decades. Some, like the economist Maynard Keynes and the novelist E. M. Forster, maintained international profiles of considerable importance while living in college. What's more, H staircase is the staircase nearest to King's Chapel, one of the great buildings of Europe. The role of religion, except as a repressive force, is often left out of the history of homosexuality (as we can call the field to which this short book is a contribution, despite the historical difficulty of transferring such vocabulary across time, nations and culture). The role of chapel and the fellows' connection with the Anglican church is a more complex thread of influence, however, and the immediate juxta-position of the door of H staircase and the south door of the chapel, ten metres apart, is an eloquent reminder of the place of the church in the life of many of the leading characters of this story.

For many of the figures we will meet, however, who shared the space of college life, *being homosexual* inevitably marked them as not fitting into the cultural expectations of the time. Often with a longing look back to ancient Greece, they were aware of their separateness, even as the college made a home for them. This dislocation and untimeliness is both the condition for and a contrast with the sense of community formed in the very particular space, a community which was widely recognised, as we will see, for its specialness, even for its queerness. As Sir Dennis Robertson, fellow of Trinity College, colleague of Maynard Keynes at the highest levels of financial think-ing, and, most relevantly, lover of Dadie Rylands, was heard to say, 'to come into King's is to enter heaven'. The Porters actually thought Robertson was a fellow of King's, he spent so much time there. It was for Robertson – coming from just down the road at Trinity College – a transformative act of the imagination and of lived experience to participate in this college community. As we will see, he was not alone in this.[1]

In the time period of this book, King's itself was trans-formed. In the 1860s King's stopped being a college solely for boys from Eton and in 1871 allowed Nonconformists to enter its doors too. Over the following decades the college would grow in size – from years with an intake of only fifteen students into a college with nearly three hundred under-graduates and a hundred postgraduate students – and become thus a far bigger and more mixed community (though when you start from admitting students from only one elite school, it would be hard *not* to become more mixed ...). As the college grew in size and in its strangeness to itself, it discussed these changes insistently, and con-sciously worked to form a community, with specific values and principles, and a repeated concern for institutional tradition. At the same time, how male relationships with other males could or should be performed – comprehended, eroticised, denied – was also a subject of compelling focus, in King's and more broadly in society, not least through the development of psychology, sexology and, as today, through media and legal panics about sexuality. To know oneself as a person and as a community were overlapping fascinations. What is more, the social demand of the concealment of desire, highly exacerbated for the queer man, whose desire was so stridently denigrated in public, always put a premium on who was in the know. The work of self-definition became a shared, complicit process with its own 'epistemology of the closet'.[2] It was a community of men coming into being, at the same time as homosexuality as a developed idea was coming into being, and this matrix provides the overheated condition for the stories of this book. For many of the men we will meet in this first chapter particularly, to (seek to) know oneself was a constant and destabilising anxiety, often translated into a wish to analyse others, and to join in anatomising relationships – which is mirrored (with differ-ent consequences) by our desire to understand – to know – them. This chapter's title, 'The Discovery of

Homosexuality', is meant to indicate not just that homosexuality was first outlined by theorists as an idea and a word
in this era, but also that homosexuality was something to be
discovered in oneself and in others.

There is a long cast list in this history, of major players
who strut across the stage, and others in the supporting
cast. I want first to introduce five of the founding
members of the community. Each is chosen because they
are so talked and written about by their contemporaries,
figures who fired the imagination, characters through
which to imagine the world's possibilities. They are men
who became nationally known, and who are also intimately connected with each other. It is a network, a community in formation. We will meet them in turn, along
with their admiring friends. We can start with the arrival
in college of **J. K. Stephen** (1859–92) (see Figure 3),
whose rooms were H1.[3] Stephen came up to King's from
Eton in 1878, graduated in 1882, and was appointed a
fellow in 1885 – a standard career path of elect excellence.
The year 1885 was also when all forms of sexual behaviour between men, thanks to the category 'gross
indecency', were made illegal in English law. I start here,
then, with purpose: a moment of national change.

The connection between King's and Eton was still
close in these years. Until 1861, not only could pupils
from Eton alone attend King's, but the right to hold a
fellowship was also reserved for Etonians (and it could be
held for life). Although by the 1880s there was a mix of
students and fellows from different schools (all male still,
of course), the ability to move between Eton and King's
was still strongly in evidence – several of our characters, at
least in the first decades of this story, move between being

THE CAMERON STUDIO.   70. MORTIMER ST. REGENT STREET.

FIGURE 3 J. K. Stephen, bullish, powerful, a 'great mad figure'.

a pupil at Eton, a student at King's, returning as a teacher to Eton, and then returning to King's as a fellow. There was still an 'Eton set' at King's, a clique of boys and men who had known each other for some years already. J. K. Stephen made a deep impression on everyone he met, 'certainly the most marked man of the younger generation'. Arthur Benson, whose huge set of diaries and published reminiscences, as well as his career between Eton and Cambridge, make him a key witness for the period, offers a picture self-consciously touched by the glow of a lost time. Benson was in the year below him at school and at King's, and he looked up to Stephen:

J.K. Stephen was a young man of quite extraordinary brilliance and power. One sees the old days in a golden light, no doubt, but yet I do not think I ever heard talk of such range and quality as his; he could be serious, dry, severely intellectual; but he also had a sharp and keen-edged wit, together with a broad, fanciful and quite irresponsible humour. He enjoyed almost more than strenuous discussion the society of appreciative, friendly perceptive men, in whose company his talk could ebb and flow with his restless mood.[1]

Notice the word 'irresponsible': Benson, even as he revels in Stephen's personality, cannot help marking his sense of danger or transgression, a certain lack of restraint – 'restless' – in Stephen. Other stories of Stephen's wit abound (biographies of the period love to record the put-downs and *bon mots* of its heroes): on his one visit to King's, we are told, Oscar Wilde and Stephen swapped repartee like a pair of tennis players. Virginia Woolf (née Stephen), J. K. Stephen's cousin, was less sanguine, however, and saw his displayed masculinity in a different light:

This great mad figure with his broad shoulders and very clean cut mouth, and the deep voice and the powerful face – and the very blue eyes – this mad man would recite poetry to us; "The Burial of Sir John Moore," I remember; and he always brings to mind some tormented bull; and also Achilles – Achilles on his pressed bed lolling roars out a deep applause.[5]

It's hard to match 'tormented bull' with 'fanciful and irresponsible humour' – but Stephen had very different relationships with men and women. And even Benson, with his characteristic veils of restraint, indicated that already at school there was a worrying aspect to Stephen's personality. He was, writes Benson, 'of an emotional nature always, but found it very hard to express his feelings', and adds: 'I was aware in those days, especially just before the time came for him to leave [Eton], that there was some hidden flow of feeling about him, a heart-felt craving which he could not express even to himself.'[6] This coded language of craving and inexpressibility – 'hidden ... feeling' especially – hints at two sides of Stephen's life – the mental illness which led to his young death, and his sexuality. Stephen was deeply unstable (retrospectively diagnosed as bi-polar), and an accident on a boat, when he was hit on the head, was thought by his friends and family to have exacerbated his symptoms. After a psychotic incident, when he was found naked and ranting in Cambridge, he starved himself to death in a sanatorium. He had earlier been arrested in Paris for *escoperil* (financial fraud / unpaid debts), and was released thanks to the intervention of the British Ambassador, who pleaded Stephen's insanity. Stephen's father, one of many threatening and unsympathetic fathers in this history, did not know which was more of a disgrace, the charge of *escoperil* or the defence of insanity.

Stephen's school life is also salient, and will introduce us to the interconnected lives of many of the figures of this story – Stephen's clique, the 'Eton set'. Stephen had been taught at Eton by Oscar Browning, of whom *much* more shortly. Browning, always known as O. B., became an international celebrity, especially in his own mind. He was an extremely popular housemaster at Eton who in 1875, at the height of his success as a schoolmaster, was sacked by the headmaster, Hornby. The explicit reason was that Browning had admitted forty-three pupils into his house, rather than the statutory forty. The case was a widely publicised scandal, and questions were even raised in Parliament by a disgruntled parent (and MP). Denials

43

that there had been any immorality involved only increased suspicions. In later Victorian Britain anxiety about morality in the public schools was intense, embodied in increasingly shrill denunciations of masturbation and carefully veiled insinuations of homosexual behaviour. Not long before Browning's dismissal, another teacher, the equally charismatic William Johnson (1823–92), formerly an undergraduate at King's, had also been sacked from Eton for encouraging a culture of 'romantic friendship' between the boys and for having his 'favourites', including Oscar Browning, whom he taught. Johnson changed his name to William Cory and became a successful poet, one of the Uranians, whose poems and journals were read avidly by self-recognising gay men in particular. (In turn, the sociologist Edward Sagarin chose Cory as his pseudonym for his groundbreaking 1951 book, *The Homosexual in America*.)[7] That Cory's journal in particular became such a lure for the imagination of young men seeking to understand their own desires did not thrill the authorities at Eton – not the sort of teaching they wanted to be associated with their school. There was in Eton a tradition – loaded word! – of anxiety and excess in relations between teachers and pupils. And a network in place: Cory, Browning, Stephen, Benson … a network which, as we will see, was incremental and expanding. Through poetry, scandal, essays, reminiscence, their intimacies became part of a national discussion. These men knew they were at the eye of a public storm.[8]

The headmaster in his disciplinary meeting with Browning had mentioned to Browning that he was spending too much time with a good-looking boy from another house, George Curzon – who in adulthood would rise to rule India for the British Empire as Viceroy.[9] Browning was incensed by the insinuation that his interest was based on looks (incensed not least because of the accusation's truth). The politics of the case for dismissal remain murky: the headmaster also disliked Browning both as a person and as a liberal reformer; but the accusations that Browning had a sexual interest in young men was, as we will see, well founded, even if he was, while a schoolmaster, a strident campaigner for moral uprightness in schools. Browning, who had been forbidden by Hornby to have any further contact with Curzon, went on to take Curzon very publicly on a holiday to Europe with him, and a much re-circulated formal photograph of Browning and Curzon together comes from this trip (see Figure 4).

Curzon had been violently abused as a child by his governess, events vividly described later by Curzon himself as savage, brutal, vindictive, insane: Browning offered him the adult care he had lacked as a child. In a way that would be inconceivable today, Browning also took J. K. Stephen on holiday with him – they spent the best part of *a year* abroad together – when Stephen was sixteen years old, and still had two years to go at Eton. What was such a holiday like? Another student who also went on holiday with O. B. when he was seventeen gives us one side of what might be expected: 'O. B. used to talk to me about everything and I became the depository of certain most intimate secrets. No doubt in many ways it must have been bad for me, but in others it was excellent ...'[10] O. B. was indiscreet, suggestive and explicit, it is implied, and the ambivalence of the boy is clear enough: he was excited by the revelations ('It was excellent ...'), but knows it must

FIGURE 4 Curzon, future Viceroy of India, with Oscar Browning, his teacher, on holiday together. Browning's hand is on Curzon, who looks away from Browning.

be marked as inappropriate and morally dodgy, even if he does not quite credit it as such: 'it must have been bad for me …'. We will pick up the consequences of this later. Stephen was very much part of this world of suspiciously emotional 'romantic friendship' between boys, and between teachers and boys. O. B. went back to King's as a fellow, after he had been sacked from Eton, and Stephen duly joined him in college. To O. B., with his customary overstatement, Stephen was 'the most brilliant young man with whom I ever came into contact, and was regarded by all his contemporaries as an intellectual giant' – difficult though this is to imagine from Stephen's published writing, none of which is coruscatingly brilliant.[11] Stephen travelled with Browning – round Europe; from Eton to King's; in the transition from pupil to young man. This transformative intimacy is typical of the journeys I am following.

As an undergraduate the charismatic Stephen was elected into the Apostles, the semi-secret society of elite, self-selected men, well known to Bloomsbury scholars as a hotbed of sexual conversations and occasional activity. He was elected a fellow of King's in 1885. He had already been invited in 1883 to become the tutor to Prince Albert Victor, Edward VII's son and the heir to the throne (see Figure 5).

Rumours about Prince Eddy, as he was known to his family, became international news during the Cleveland Street case. A male brothel on Cleveland Street was raided by the police, and in the consequent pursuit of clients, a 'member of the royal family' was implicated. There was certainly a good deal of pressure brought on the police not to continue the case – ultimately, no clients were prosecuted – but any direct evidence concerning Albert Victor is absent, though recent scholars have collected circumstantial material of varying persuasiveness.[12] Nor, despite continuing fantasies and accusations, was either the prince or J. K. Stephen a credible suspect for Jack the Ripper, as was once feverishly suspected – though J. K. Stephen's performance in the first Greek play in Cambridge in the character of Ajax, a hero who goes mad and tortures and dismembers sheep, has proved grist for the mill of such misapprehensions. Albert Victor died of influenza the same year as Stephen starved himself to death. Stephen and the prince were close friends; many of

FIGURE 5 Prince Albert Victor, 'Prince Eddy', liked dressing up.

their friends and acquaintances will reappear in this history; they were part of a community of young men in Cambridge, many of whom provide more overt evidence of their homosexual activity and preferences. Much as Browning tutored Stephen, Stephen tutored the prince. J. K. Stephen's modern biographers consequently see him as a discomfortingly misogynistic, gay man, whose internal conflicts combined a mental instability with a tortured sexual self-awareness in a disastrous compound. He also matters because his relationship with the heir to the throne threatened to bring into public life that which should not be known, not publicly.

I start with J. K. Stephen in H1, however, also because his case is paradigmatic of how complex the archive for this history will repeatedly prove. H1 marks the space of Stephen's transition from school to adulthood, from bright pupil to man about town. King's became his home. Stephen was very much an iconic figure – a star – in a community that can be called, at the very least, homosocial; it was a community that moved between Eton, King's at Cambridge, London – and trips together abroad – and which linked generations. It recognised romantic relationships both between men and between men and boys (the category 'boys', we should remember, has an age range up to twenty, or thereabouts: pupils often stayed at school until they were nineteen or more). Yet when sexual activity between males was socially unacceptable and, from 1885, newly illegal, there is also a careful silence in much of the evidence. In a way that is surprising to today's expectations, passionate kissing, hugging and lying in bed together, along with naked swimming, could be regarded as decently separate from sexual

49

activity, though its erotic charge could certainly also be manifest (not least to those lying naked together on the sand). As we will shortly see, there is another strand of evidence from only slightly later which is intensely explicit and direct about sexual behaviour. But it is important not to translate simply between these bodies of material: it cannot be assumed that because we know that one group of friends were intensely physical, the same must be true of others, when the evidence is lacking. It is, for example, quite clear that at a school like Eton or Marlborough or Harrow, there were boys who actively and openly pursued sex with other boys; there were also boys who knew about such behaviour while not themselves involved; and there were boys who went through school oblivious to such scenes, and whose shocked denials that such things even took place should be taken seriously as truthful records of their own experiences. They later worked out what they had not seen, and tell us so. This mix of explicit, even swashbuckling behaviour, and an unaware or willed blindness towards it, and a politic refusal to recognise publicly what was known privately, continued into university life and beyond. This – not to mention the class-based and active concealment of explicit material – leaves Stephen's bedroom in an obscurity of willed decency. This sketch of Stephen has drawn on the private and public descriptions of him by his contemporaries, the essayist Benson, the novelist Woolf, the poet Cory, the historian Browning, Prince Eddy, and so on: his network. These judgements, however, never turned to the language of sexuality to express Stephen's violent dissatisfactions. It is not merely discretion; it is also the lack of an adequate shared public vocabulary. The normative range of explanation did not yet include a pathologised sexuality. It is not just the lack of evidence that makes it so hard to know how Prince Eddy and Stephen would have described their relationship when they were alone.

The second leading actor in this story is **A. C. Benson** (1862–1925).[13] I have already quoted from his public and private memories of J. K. Stephen. Arthur Benson moved into J. K. Stephen's rooms first at Eton, and then followed him to King's where he took over H1. In contrast to the case of Stephen, we have all too much evidence about Benson's life. He left 180 volumes of diary, from his time as an Eton schoolmaster, then in Windsor Castle as the editor of Queen Victoria's letters, and finally as a fellow and then Master of Magdalen College. (I am, it seems, the only person alive to have read through them all.) He started his diary only when his father died, and continued writing till the very day of his death, when with graphomaniac zeal he recorded his heart attack as it was happening, rather than call for help. He also wrote autobiographies; reminiscences of his friends; a biography of his father, and other biographies of his brothers and sisters. He wrote dozens of volumes of essays, all of which project an image of the civilised but melancholic don's perspective on life and its transitions. He revelled in the compelling complicities of the oppressive intimacies of college life. He was also a major public figure – his books were huge best-sellers – and, in turn, he appears in many a diary and volume of reminiscences. Benson gives a uniquely rich portrait of Cambridge between the 1880s and 1920s, and of his place in it, and of his self-recognition and anxiety about his own desires and those of his friends. A *very* detailed biography could well be written of this maven of life-writing.

Hı and King's played a major role in Benson's self-understanding. Something happened to him in these rooms in 1882, his second year as an undergraduate: 'It was in these rooms that I passed my darkest hours – it hardly does to think of now – and yet it was so fantastic and unreal' (this, twenty-one years later).[14] He assiduously marked the anniversary of 'my great misfortune' in his diary, year on year, on 9 November. Benson never tells us what this event was. But his first published novel, which is thinly disguised autobiography in many an incident, tells the story of (another) 'Arthur' who formed a relationship with a 'weak but singularly attractive boy' at school – a relationship described as an ideal of intimacy that transcended even the bond of a married couple. The boy later visits 'Arthur' in his rooms at university on 8 November, which is commemorated with a prayer for salvation in his diary of 9 November (the autobiographical hints are very precise). 'What passed I cannot say', says the reticent narrator, reading 'Arthur's' letters, but 'I can hardly picture to myself the agony, disgust, and rage (his words and feelings about sensuality of any kind were strangely keen and bitter), loyalty fighting with the sense of repulsion, pity struggling with honour, which must have convulsed him when he discovered that his friend was not only yielding but deliberately impure.'[15] Arthur writes of 'Arthur' but cannot say what happened; the feelings of agony and disgust at sensuality are recorded; the horror at deliberate impurity stressed. The vice that cannot speak its name is performatively silenced or put under erasure not just because of the legal restraints on such behaviour, but also because its name is indeed still under construction: sexology, psychology, medicine were fields struggling to find an authoritative and agreed vocabulary – and diagnosis, beyond criminalisation – for male desire for males. The map of sexual naming is shifting and hard to control in this period. What's more, Benson is well aware that he is not quite up to date with this language: he feels himself out of sorts with the time. He is also a deeply reticent man who can praise frankness but always privileges discretion. Benson's diaries have hundreds of pages in which he struggles to find his position on the map of desire. He idealises the pure, chivalric relations of boys at school, and hates the corrupt recognition and acceptance of impurity – the physicality of desire. But he lives constantly in the grey area between these polarised values. He goes on holiday with men who kiss and flirt in front of him, to his dismay, while he can lovingly describe his own evening sitting with a boy resting his head on his lap, reading William Cory's journal. He courts and listens to boys' confessions of desire, but is equally fascinated and horrified by their openness. He upbraids his friends for their sexual perversion, but calls them 'pure and good'. The awkward paradoxes and painful tensions in his self-understanding and self-description multiply over the thousands of pages of self-reflection in his diaries.

So, Benson can look back at his time as a teacher at Eton (see Figure 6), recalling his fixations on the young objects of his desires: 'Then there was the Arthur Mason adoration ... and Reeve ... and Martin ... and the opening up of Eton life. How utterly purposeless one was then. I know what I want now, though I can't get it.'[16] Desire, when recognised, is still barred. Desire remains terrifying. 'Can one trust <u>any</u> boy not to lapse into animalism? No,

FIGURE 6 Arthur Benson as schoolmaster at Eton surrounded by the boys of his house. Percy Lubbock (see also Figure 12) is at the top right corner.

one can't: and I can forgive a sudden fall, a distortion of passion, even a habit of evil; but when this is added to a foul and ugly shamelessness of vice, the most corrupting of things, it makes one wonder that the brimstone does not fall down.'[17]

In a way that helps explain the H1 incident, Benson can imagine and even forgive a momentary lapse, even several such moments ('a habit of evil') – but cannot forgive a lack of crippling guilt, seen as aesthetic ('ugly') and moral ('*shamelessness*') corruption. The religious language here is unmistakable: lapse, fall, evil, brimstone (the punishment of Sodom and Gomorrah). Benson's father was Edward White Benson, Queen Victoria's Archbishop of Canterbury, a fiercely committed and passionate Christian whose influence on his children was strikingly intense and feared (none of his six children ever had heterosexual intercourse). Benson started his diary the day his father died. It contains not just long reflections on their relationship but also single sentences that seem to echo his father's religious authority with a sad horror: 'I woke early with a repugnance of the flesh.'[18] Benson – and here the symbolism seems too painfully clear – had a picture on display in H1 of a kneeling naked man, painted blue, illuminated by rays of sun. It was inscribed in Greek *phos etheasamên kai emphobos ên* – 'I beheld a light and was afraid'. The learned and inescapable religious background here is crucial. On the road to Damascus, according to the book of Acts, Paul sees a great light and hears a voice from heaven asking him, 'Saul, Saul, why do you persecute me?' His companions 'beheld the light and became terrified', *to phôs etheasanto kai emphoboi egenonto.* (Or, if you can allow the briefest of professional philological detours, so at least they do in the Textus Receptus, the standard Greek text from the Renaissance onwards; the Revised Standard edition of the Bible, as edited by Westcott and Hort, and published in 1881, the year Benson came to King's, deletes the second phrase, although it is already present in the early if inferior Codex Beziae – Westcott, the editor of the Revised Standard edition, was a great friend of Benson's father, and a student at King's.) Benson has done three shocking things to the well-known scriptural quotation, as perhaps only the disaffected son of an archbishop could. First, he has turned it from the plural to the singular. Benson, who is so often the observer, especially of scenes of desire, rather than the actor, does not quite place himself amid the companions who are witnesses only to the visual aspect of Paul's traumatic experience, but rather makes this a personal confession. He is the hero of this singular story of fear. 'They looked on' becomes 'I have seen'. Second, he has left out the definite article. '*The* light' is a crucial part of Christian rhetoric over the centuries, an expression of the immutable truth. 'A light' allows for multiple lights, and refuses to specify the all-embracing religious truth. Benson has seen something else. Third, what he offers as the object of sight is a naked, kneeling man, in blue. The naked man may seem shocking enough (there is no suggestion that this is St Paul). Is blue significant? John Addington Symonds, whose life as a gay man has been so exhaustively and insightfully discussed in recent years – he floats through certain moments of this history too – had published his essay 'In the Key of Blue' not long before, an 'open love letter', which many read with intent. As modern critics outline, blue 'epitomises the mix of fascination and revulsion with which Symonds describes his desires'.[19] For Richard Tyrrwhit at least, a contemporary art critic and scourge of unmanly art, Symonds' blue was in a nasty lineage: 'We have all heard of the famous symphony in blue, and of the *Closet Blue* and here is the *Key of Blue*', he wrote dismissively in 1893, following his excoriating essay against such Greek corruption in *The Contemporary Review* of 1877. In a line with (mistitled) paintings of Whistler and Rossetti, Symonds' prose, in Tyrrwhit's eyes, is the equivalent of dangerously modern and louche art, 'fleshly aesthetics'. Indeed, the novelist George Egerton, the male pseudonym of Mary Bright, received a letter from a stranger, fascinated by 'his' novels of female experience, who asked 'Are you blue?' Blue, it seems, could be a coded word for sexual inclinations. (And this must have been a very forward question!)[20] So perhaps Benson's blue man is coloured with a modern suggestiveness. Typically for Benson, the picture he displays in his room imagines a naked man but immediately and sophisticatedly glosses it within a religious notion of a transformative vision, but a rewritten religious framework, to note that he has beheld – and *is afraid*. A parody of Benson's writing in *Punch* was hilariously and all too precisely entitled 'At a Safe Distance'.[21]

H1 was Benson's dangerous and beloved personal space. He also describes the public scene at King's in an equally memorable way. When Benson comes back as a fellow of Magdalen to King's for a feast, the Founder's Feast of 1909, he marvels at what he sees among the students: 'The public fondling and caressing of each other, friends and lovers sitting with their arms enlaced, cheeks even touching, struck me as curious, beautiful in a way, but rather dangerous.'[22]

The move here from fascination ('curious') to explicit recognition ('friends and lovers') to envious admiration ('beautiful in a way') to concern ('rather dangerous') is an archetypal transition from emotional longing to self-policing – as well as an extraordinary picture of what dinner might be like in Edwardian King's. Not everyone agreed with Benson's longing view. Leo Maxse was particularly disgusted at what he saw as a culture of effeminacy in King's already in 1886. He wrote his outrage to the Provost, M. R. James, in the strongest terms: 'King's is damnable, there is no other word for it, a cesspool of all that is abominable with a thin diminishing layer of something better.'[23] Maxse, who took no degree at Cambridge, went on to become an influential and *very* right-wing member of the Conservative Party and a journalist who edited the *National Review* for years (his father bought the journal for him). Maxse bitterly opposed the formation of the League of Nations, with which, as we will see, the 'cesspool' of King's fellows were deeply involved. But – to keep the network working – he married Kitty Lushington, who was the model for Mrs Dalloway in Virginia Woolf's novel, and a great friend of the Stephen family. But even to those on the inside such dinners could seem wildly surprising and shocking in their public display. The young Maynard Keynes was at the same dinner in 1909 as Arthur Benson, but gives us a quite different insider perspective. It was his first year as a fellow, and he writes excitedly to his lover, the artist Duncan Grant, about the occasion: 'Yesterday evening will always mark an epoch, I think, in the history of King's manners. If there was debauchery, it was private. Manners not morals gave way. Quite suddenly our rigid rules of convention that one kisses no one in public utterly collapsed – and we all kissed! The scene really can't be described' – and adds, a concern destined not to be fulfilled, 'We've never behaved like this before – I wonder if we ever shall again.'[24] What for Benson was dangerous was for Keynes a thrill. The move from 'manners' to 'debauchery' was a shift in public display, but not in 'morals': again, note, the language is not about identity or sexuality, but what can be seen and said. Suddenly, everyone could be in the know.

Benson was hospitalised in London for acute depression for several years (his diaries, desperate to read, trace his collapse and then are silenced for a while), before returning to take up his post again as Master of Magdalen. I have tried elsewhere to trace the intricate dynamics of social, psychological, familial and intellectual tensions which contributed to his mental illness.[25] But Benson offers a quite different picture from J. K. Stephen, although they are contemporaries. Benson does use the word homosexual – hyphenated and marked by inverted commas as newfangled: 'homo-sexual' – but only twice and in the last year of his life, 1925. He never uses it nor indeed the vocabulary of sexuality itself of *himself*. Otherwise, he calibrates male desire – other people's sexuality – in a fascinatingly different manner. He is fiercely moral, but about physicality – the flesh – rather than the object of desire, though he warns his friends off any interest in the young choirboys of the college. He says – aged fifty – that he has never been kissed, and his 'repugnance of the flesh' is evidently linked to his response to his religious upbringing, and his father's overwhelming and insistent moralism. Despite a love of beauty, he is very sniffy about men who are motivated merely by the visual: for him, conversation and intimacy are all – but too much intimacy is always a threat to his need for reticent decency. Yet he repeatedly and avidly spends time with a more patently and explicitly sexual crowd, watching with fascinated dismay the freedom he cannot allow himself. Benson, one of the men who came back repeatedly to King's, will reappear in scene after scene in this history, either as commentator or as participant. He was supremely well connected. Benson – who dined with Queen Victoria – records that his final longing relationship was with the young Dadie Rylands, who was still in King's in the final year of the twentieth century. Above all, Benson watched, talked and talked, and wrote and wrote obsessively about the male desire he saw all around him and felt inside himself. He is a key witness to what it was like to live through the decades-long invention of homosexuality as a named, modern pathology.

Our third protagonist is **Montagu Rhodes James** (1862–1936).[26] When Benson left H1, the room passed to Monty James, who had been in the year below Benson at school, and at the same prep school, Temple Grove. People were well aware whose rooms they were moving into and the construction of a lineage. So, Arthur Cole dashes off a note to Jack Sheppard in 1906 (both men will appear later in this book): 'Do tell me whether you are staying in your old rooms: and who else are coming onto the staircase: my rooms are to be Truscott's old ones: I am a very unworthy successor to such a leader of fashion as he.'[27] Both James and Benson describe the blue painting of the kneeling man in H1 (James with a surprised distance, Benson with a slightly embarrassed recollection). James met J. K. Stephen for the first time in a box at the Opéra Comique in Paris, when James was still at school and Stephen was already an undergraduate. The three men were closely interconnected, part of the network.

James was friends with Benson throughout his life; like Benson he returned to Eton, but not until he had spent decades as a fellow and then Provost (head of the institution) at King's, and returned to Eton to take up the role of Provost there. James, who lived more than fifty years in the two institutions, encapsulates the connection between the two foundations of Henry VI, Eton and King's. He was an institutional man (see Figure 7).

When James came to King's in 1882, there were only fifteen undergraduates in his entering year (there were usually a few more, though the whole college had only sixty-seven students) and he was the only Etonian in his year. The scale of the college in these years was oppressively intimate. To Benson, James was conservative and old-fashioned. James' memoirs, *Eton and King's: Recollections Mainly Trivial*, are indeed deeply dull, not least for their refusal of any risky gossip or recollection of any crisis, transformation or emotional upheaval. But there is one story that at least shows the effort of concealment tellingly.

M. R. James is now best known for his ghost stories, often uneasily fashioned out of materials from his scholarly life, which have been repeatedly printed, staged and turned into films. He used to read them at Christmas, in the dark, to an audience of students and fellows in the Provost's Lodge. (Another philological note: his scholarly work on the manuscript tradition of apocryphal texts of the Christian canon is still important, however, at least to those who work on the apocryphal texts ...) In *Eton and King's*, he records that there was a story of a ghost on G staircase, though he claimed not to have heard its lamentations himself. He tells us – making the story as uninteresting as possible – that he asked two elderly fellows about it, and they revealed the story which he

FIGURE 7 Monty James, the figure of institutional and scholarly
authority: he grew into this image.

will not repeat out of respectfulness. We know, however, from letters in the archive that one of those fellows was Frederick Whitting (1834–1911), who had been Vice Provost of the college and lived on the top floor of G staircase for many years. He had a particular fondness for the choir and its choirboys. Rather creepily, he left money in his will for the choirboys' entertainment and asked that his portrait be thanked by them each year. Whitting (his name oddly is pronounced Whiting, like the fish), we know, told James that the dead fellow was a former bursar, one Thomas Brocklebank (1825–78), who had killed himself in his rooms on G staircase. (James says no more than 'a man who died in 1878'.) The cause was a revelation of 'copulation'. Whitting had been Second Bursar under Brocklebank. Brocklebank was ordained and single and there is little doubt that the charge was sex with another male. If the story was true, the death was covered up, as James also silences it, because Brocklebank is buried in Mill Road Cemetery, consecrated ground forbidden to a suicide. James published the barest hint of this story. But the next year he received a remarkable letter from Father Oliver Vassall-Phillips, then a military chaplain who had read *Eton and King's* on his way to his regiment in India. Vassall-Phillips wrote to ask if the ghost might not be his friend James Wilson, who had committed suicide 'in ghastly circumstances arising out of a visit to me at Oxford' – a bizarre competitiveness to claim the ghost of past shame.[28] Wilson had thrown himself in front of a train near Taplow in Buckinghamshire (there is no immediate explanation of why the ghost would have migrated to King's, Wilson's college, except to haunt Vassall-Phillips). Oliver Vassall-Phillips was a Catholic convert who published several books on his religious faith and was regarded as a

good and holy man. Vassall-Phillips does not specify what
had happened with Wilson, but he writes at length (instead) –
a revelatory displacement – about how Oscar Browning had
been sacked from Eton because of his relationship with
Curzon and explains that Wilson wrote 'a terrible and most
pathetic letter … Forty-eight years have passed since then,
but every word of that letter burned its way into my heart so
that I can never forget it as long as I remember anything.'[29]
Vassall-Phillips was the pupil I cited earlier, who, when he
was a seventeen-year-old boy at Eton, had himself gone on
holiday to Rome with Oscar Browning; and, when Browning
was sacked from Eton, wrote to him 'Altogether I miss you
DREADFULLY.'[30] Wilson, in turn, had also been a very
close friend of J. K. Stephen from school and King's. John
Addington Symonds, coming back again into this story,
wrote a poem about Wilson's death, which he sent privately
to Oscar Browning (here we see the network of community
at work again). It begins with a familiar appeal to 'Greek
Love':

> He loved & thought no shame;
> But spake divinely bold;
> Simple & void of blame
> As were the Greeks of old.

And its final verse makes Wilson a martyr of purity:

> Too pure to brook a stain,
> Too proud his wound to hide,
> Under the rushing train
> He laid him down and died.[31]

The connections cry out to be made. The network
widens to add Wilson to Stephen and Symonds, and

Vassall-Phillips to Browning and Wilson. The only possible hint of Vassall-Phillips' own desires in his autobiography – primarily the tale of his conversion – is a footnote which records 'Poor Oscar Wilde ... was a friend of mine during his last year at Magdalen.'[32] As Darryl Jones smartly writes, 'And so Father Vassall-Phillips wrote his own desperate letter to MRJ, in the hope that he could help him somehow to lay his own ghosts.'[33] For a Catholic priest, writing in the 1920s, and recalling in profound guilt and shame a trauma of past and destructive sexual experience of whatever form, he could tell his story only through a ghost story to the master of ghost stories. When a story of a horrific self-inflicted death is tied so closely with the dynamics of the will to conceal and the passion to reveal, it is no surprise that the result is ghosts. They haunt the history of homosexuality.

M. R. James was not ordained, but he wrote about scriptural texts his whole life, and obsessively visited cathedrals on his holidays in France. It would seem that he was celibate, though a subject of gossip to his friends as such. Benson went on holiday during the First World War with Frank Salter, a colleague at Magdalene, and Oliffe Richmond, a classicist at King's who lived in E5 (the office I have been in for thirty years). Richmond, nineteen years younger than Benson, was the friend whom he warned off the choirboys: 'O. R. has a morbid predilection for boys – it is a sort of sexuality, an erotic mania, though wholly pure and good' ... 'I told O. R. he must drop these boys or that he would be misrepresented' ... 'I told him today that it was a sexual perversion.'[34] Such judgements are poised between a modern pathology of sexuality and an older definition of sexual transgression based on activity. So Benson can call Richmond's predilection a sexuality, an erotic mania and a perversion – which all imply a form of pathology, though they are terms that Benson would never apply to himself – but he can also determine that Richmond is 'pure and good', because, presumably, there was no specific physical contact between Richmond and the boys. (To be a sexual pervert who is pure and good has become even less imaginable, I suspect, at least in the popular press.) On their holiday, the three men spent the evenings 'composing limericks and discussing Monty James's mysterious love life'. (James was particularly fond of one James McBryde [see Figure 8], ten years younger, an illustrator – and very good looking – who died young, while illustrating James' ghost stories: they holidayed together.) Benson had his view: 'I don't myself think that Monty is at all marriageable' – a term which encodes (and conceals its explicit) meaning clearly enough. Richmond was less sure, and thought he might have been on the verge of marriage before. They agreed that 'these things are mysterious'.[35] They knew that James was celibate, but were fascinated by the question of what sex he wasn't having. This scene vividly captures some of the complexity of sexual self-positioning. Benson himself was celibate, but his embedding in an erotic world with his (mis)recognitions of his own passions makes him feel and express himself quite differently from the celibate James. Celibacy has recently been reclaimed as 'queer', but this is to misrepresent its history as a proclaimed and enacted *virtue*, along with chastity and purity, not least in the late nineteenth century with its purity campaigns. Even Havelock Ellis, of all people, the most influential and shockingly open of

M. R. JAMES

LETTERS TO A FRIEND

FIGURE 8 A turning point in the life of M. R. James (on the right).
He loved James McBryde (far left), who would die young, only four years
after this photograph. In the same year as this posed studio picture was
made, William Stone (in the middle) emigrated to work in the church in
Sri Lanka. M. R. James stayed in Cambridge another seventeen years.

67

sexologists, could write that sexual abstinence is 'a virtue because it is a discipline of self-control, because it helps fortify the character and self'. He would have recognised 'erotic chastity' in Benson.[36] Monty James provides one pole in the ongoing discussion of these men about how to understand their feelings. Not only was he a mystery to his friends for his apparently asexual life – a very different sort of celibacy from Benson's 'productive sexual continence'[37] – but also in contrast with Benson's obsessive talking and writing about desire, James as Provost insisted on no public, or, it seems, private exploration of such ideas. When a serious conversation started in the Provost's Drawing Room, 'The Provost rapped sharply on the table with his pipe', recalled Nathaniel Wedd, 'and called out "no thinking, gentlemen, please."' That is one response to the potentially exposing awkwardness of social life … Oscar Browning liked to declare 'James hates thought.'[38] Unlike the wild and self-destructive Stephen, or the voluble, erotically tortured Benson, Monty James provides a self-concealing, silent refusal of desire at the centre of the institution, a man who writes of ghosts and the texts excluded from the canon of the passion. It is as if he doesn't want to know.

One of his last ghost stories is called 'An Evening's Entertainment' (1925).[39] James contrasts the glassy certainty of modern science with the old days of dark tales, and, as an example, imagines a grandmother, by the fireside, telling her grandchildren of a strange couple who met a grizzly end. A Mr Davies lived in a cottage with a younger man, back in the days: 'One day he came back from market and brought a young man with him' – we will see plenty of stories like this later in this book, though in this case 'nobody seemed to know' what the relationship was. The granny comments, 'Well, now, what did those two men do with themselves? Of course I can't tell you half the foolish things that the people got into their heads, and we know, don't we, that you mustn't speak evil when you aren't sure it's true, even when people are dead and gone.' The younger man, never named, is found hanged from a tree in a strange, white robe, with a bloodied axe beneath him – the two men regularly went together to an ancient chalk-carved man in the hills, to perform, it is hinted, pagan rites – and Mr Davies is subsequently found with his torso hacked apart in the house. The villagers are disgusted and horrified, and bury the men far from sanctified ground – and nobody, the grandmother warns the terrified children, should ever go near the fruit bushes that grow from the still bloody soil. An odd male couple, about whose life together in a cottage one dare not speak, whose bodies are mutilated in mutual death, with a strong hint of pagan affiliations, and who the villagers fear and mistrust and bury – does one need Freud here to wonder what this tale is (not) saying about James himself, his dark (un)thinking, his own haunting, from around the fire? As the ghost-story teller says, 'we know, don't we'... not to speak.

Between ghosts and 'no thinking', James captures how the desire that dares not speak out can haunt a life, not quite silently, however silenced.

It is time for the fourth leading figure of the story, who characteristically has already demanded attention. For if there was one fellow who raised Monty James' hackles it was indeed **Oscar Browning** (1837–1923) (see Figure 9).

Browning was everything James was not and did not wish to be. Flamboyant, gossipy, outrageous,

FIGURE 9 Oscar Browning, depicted as he would have wished, in a portrait from a society magazine – a cartoon and thus a figure of fantasy.

self-aggrandising, proud, social, arrogant, silly, snobbish ... Judgements on O. B. flew around Cambridge and elsewhere. Fred Benson, Arthur's younger brother, called him, sharply enough, a 'genius flawed by abysmal fatuity'; Shane Leslie, more theatrically, called him 'Falstaff playing Hamlet'. Edward Dent, who would become a pioneering professor of music – and is a key figure in Chapter 3 of this book – waxed lyrical: 'The strangeness of the creation of such a man, so fine, so gross, so public-spirited, so mean, so intellectual, so dull, so great, so little, is a perfect mystery ... I cannot defend him and yet I admire him; I cannot respect him and yet I like him ... There is no theory of God which will explain the existence of a man like him.'[40] O. B. published two massive volumes of autobiography – full of self-serving stories – and he became a figure of ridicule and even disdain over his time in King's.[41] Benson at O. B.'s memorial service reflected that there was nobody who really cared that he had died (Browning was twenty-five years older than Benson and had lived his last fourteen years in Rome). Goldsworthy Lowes Dickinson (a contemporary of Benson whom we shall meet shortly) seems at least to have enjoyed writing O. B.'s entry in the *Dictionary of National Biography*: with an amused, plausibly deniable slur that O. B. himself would have loved, he wrote that O. B. 'assisted young Italians, as he had young Englishmen, towards the openings they desired'. Yet it is clear that also for many years his rooms on A staircase were both a hub of social life at King's and a mecca for young men. His room became the stage for the performance of his public persona. He held regular evenings both of serious debate – he was passionate about promoting history as a university discipline – and of raucous music, drinking and partying. Student after student described the shock and delight of the first time they entered those rooms. He was so well known and, even more, notorious in Cambridge, that the student-edited magazine *Granta* self-defeatingly announced that it intended to publish an edition in which it would refuse to mention his name.

As a teacher at Eton, we have seen, Browning travelled with favoured youths, and was blatant about his interests in particular young men, while actively campaigning against sexual immorality in schools. The full scale of the tensions in Browning's personal life have been explored in greatest detail by Ian Anstruther. Browning, bizarrely for a fellow, owned a Turkish bath, where he regularly also went with young men, as, in summer, he frequented the naked bathing pool on the River Cam. 'He was the first tutor to establish an elaborate bath in his rooms and its protocol was observed by a series of boys who served as his attendants in the daily ritual of O. B. as Roman emperor.'[42] As one colleague noted without further comment, O. B.'s 'corpulent person was constantly to be found in the state of primitive nudity'.[43] He also actively worked against the admission of women into the university (or his own circle). As Jane Marcus puts it, with sharp and well-placed disdain, 'Browning held the unofficial Chair of Applied Misogyny at Cambridge for many years.'[44] Most tellingly, for a man who loudly protested his purity with young entitled men in the many cases when it was doubted, O. B. also left thousands of letters to him from young, poor men. Many record small acts of charity, where O. B. provided money to those in need. But, according to Ian Anstruther, who is the only person to have worked through the massive collection, many indicate more physical relationships, and an 'unpleasant homosexual appetite'.[45] John Addington Symonds' encounters with soldiers and others on the streets of London have become iconic for a style of 'a distinctly *urban* queer culture' in the period – where for working-class males, 'Men neither understood themselves, nor were labelled by others, through their choice of sexual partner' to the extent that '[e]ngaging in homosex or an intimate relationship with another man was not incompatible with definitions of masculine "normality"', especially when financially advantageous.[46] Such 'sexual slumming' was called by Oscar Wilde 'feasting with panthers', as we noted in the introduction, and the practice, dwelled on by the lawyer, clearly shocked the jurors in Wilde's trial who were not unreasonably unconvinced by his defence of 'a passion to civilise the community'.[47] For Browning, however, although it was a culture in which he was evidently at home, and he took advantage of it, such interactions were repeatedly imagined through the language of charity, education and social care, rather than the more obviously commercial or hedonistic exchanges of Symonds. ('His ideal was higher than his practice', commented Sir John Sheppard with a knowing dryness.)[48] And Browning conducted this side of his life with immense and open flair. As Anstruther sums up, 'The way in which he continued to collect young men, take them about and show them off after Wilde's imprisonment is quite astounding. Every other man of like temperament fled the country or went to ground at that moment, but Browning – dangerously called Oscar, too – continued to flaunt his inclinations with such an air of innocence that even his enemies were left breathless with astonishment.' Benson – of course – was deeply unimpressed by such showboating: 'It is an awful picture – So greedy, vain, foul-minded, grasping, ugly, sensual a man on the one hand; & on the other, the traces of an old glory about him, like faded and tarnished gilding. A youth, a spring, an energy, a love of beauty – so sweet in themselves, yet harbouring still in this gross & tun-like frame.'[49]

Our first four figures at King's – three from H1, one from A staircase – bring to the fore, first of all, the question of publicity and the love – or vice – that dare not speak its name. J. K. Stephen, not least in his contact with the heir to the throne, struggled between his very public wit and charisma, his necessarily private relationships, and the silencing of scandal that followed his transgressions. Virginia Woolf heard his bellowing as torment, but even his collapse and suicide were carefully edited and repressed by his family. Benson, who obsessed about the dynamics of frankness and discretion, talked and wrote about others' more open and physical relationships, and drew and redrew a map of sexuality on which he could not ever quite find himself. He became a centre of gossip, reflection and serious debate about male desire, especially for younger men as he grew older, while maintaining his own distaste for the fleshliness of physical contact. For him, the boundary of what was concealed and revealed was constantly being renegotiated, not least in the contrast between his diary, his conversations and his public life as an internationally successful author, whose self-image was carefully curated and veiled: it was Benson, after all, who wrote the words for 'Land of Hope and Glory', still sung with flag waving at the last night of the Proms (perhaps a queerer celebration than it knows). Monty James, by contrast, demanded 'no thinking'. He seems to have refused to enter the space Benson inhabited, despite their long friendship. Even when he comes across a story of sexual crisis he can only perform its silencing, precariously: his unwillingness to name Brocklebank summons the ghost of Wilson, friend of Stephen and Symonds. For his friends, his very blankness becomes a source of mystery and imagination: could an internal life really be so unspoken? Browning, however, hid in plain sight. Protesting his innocence, importance and notoriety, he paraded his own nakedness (physical and moral) – and yet his behaviour with young men from the working class remained hidden or at least undiscussed by his contemporaries. Indeed, in a paradigmatic scene for the complex dynamics of revelation, R. C. Jackson, a very minor poet, wrote to Browning after the Wilde trial, unable to name Wilde, but desperate for some sort of comfort after the shocking truths he has heard from Robbie Ross: 'My beloved Browning, today I lunched with Mr. Ross ... & he made terrible things known to me, respecting the person we spoke about ... He appeared to think nothing of such foul enormities, saying "Michael Angelo, Shakespeare, J. A. Symonds, Pater and many others were equally admirers of the same sort of thing".'[50] Browning's reply is not recorded. The 'love that dare not speak its name' is a phrase that conceals very different possible negotiations of expressibility within the same community of men. Without an established vocabulary of male desire for males, each of these men wrote and performed a fugitive discourse, struggling to articulate their sense of self – however flamboyant the performance – in and against the institutional lives they inhabited.

Our fifth star of the Gibbs Building is Arthur Benson's brother, Fred, best known today as **E. F. Benson**, the author of the 'Mapp and Lucia' stories, still a staple of period drama at the BBC.[51] He came up to King's six years after Arthur in 1887, but was quite a different character from his brother. (See Figure 10 and Figure 11.)

He moved into E1. For Nathaniel Wedd (whom E. M. Forster described as 'a cynical, aggressive, Mephistophelean character who affected red ties and blasphemy'),[52] Arthur Benson had been the *arbiter elegentiae* at King's. Wedd divided the college into 'the best set' and

FIGURE 10 Fred Benson at nineteen, between school and college.

FIGURE 11 Fred Benson at twenty-two, now a budding man about town.

'scallywags'. 'The dominant personality in the best set was Arthur Benson. He decided who was, and who was not, to be known, and his word was law in the best circles. His criteria were not those of the ordinary conforming conservative, either in speculation or in the conduct of life. He was, indeed, something of a heretic …'[53] Fred Benson was very much part of the same set as his brother had been, but was involved in a prank which turned violent and became scandalous (something Arthur would have avoided at all costs), and which acted as a catalyst for change in the college's social life. The prank was that the undergraduate Robbie Ross, certainly one of the scallywags, was thrown into the fountain in the front court of the college. He became famous later as the friend and literary executor of Oscar Wilde, and produced the first edition of Wilde's poem *De profundis*, which proved so important for the image of the martyred homosexual in the twentieth century. Ross became ill with pneumonia from his dunking. But the real shock was that the Junior Tutor (what would be called a dean in the United States), one Tilley, was actively involved in instigating the student response to the openly effeminate and aggressively unmanly Ross. (Tilley lived on H staircase too, in the rooms above M. R. James.) This dunking might sound like no more than a homophobic attack, dressed up as student high-jinks. But the boundaries are actually much harder to draw. Fred Benson had already fallen in love with his room-mate in E1, the rather glamorous Vincent Yorke. 'I feel perfectly mad about him just now', wrote Fred in his diary, 'But I hope and believe it will soon be all right. Ah, if only he knew, and yet I think he does.'[54] (Who is in the know?) At school, he had reacted to his

77

sexual feelings for one Glennie rather like his older brother: 'There are some feelings morbid and sensual what next'; 'what it might lead to if indulged I don't dare think'; 'I hope that sometime Glennie will know all that I have felt'.[55] (Who knows, and when ...?) But Fred responded to his father's overbearing Christianity and discipline quite differently from Arthur: he became a leading figure skater – a hobby bound to outrage his evangelical father; he wrote flippant society novels; he holidayed on Capri; he affected to have no knowledge or interest in the church or in religious dogma. His sense of physical pleasure too was quite different from Arthur's. Like E. M. Forster in the Middle East and India, he revelled in the otherness of the Italians he met on Capri: 'They were quite without moral sense, but it was ludicrous to call that wicked. Pleasure sanctified all they did; they gave it and took it, and slept it off, and sought it again. How different from the bleak and solemn Northerners!'[56] This is from a novel, *Colin*, but it is easy to see how this sexualised Mediterranean world would challenge his father's and brother's different views of the order of things, not least in the amusingly naughty use of religious language, especially the idea that pleasure could *sanctify* behaviour (a truly scandalous assertion – 'if it feels good, it's *holy*' – which also mocks the grander aesthetics of Walter Pater's love of the deeply felt moment). When Fred helped throw Robbie Ross in the fountain it was not simply because Ross was a 'homosexual' but for a probably unexpressed mix of motives, including the recognition that he was not the right *sort* of homosexual, was too open, too effeminate, too performatively sophisticated, too foreign (French mother, Canadian father) and wrote

journalism in the student newspaper that was too provocative (he suggested Oscar Browning should be Vice
Provost of King's). And – inevitably – because he went to
the wrong school.

But it is also as a guide to schoolboy life and memories
that Fred Benson is most significant for this history. Fred
Benson wrote novels about schooldays which became
best-sellers during the First World War, as the young
soldiers looked back to an imagined golden and peaceful
era of happiness before the war. His hero, David Blaize,
acts out his innocence in a way which the reader can't
share:

Hughes used to be a ripper, but he's different somehow now.
He asked me the other day if Maddox had become a saint, and if
I'd converted him. What the devil was he talking about? I don't
like Hughes as much as I used. He told some filthy tale in
dormitory the other night, and some of the fellows laughed.
I laughed too. I supposed it was polite, but I didn't see a hang of
what it all meant ... He wanted to explain it to me; came and sat
on my bed and wanted to explain. But just then Maddox came
to bed: he'd been sitting up late working, and he hoofed
Hughes out again in less than no time. It was the day after that
that Hughes asked me if Maddox had become a saint.[57]

David fails even to recognise that Hughes (amusingly
named after the author of *Tom Brown's Schooldays*) is
attempting to lead him towards some sexual activity –
but Maddox saves the day. The reader is encouraged to
respond knowingly.

Benson's display of knowing innocence passed without
comment. The same was not true for other novels of the
era. In the same year, 1916, Alec Waugh's *The Loom of*

Youth caused a scandal. A boy tells his friends that he has been expelled:

"But … what the hell have you been doing?" "Chief's found out all about me and Fitzroy, and I've got to go!"

"But I never thought there was really anything in that," said Gordon. "I thought – ".

"Oh, well, there was. I know I'm an awful swine and all that – Oh, it's pretty damnable; and the Three Cock, too! I believe I should have got my House cap!"[58]

The boy has been engaging in sexual activity with Fitzroy. His friends knew about it, but turned a blind eye or refused to believe it was actually sexual ("I never thought there was really anything in that"). The sex is passed off with insouciance – "I know I'm an awful swine and all that" – but the anguish is reserved for the boy being unable to win his cap at football (the 'Three Cock' is the big game): there is no apparent sense of shame. As he concludes, the punishment is unfair because his school has educated him into what he is: "'Unfair? Yes, that's the right word; it is unfair. Who made me what I am but Fernhurst? Two years ago I came here as innocent as Caruthers there; never knew anything. Fernhurst taught me everything.'" Later in the book, its hero, the once young and innocent Gordon, learns to accept that his room-mate is having an affair and gives him time alone with his lover – and, in turn, asks for time alone himself: we see how the school teaches … Schoolmasters, past and present, and schoolboys, past and present, wrote feverish letters to the press denying that Waugh's book represented any form of truth. Many more bought and read the book. The boy's friends *know* and *don't know* what is going on ("I never thought …"); the boy himself *knows* ("I know …") – but it is knowledge disavowed with a mocking self-judgement; but when the headmaster *knows* ("found out"), the boy must be removed – but he defends himself because it was the school that gave him the *knowledge* he has – which moves the readers to respond with what they know about school sexuality … Who or what is to be *found out*? The epistemology of the college in action.

The literary imagination of schoolboy emotions focused largely on boys among themselves at school, and on the precarious innocence or corruption of such sexuality. Such books were something of a response to 'the later Victorian moral hysteria about schoolboy homosexuality [which] was inseparable from the ideological push to redefine the nature of adolescent citizenship and education'.[59] Edward Lyttleton, at Eton, was only one distinguished teacher who published long pamphlets on how to control the threat of masturbation, and how to inculcate a proper sexual morality in children, as part of his project of reforming education.[60] Typically, Monty James wrote that 'Farrar's *St. Winifred's* had served to form my expectations of school life' – the most mawkish of moralised narratives, to which he seems to have lived up.[61] With a wonderful and predictive self-reflectiveness, Waugh's book describes the reception of Arnold Lunn's brutally unidealistic book *The Harrovians*, which prompted Old Harrovians to write to the papers 'saying that they had been at Harrow for six years, and that the conversation was, except in a few ignoble exceptions, pure and manly, and that the general atmosphere was one of clean, healthy broadmindedness'. The response of the hero of Waugh's book is more aware: 'Gordon fumed. What fools all these people were!'[62] The tension between books like the chaste *St. Winifred's* and the explicit *The Harrovians* made schoolboy fiction a place to angst about the expression of sexual feelings, let alone sexual activity. E. F. Benson was one of the prime figures in this space: he helped form the public imagination of how schooldays should be valued.

But relationships between older and younger men were equally in evidence at school and university – and this needs some careful discussion. Here we can turn to Benson's circle of friends and intellectual colleagues. Howard Sturgis was a great friend of the Bensons, of Monty James – and of Henry James and E. M. Forster (as the network broadens). Sturgis' long-term lover, William Haynes-Smith, was known to everyone in their circle as 'The Babe', and, as I have already mentioned, Fred Benson wrote a novel set in Cambridge student life called *The Babe, B.A.* starring 'a cynical old gentleman of twenty years of age who played the banjo charmingly', and which has a chapter-length parodic description of a fellows' dinner at King's.[63] Sturgis, for his part, also wrote a widely read schoolboy novel, *Tim*, which depicts a sentimental affair between boys at school. Arthur Benson, like Henry James (and unlike Edith Wharton), rather despised its sentimentality, but Havelock Ellis, theorist of sexuality, and another friend of Arthur Benson as well as of Symonds, commented that it was written 'in order that the emotional and romantic character of the [homosexual] relations described may appear more natural'.[64] Ellis, one of the founders of modern sexual psychology, was also being educated by his friends, and by their novels as well as their experiences. (And the 'natural', note, is what is at stake.) The network of writers and readers – novelists, sexologists, teachers, gentlemen about town – spreads and interconnects around a story of how young males desire. It was Sturgis kissing Percy Lubbock when on holiday with Benson, 'a long and lover-like kiss', that prompted from the diarist another outburst of disgust at such 'emotional flirtations' where his friends kept 'making little overtures and whinneyings, like dogs and horses' to each other.[65] Lubbock was twenty-four years younger than Sturgis (and had been at Eton and King's, where he lived in G2) and would go on to edit Arthur Benson's papers, as well as becoming a literary critic of distinction. Percy Lubbock became friends with Howard Sturgis when Lubbock was a boy in Benson's house at Eton. Benson, Lubbock's housemaster and teacher, comments on the potential of such a 'romantic friendship': 'I think it will do him good – he wants sympathizing with.'[66] There is no suggestion that it was in any way inappropriate for a schoolboy of nineteen, as Lubbock then was, to have such a relationship with a much older man under the eyes of his teacher – and the three men remain friends – gossipy, flirtatious, caring – for many subsequent decades (see Figure 12).

But relations between teachers and pupils, as Oscar Browning found out, were generally more worrying. At Rossall School where many of the teachers were 'confused, alarmed and obsessed by sexual matters', it was a rule that 'no master was allowed to have an unaccompanied boy in his room for more than ten minutes at a stretch, during which time the door had to remain open'.[67] So much for attentive pastoral care. As Joe Ackerley later recalled with his brilliantly incisive wit, this set of regulations scarcely controlled boyhood sexuality (let alone 'the

FIGURE 12 Howard Sturgis (b. 1855), A. C. Benson (b. 1862) and Percy
Lubbock (b. 1879) enjoying a gossip in the garden.

school tart'). Yet there were also scientific, medical voices
raised *in support* of relations across the generations.
Following German sexology, Symonds defined himself
as a 'Mittel-Urning or Zwischen-Urning', which meant
the object of his desire was 'healthy young men in the
bloom of adolescence between nineteen and twenty'.[68]
G. Stanley Hall became a new authority with his book
Adolescence (1925), in which he took Socrates as a model:
'[T]o love boys is the key ... All who strive are lovers; and
the only true love is of knowledge and virtue' – and
concluded that 'Attachment for elders or for well-
developed specimens of the same sex' is a social good.[69]
Again and again in the history of H staircase we come
across relationships between students and fellows or other
older men. As we will see, these are often explicitly sought
out by the younger men – though on occasion profoundly

unwanted, sometimes confusedly and temporarily accepted if not welcomed. But they remained integral to college life.

Such accepted relationships – we will see opposition to them later – contrast starkly with the familiar modern liberal insistence on age and status as the determinants of power relations and power relations as destructive of appropriate relationships based on equality – and consequently have raised serious and awkward issues for the history of homosexuality, especially in the educational environment of the university. As Jennifer Ingleheart has discussed most saliently, even with Uranian poets, a group which actively promoted the love of boys, the process of self-definition or cultural recognition is not easily determined: 'The boundaries between Uranian and adult homosexual desires were not as clearly demarcated in the late nineteenth- and early twentieth-century eras ... this may be a politically inconvenient fact for modern gay men, who are understandably keen to distance themselves from damaging imputations of paedophilia, but it remains true.'[70] It might be better to say that when the language of desire has not yet been formalised and institutionalised into its current modern pathology, the range of relationships between men are not collectively referred to as one category ('homosexuality'). Rather, there is a range of difference and calibration that is contingent and situated. A man like Arthur Benson can denigrate desiring choirboys ('a perversion'), while also allowing its potential purity in his friend's case, but would not balk at desiring 'boys', that is, slightly older young males. He wrote about Symonds – a marvellously tortured judgement – that he had 'the courage to bear up against

85

the feeling of being so corrupt and dirty minded'.[71] For others, like Symonds or Edward Carpenter, class (with associations of manliness and physique) might be a determinative factor in the object of desire, but these partners might be referred to also as boys – and these 'boys' might not see themselves as in any way perverse but as decently and fully men. Such categories can slip and need recalibration. And of course, as we will shortly see, many men who found their desires most powerfully addressed towards males, also married and had children – and debated to what degree sexuality could be defined as a singular category according to the object of desire. This fluidity of sexual self-definition and social categorisation of sexuality may seem to some modern readers a surprising characteristic of Victorian and Edwardian Britain. Such are 'the labor pains of a newly public "homosexual identity"'.

What such age distinctions meant was openly discussed at the time, of course. Charles Sayle (1864–1924), a Uranian poet and one of those men who were regular visitors at King's, who had his own 'salon' in Cambridge, had had to leave Oxford not only because of an affair with another boy, but also because he published rather too explicit poetry about it ('I the man fulfilled of sin and shame …', 'What made you kiss me then, Brother and friend as thou art? Ah! I kissed you back again …').[72] He continued to be too open and troublesome in his affairs (Arthur Benson thought) and was regarded by even his friends as rather fussy, boring, with 'an undercurrent of sadness and even dreariness'. He wrote, however: 'We old folk have to learn our lesson not to interfere with the pleasures of the young, not to expect anything of the young, to remember that all things pass' – aged thirty-nine![73] This did not stop him pursuing younger men and, on occasion, girls. Edward White Benson, the severe archbishop father of Arthur and Fred Benson, by contrast, had proposed to his future wife, Minnie Sidgwick, when she was twelve and he was a twenty-three-year-old teacher. The story of the courtship and marriage is deeply unsettling, but the contemporary response to the engagement was unconcerned about the age gap: 'it was rather romantic', commented an aunt, 'there was something very pure and unworldly about such an affection'. What would be denigrated today as grooming is explained as 'very pure and unworldly'.[74] (Minnie Sidgwick's desperately sad description of the wedding night is anything but very pure and unworldly: 'How I cried ... The nights! I cant think how I lived.')[75] Benson was not alone among clergymen in forming such an alliance with a much younger woman, and he became archbishop without any eyebrows being raised about his courtship of a child. With such privileged marriages in the public eye, it was much less surprising that relations between teachers and their younger students could be normalised, certainly in their own eyes.

Michel Foucault, modern maven of sexuality, found an especial delight in the possibilities of anonymised, anti-heteronormative sex with young temporary partners; and generalised this delight:

But two men of noticeably different ages – what code would allow them to communicate? They face each other without terms or convenient words, with nothing to assure them about the meaning of the movement that carries them toward each other. They have to invent, from A to Z, a relationship that is still formless, which is friendship: that is to say, the sum of everything through which they can give each other pleasure.[76]

Nothing could be further from the late Victorian and Edwardian King's College. Older men and younger men spent a long time precisely testing and sharing a vocabulary, a mode of practice, a politics, as the values of one generation were passed on to the next through the institutionalised shared spaces and shared time together – and challenged and changed from within by the younger men. Edwardians were especially aware that the Victorian era was another time, another country, and especially after the First World War, the expectations of Victorian moral certainty could be observed only across an abyss of difference, 'a real gulf, vastly sundering, ... that lies between the two eras', as Fred Benson expressed it: he had, after all, crossed that gulf.[77] Stories of a previous generation's experiences were translated into ready anecdotes and parables and, precisely, codes – and rejected as being out of date. The young man who arrived as a 'boy' at Eton and then King's before the war might become the older man receiving the next generation after the war, as he had been received, a process stretching over decades. The intergenerational interaction, sexual, cultural, intellectual – its dynamics of continuity and change – is absolutely integral to this history of homosexuality. Foucault's relationships are described (and celebrated by him) only from his point of view, and only in the brief moment of their temporary flowering. Even Oscar Browning's manipulative and temporary engagements with working-class youths are framed by long-term relationships, and the group around Benson is deeply enmeshed in their shared histories, shared conversations, shared memories, over time and across the shifting possibilities of positionality such a passing of time demands.

Network theory would help map the complex set of relationships that make up this community: **J. K. Stephen** was friends with **Arthur Benson** and **M. R. James**; all three, from H1, were intimate with **Oscar Browning** who had taken Stephen on holiday; Stephen tutored the prince; Benson edited the prince's mother's letters (to keep the royal connection going); **Fred Benson** dumped Ross in a fountain; Ross was friends with Oscar Wilde, as was Vassall-Phillips who also travelled with Browning, and was intimate with Wilson who was close to Stephen, and celebrated by Symonds. Arthur Benson's mate Sturgis had a lover who provided the name for a Fred Benson novel; Sturgis became close to Percy Lubbock, when Lubbock was a pupil of Arthur Benson: Lubbock went on to edit Arthur Benson's diary (and reputation). Both Bensons were chums with Henry James, who read Sturgis' novel … And so on. The intimate Cambridge college network has links out into the royal family, the royalty of literary culture, the scandal of Wilde, the church, the medical establishment, the musical and theatrical scene. Indeed, the five men on whom I have focused are major public figures: the tutor to the prince, a leading public intellectual, a celebrity academic, a famous and best-selling novelist and the head of two of the most influential educational institutions in the country – an establishment man if ever there were one. Their understanding of intimacy fed into public, national debate. This was a period that was searching for its experts. How was sexuality to be understood and regulated, as it underwent such a sea change

89

thanks to scientific theories, religious tensions and legal interventions? Which authorities were to be trusted? What were the lineaments of self-understanding to be? The fostered, intimate connections of college life became part of the public life of the broader national scene, as the search to find the map of desire for these men became part of how modernity came to understand itself as modern.

This college community, formed across generations by such intergenerational interaction – that is, by the transfer of knowledge, of values, and of the tacit assumptions embedded in the stories as much as in the regulations that make up the tender of social interaction – was especially self-conscious that it stood against the standard normative values of society, and consequently required more than usually acute and careful negotiations of the dynamics of display and publicity, action and concealment. Central to this community was an age discrepancy in many of its most intensely felt relationships – relationships which might, as with Benson and Lubbock, last over many decades. In this asymmetry of age and authority, such relationships did not differ greatly from heteronormative relationships in broader society, and found a ready and privileged model in 'Greek love' – the alibi of classical authority – a model which expected an older man to desire a younger youth. To understand the dynamics of this very particular community, then, we have to appreciate two different but interlinked trajectories: first, how each person saw themselves in time, in a tradition, moving through time, changing: what is it to be of one's generation, of a particular time, of a particular time of life? – an obsessive topic of conversation for the men we have been focusing on. Second, how does the institution itself change over time, and manage its transitions through time? – an equally pressing historical concern for those who inhabited the institution, as it did transform. 'Queer time', if it is to have the richness necessary to comprehend these men's lives, needs this intricate framework of lived experience. Each of these men, with the exception of Stephen who died young, lived through the social changes brought about by the First World War; the transformation in the public recognition of homosexuality, signalled by the Wilde trial and the new vocabulary and institutions of medicalisation of sexuality; and their own transformative dynamics of self-understanding prompted by such broad cultural shifts, as they went through their lives, growing older and changed by experience. And they did it together, talking all the while, and writing in private and to each other, and, through the thickest of veils, in public. This history is what I mean by the discovery of homosexuality.

2

The Politics of Homosexuality

~

But we can also start somewhere else. And this will produce a different narrative and cast of characters. Let me
begin, again, now with **Goldsworthy Lowes Dickinson**
(1862–1932), who was born the same year as Arthur
Benson and Monty James, and was an undergraduate at
the same time as Benson (James who left school at twenty,
the oldest boy ever at Eton, started the year after). Lowes
Dickinson was elected a fellow in 1887, and stayed in
college until his death in 1932, first in H2, on the ground
floor opposite H1, and then on the top floor of
G staircase, where Whitting had lived for many years.
(See Figure 13.)

Nathaniel Wedd, again, summarises with an easy certainty the college's role in Lowes Dickinson's life:
'Dickinson's debt to King's was great. It gave him the
surroundings and the freedom that he needed for his
special development …' (the code is again there, of
course, in 'special development').[1] His rooms in the
Gibbs Building were where Lowes Dickinson held court,
the realm of his influence in college. But Lowes
Dickinson is not like the fellows and students we have
been discussing so far, and this story will take us towards a
far more politicised sense of sexuality, and a more explicit
and enacted sense of physicality, as the twentieth century
advances. Lowes Dickinson may have been born the same
year as Benson and James, but in many ways he looks

FIGURE 13 The young Goldie, sketched by his admiring friend,
Roger Fry.

forward in time in a strikingly different way from either of his colleagues. I have separated the stories into these two chapters: but the fact that they run side by side, in the same space and time, is integral to the complexity of this history.

Goldsworthy Lowes Dickinson left an autobiography, along with some further secret chapters, separately enveloped, which contained material of a sort rarely seen even in more modern autobiographies. E. M. Forster (1879–1970), who was his literary executor and friend for thirty years, wrote a biography of him after reading the manuscript, but left out almost all of what Lowes Dickinson had carefully archived of his sexual past. It was left to Sir Dennis Proctor (1905–83), the fifth of Lowes Dickinson's great loves, and the only one to have been in such a relationship after the autobiography had been written, to publish the whole manuscript in 1973, with a preface by Noel Annan (1916–2000) and his own intimate introduction.[2] Proctor was a senior civil servant, and although he was close to both Guy Burgess, from whom he said he had 'no secrets', and Anthony Blunt, two of the most notorious of Stalin's Cambridge spies, he was cleared of any involvement with spying for Russia. He felt free now, as he explains in his introduction, to be as open and even indiscreet as he wanted to be. The story of Goldie, as he was widely known, who lived in King's for around fifty years, thus comes to us curated by three other fellows of King's, all with homosexual histories of their own.

Lowes Dickinson's politics takes three major forms, none of which would find Arthur Benson or Monty James as sympathetic fellow travellers. First, in his early years, he published *The Greek View of Life* (1896) – yet another turn to the privileged origin of Greek society. J. A. Symonds' *A Problem in Greek Ethics* provides a vivid and salient contrast to the impact of Lowes Dickinson's work. Symonds' provocative essay started life in the 1860s as a private pamphlet, circulated among friends. It was finished around 1873, but not printed until 1883 – and then only in ten copies, which circulated cautiously, hand to hand, among a very selected readership. It appeared as an appendix in Havelock Ellis' seminal book, *Sexual Inversion*, in 1897 (a year earlier in German translation, as a chapter), and as a stand-alone volume finally in 1901, with a subtitle, *Being an Enquiry into the Problem of Sexual Inversion, Addressed Especially to Medical Psychologists and Jurists*. There was no publisher given, as fear of prosecution continued to dog any such discussion, even when explicitly if disingenuously aimed at medical and legal experts. It was not easy for Symonds to speak publicly on this of all subjects, and at each stage his publication was hedged with anonymity, defensiveness and restrictions of readership. For those that were in the know, however, it proved a secret eye-opener, a talisman of knowingness. This very brief history of Symonds' contribution highlights the impact of Lowes Dickinson's work. His was a book published by a respectable house, Methuen, by a Cambridge don; it was addressed to a general public – and indeed went through more than twenty editions in the twentieth century. Its careful discussion of sexuality is embedded in a history of Greek culture and values, and protected by the privilege of the classical and educational framing of the book. It was, however, immediately recognised as inspirational. Goldie went on to make successful radio broadcasts about Plato, and was an instrumental figure in keeping the role of classics at the fore of public life, in a period of increasing challenge to its continuing dominant role in education.

The effect of the book is perhaps best judged by its opponents. G. K. Chesterton, a powerfully influential writer, broadcaster and religious apologist – best known today for his Father Brown detective stories – included his attack on Lowes Dickinson, entitled tellingly 'Paganism and Mr Lowes Dickinson', in his polemical book of 1905, *Heretics*, which quickly went through twelve printings. He was clear about the genealogy of Dickinson's work: it is an example of what was 'preached flamboyantly by Mr Swinburne or delicately by Walter Pater' (the sexual slur of degeneracy is patent, along with the slurring of Swinburne's 'flamboyance' and Pater's 'delicacy', carefully chosen stereotypes of insufficient manliness). This line of writers 'are envied and admired as shamelessly happy when they had only one great sin – despair' (and Oscar Wilde, to complete the roll call of heretics, is also singled out for *his* 'philosophy of despair'). 'Shamelessly' is another pointed adverb, designed to raise the spectre of the shame they should suffer (but don't). But Dickinson causes Chesterton greater concern than his predecessors because he is 'too solid' – not flaky or a mere hedonist like the others he names.[3] This leads Chesterton to construct a long argument in which he not merely defends Christian hope against the empty despair of a *carpe diem* philosophy, but also attempts to deny that the contrast between Christian asceticism and Greek gaiety and pleasure has any purchase at all. This leads him into a historically ludicrous, if exuberant rhetoric of denial: 'I say that St Simeon Stylites had not his main inspiration in asceticism. I say that the main Christian impulse cannot be described as asceticism, even in the ascetics.'[4] This absurd claim is prompted, it seems, by the dangerous persuasiveness of Lowes Dickinson's picture of Greece, where the claim of pleasure – code word for a sexual as well as moral liberty – is deeply threatening to Chesterton. It is indeed 'the Greek view of life' that Chesterton wants to crush. What makes Lowes Dickinson's work intensely political is that it is a public, authoritative, quietly transformative and successful promotion of a perspective so conducive to living a life other than the normative demands of his contemporary British society. 'Greek love' – in various iterations – had been code for male desire for males for many decades: Goldsworthy Lowes Dickinson was an instrumental force in making such language more publicly comprehensible and expressible. He was – eventually – on the radio. No wonder Chesterton ranted, loudly.

The second strand of Lowes Dickinson's political contribution can be expressed more briefly, but is nonetheless important. Goldie was both a pacifist and an internationalist, and he not only wrote about such matters profusely, academically, in policy circles and in the public sphere, but also was actively involved in political process. During the First World War he was a founder member of the Bryce Group which was part of the formation of the League of Nations. He wrote several policy statements for the fledgling international organisation, which is perhaps best seen now as a precursor to the United Nations. His engagement was also motivated by an intense awareness of the social cost of poverty and injustice. His book *Letters from John Chinaman* is a remarkable testimony to his imaginative internationalism. Written in response to the Boxer riots and European attempts to control trade with China, and written as if from the perspective of a Chinese official, the letters were particularly widely read, especially in America. For a short while, it was even wondered if these were actually written by a Chinese official; but even when the author was known, the picture of British imperialism from the other side, as it were, proved extremely provocative. There is quite a tradition of writing social critique as if from the outside – a tradition that goes back to the Greeks who imagined Anacharsis, a wise Syrian, mocking their beloved customs like naked wrestling – but how Lowes Dickinson was an outsider is certainly made more complex by his own self-aware queerness. Lowes Dickinson, like so many of the figures in this history, was a maven of the 'as if'. The *Letters* were written, however, in King's College Garden, he tells us, a comfortable enclave far away from the action they commented on. In a bizarre twist, one early printing of the book had a grotesque portrait of a Chinaman on the cover, which Goldie hated, not least, one suspects, for its racial distortion. It was removed in later editions. The illustrator was G. K. Chesterton.

Lowes Dickinson worked for international peace at a time of passionate commitment to international war, and stood against European colonial violence at a time of jingoistic imperialism. The contrast of this political activity with, say, Arthur Benson, who edited Queen Victoria's letters and wrote the words for 'Land of Hope and Glory', could not be more sharply etched.

The peaceful, polemical socialism of Lowes Dickinson's political activity leads directly to the third political vector. He was good friends with Edward Carpenter, and visited him often and corresponded with him frequently. Carpenter (1844–1929) was a Utopian socialist, who left the comfort of bourgeois life to live in rustic self-sufficiency, backed by an inheritance from his father.[5] He had attended Cambridge, and entered the church; he left the ministry to take up a position as an outreach lecturer in deprived communities, and after a repeatedly restless search for a career, he moved to Milthorpe in Derbyshire, first with his lover Albert Ferneyhough, a scythe-maker, and then for many years longer with George Merrill, a working-class man, twenty-two years younger than himself. There, supported by the financial security of his inherited wealth, he wrote essays lauding the 'simple life', vegetarianism and sexual liberation. A pilgrimage to visit Carpenter became a stop in the journey of would-be literary intellectuals, and, for some – including E. M. Forster, D. H. Lawrence, Edward Dent, Havelock Ellis and the Garden City architect, Charlie Ashbee, all of whom appear in this history – his influence was lasting and significant. Carpenter was a radical, influenced politically by Marxism, and aesthetically and physically by Walt Whitman, though his thinking was eclectic and individual, with a set of long, published manifestos. Carpenter provided one of the key test-cases for Havelock Ellis' pioneering study of homosexuality. For Goldsworthy Lowes Dickinson, Carpenter was someone to talk to, write to, who understood his desire, encouraged its intellectual and physical expression, and allowed him to connect such desires to his political drive. Carpenter offered the possibility of a way of life in which homosexuality was integral and open.

Yet Lowes Dickinson's sexual life was a long-running failure. He called his autobiography 'The curious, passionate, unhappy, ecstatic story of my love and loves'; to a modern critic it was simply 'agony and gloom'. He did not think of himself as a homosexual in his early years. He recalls a scene from his schooldays at Charterhouse that matches the grimmer schoolboy novels but indicates no stimulation or self-recognition from it: 'As I write, there comes back to me a picture, in the room where we changed for exercise, of a bigger boy masturbating against a smaller, amid a crowd of admirers.' It was a much later encounter with a student talking about Plato that turned him towards self-recognition: 'Then, one evening, in a talk with a student of classics, I discovered that the Greek love, as I had read of it in Plato, was a continuous and still existing fact.'[6] 'The Greek View of Life' found its myth of origin here. Throughout his adult life, Dickinson had a fantasy – a fetish, perhaps – about being walked on by men in boots; his first sexual experience was masturbating over his father's shiny boots. He declares in his autobiography that if he cannot fulfil his desire with a man, then masturbation is preferable to a repressed abstinence. (True to his early education, with its paranoia about such things, as a young man he consulted a doctor about the dangers of such a practice. After forty years' experience he feels capable of asserting his own authority: 'I commend it to whoever may have to adapt to the same circumstances' of frustration.) He summed up his desperate failure in a poem, the last two lines of which cry out to himself:

> How could you, so supremely misendowed,
> Hope to attract the sensitive and proud?[7]

But this history of mismatched desires is more complicated than it seems at first sight. His first great love was the artist and art critic Roger Fry (with whom Arthur Benson had edited a student magazine, and who will reappear as a friend of Lytton Strachey's shortly, and then in Chapter 3: Fry moved into G staircase in 1897 and his paintings still adorn many rooms in King's). They bathed naked together, lay on the beach holding hands, and lounged with friends in gardens (see Figure 14).

Later, 'We slept in the same bed. And I recollect him saying to me, as we embraced, should we not go further? I said No, and did not want to. Why? I don't know. I believe I thought it would lower our love.'[8] The level of self-analysis may seem rather jejune here, but it is a programmatic scene. Fry was the first great love. Three further men obsessed him (Proctor, the fifth, is not in the autobiography). Each of these later young men had no interest in sex with males, and later married (indeed his relationship with Fry ended when Fry fell in love with a woman). Two of the four great

Lowes-D.   Dadie   RP   Roger

FIGURE 14 Goldsworthy Lowes Dickinson, with Lytton Strachey, Dadie Rylands, Ralph Partridge and Roger Senhouse, future director of the publishing house Secker and Warburg, and Strachey's last lover, all under the trees again. There are a surprisingly large number of pictures of naked men and, usually separately, naked women, in the archives of Frances Partridge, Dora Carrington and Ottoline Morrell, on the beach, in the garden, by the lakes. But these pictures are too small, too faded or too prurient to print here.

loves were about the same age as himself, the two later men much younger: as we discussed above, age difference and aging are interrelated steps in a trajectory (and Goldie writes movingly of the vexing upheaval of desire experienced as an older man, which exacerbated his melancholic anticipation of failure). With Ferdinand Schiller, physical contact was carefully staged. They went on holiday: 'Every night he kissed me goodnight. And that little ceremony, nothing no doubt to him, was a kind of sacrament to me. The place hangs all in a golden mist in my mind.' He wrote a letter about it to Ferdinand: 'To kiss you is to me a sort of opening of heaven; and to you I imagine a rather tiresome formula' – but never sent the letter, explicit as it was. The story is

similar with Oscar Eckhard and Peter Savary, and as far as
we can tell with Dennis Proctor, who wrote that 'each of us
did our best in his own way to assuage his physical desires'.
Goldie himself reflected, 'Probably, if I had ever loved a
man who returned my love in the same kind, some kind of
sexual intercourse would have resulted.' He felt the loss
deeply: 'I am like a man born crippled', but insisted that
'Whatever I feel about my life, it is not shame or humiliation.'[9] In the forty hand-written pages, marked 'privatissi-
mum' ('absolutely private'), the envelope of his secret
autobiography, he wonders at great length about the state
of his mind and body, and what it is like to have 'a woman's
soul shut up in a man's body'. Esmé Wingfield-Stratford,
who was elected a fellow in 1907 and yet another inhabitant
of H1 and protégé of O. B., is described with marvellous
baroque exuberance as 'an English historian, writer, mind-
trainer, outdoorsman, patriot and ruralist'; as he looked back
after the Second World War, he saw Goldie similarly:
'There was nothing about his personality', wrote
Wingfield-Stratford, 'that you could even remotely have
described as virile. His soul seemed to have got into a male
body by accident.'[10] The idea of a woman's soul in a male
body is taken from the theories of the German sexologist
Krafft-Ebing, but was circulating broadly; it's how Benson
describes Oscar Wilde, for example. The prose of
Dickinson's autobiographical confessions struggles, twists
and turns: he sees his life as 'sometimes tragic, but never
base' and asserts that 'The homosexual temperament must,
I think, be regarded as a misfortune, though it is possible,
with that temperament, to have a better, more passionate
and more noble life than most men of normal temperament
achieve.'[11] In his autobiography, he goes back again and

again over his affairs and other encounters, rereading letters, recalibrating his responses, and rethinking in retrospect his own feelings. Reliving his memories, again and again, and reliving how he had recorded those memories, becomes his response to the present moment. What it means to inhabit time is powerfully on show in this deeply layered, constantly rejudged expression of emotion over time.

It is also remarkable that we can view one of these relationships from multiple perspectives, in a way that is hard for most recorded examples of homosexual desire in the period, even the most intimate. Even more surprisingly, it comes from papers that were extracted by E. M. Forster from the Lowes Dickinson autobiographical archive and returned to Joe Ackerley, and consequently ended up in the library of the University of Texas, and so were never seen by Dennis Proctor. Joe Ackerley became one of E. M. Forster's closest and longest friendships. Ackerley was a prisoner of war during the First World War in a camp in Switzerland, where he came to recognise himself as a homosexual thanks to the robust questions – and follow-up bibliography – from Arnold Lunn, who was – those were the days! – organising skiing lessons for the POWs. Lunn, it may be recalled, wrote the scandalous schoolboy novel *The Harrovians*, which the hero of *The Loom of Youth* acknowledged as a good picture of the sexuality of boarding schools – though Lunn eventually converted to Catholicism and became a supporter of the Nationalists in the Spanish Civil War and of Mussolini's fascism. Lunn cut through Ackerley's tortured self-doubts and allowed him to name himself clearly and assuredly. When Ackerley returned to England and started publishing, Forster read some of his poems, befriended him and became something of a literary mentor. He encouraged Ackerley to have his first play, based on his experiences in the Swiss POW camp, published and staged, a play which was heralded as the first homosexual drama on the London stage (the cast included Robert Harris and Daniel Massey, but despite good reviews did not survive its transfer to the West End: it was staged and published finally in 1925). One of the most ecstatic reviews was from Hugh Walpole, who had been in Arthur Benson's circle in Eton and Cambridge, an object indeed of Benson's erotic fantasy: Walpole recognised the tense and dangerously expressive male relationships in the play all too well. Ackerley had previously shown his plays and poems to Benson, then Master of his Cambridge College, Magdalen, but Benson – we are here back in June 1920 – had replied with a typical anxiety about Ackerley's rawness: his work 'goes almost too deep into life & touches on a region that is hardly safe to visit'. 'Hardly safe' is a wonderfully Bensonian expression for his anxiety about the public display of emotion. 'Most people', wrote Benson, 'go to a play or a book for beauty and comfort & for illusion rather than for truth!'[12] Through Forster, Goldsworthy Lowes Dickinson met, fell in love and started a friendship with Ackerley. On their first private meeting, they sat and discussed '"the" subject' all afternoon. For the first time, Goldie was powerfully attracted to someone homosexual. 'Joe, of course,' he noted sadly in his diary, 'could not have passion, nor what one calls "love" for me.'[13] And he retreated to read and reread the poems he had written after his unconsummated affair with Ferdinand Schiller (typically reliving past feelings and his response to them as a guide to and distraction from his present). Both men write to Forster about the relationship. Ackerley, who was very attractive, was used to being pursued, and used to having flings, especially with working-class strangers, as well as 'the sort of hopeless muddle into which [his] love-affairs invariably tumbled'. In this case, the combination of Lowes Dickinson's diffidence, age – he was in his sixties – and expectation of disaster made the let-down easy: 'He managed to sublimate it', wrote Ackerley calmly, 'as he sublimated all his unreciprocated passions.'[14] Forster, Lowes Dickinson and Ackerley continued to confide in each other: another triangle in the network was formed, and rehearsed over time in shared anatomies of feeling and experience. It was thanks to Ackerley, who was then working at the BBC, that Lowes Dickinson made his radio shows about Plato – an unexpected case of failed love turned into art.

In the eyes of Goldsworthy Lowes Dickinson, homosexuality could be seen as a question of social oppression and the misjudged values of a repressive society, in and against a broader set of political principles and commitment to social justice. Homosexual desire was, for him, not just a question of personal formation, but an issue of changing society. As he wrote in the *Independent Review* as early as 1905, 'Our law on that matter [homosexuality] is a mere survival of barbarism, supported not by reason but by sheer prejudice.' The trouble was that in his personal life his frustrations, intimate failures and emotional anxieties took centre stage. His political activity was directed, committed and instrumental – but did not have purchase on his private pain. This tension remained unresolved and quietly agonising.

Lowes Dickinson's connection of sexuality and socialism did not go unnoticed outside his circle. Beatrice
Webb, one of the founders of the Fabian movement,
who regularly visited the Arts and Crafts community of
Charlie Ashbee, which we will shortly encounter, was
deeply suspicious (has there ever been a socialism without
such infighting?): 'There is a pernicious set presided over
by Lowes Dickinson', she complained, 'which makes a
sort of idea of anarchic ways in sexual questions – we
have, for a long time, been aware of its bad influence on
our young Fabians' (see Figure 15).[15]

Lowes Dickinson had written on anarchism, so her
adjective 'anarchic' was not just panicky but carefully

FIGURE 15 Goldie as guru, in his familiar cap, in his austere
office, writing.

106

chosen. The threat was that young Fabians may have their heads turned by an older man, up on G staircase: the heady brew of age difference, sexuality, education is once more disruptive, not so much to ethics as to proper political commitment. (We will see the case of such a young Fabian shortly.) Could you be a good socialist and follow Lowes Dickinson's sexual hopes? Could you be a good socialist, Lowes Dickinson might have replied, and not aim to change sexual politics?

Lowes Dickinson remained hard for his peers to evaluate. Shane Leslie, outspoken Irish diplomat, tried to capture the strange mix of political passion, hesitancy and personal charisma when he writes that Lowes Dickinson 'sought to remedy the maddening world he would not face' – though Leslie might be striving too hard for a *bon mot*.[16] It was partly through talking *about* 'Goldie', as much as with him, that students felt inspired. Lowes Dickinson named Oscar Browning as a particular influence on him (hard though it is to trace), and was himself a huge influence on his own and the next generation of students and colleagues at King's College. The construction of tradition needs its performed recognitions, its proud genealogy. **Charlie Ashbee** (1863–1942), an undergraduate who came up two years after Lowes Dickinson, became lifelong friends with him (see Figure 16).

When Ashbee graduated, he reflected on his group of friends' lives to come, and called Goldie 'the soul of us'.[17] Ashbee was the son of a famous collector of pornographic literature, with whom he fell out to the point of cutting off communication. Ashbee, through Goldie, was devoted to Edward Carpenter, and, influenced by the call to a 'simple life', became a major figure in the Arts and Crafts and in

FIGURE 16 Ashbee – young, artistic, dashing – in a photograph taken in Chicago by Frank Lloyd Wright.

the Garden City movements. He studied as an architect and city planner with Bodley, who had designed the buildings flanking the back court of King's College, and became involved with preservation and heritage in London. He too established a communal, rustic community, in Chipping Campden, a very Home Counties Cotswold village, a project which eventually failed. His impact in the world was particularly significant, however, as the first civic advisor of Jerusalem under the British Mandate, and the current city layout and regulations for building there owe a great deal to Ashbee's ordinances, many of which are still in place. Ashbee went to America to spread his particular brand of romantic socialism, and discovered a special love for the Chicago waterfront's 'creativeness ... buoyancy [and] exhilaration', which moved him, he said, more than any view, except ... standing on the back bridge of King's College. After years at a hated school, when Ashbee entered King's, 'the gates of Paradise opened before him'.[18]

On one day – a paradigmatic scene of how the lines of influence are carefully drawn and redrawn – Carpenter invited Ashbee to hear a lecture he was giving to the Fabians in London, and to bring Lowes Dickinson with him. It was, recorded Ashbee, 'a day to be written down on the tablets of ones memory & never to be forgotten'. The meeting itself was fiery, with calls for Revolution, and discussions of who would be the first to be hanged when the 'coming Revolution' came – but they were also introduced to the legendary William Morris by Carpenter. As they walked towards the station in the dark afterwards, Ashbee and Lowes Dickinson were reflective: '"And what do you think of it all?" I asked him, as soon as we were alone. "I don't know" he said: "I don't seem to feel any forrader [sic] with Socialism – do you?", "I don't know", I replied "but I believe I am more clear about one or two things – though as to the whole ... well ...!"'[19] The young men – it is January 1886, and they are in their young twenties – are struggling between their desire for change and the comfort of their privilege, between the need for social transformation and a resistance to violence. Lowes Dickinson's commitment to the politics of peace, and Ashbee's to civic restoration, are already taking shape in and against the lure of Carpenter's more radical charisma.

Unlike Lowes Dickinson, Ashbee had a more physical and experimental sex life, which was, as far as we can tell, primarily with working men, and his Arts and Crafts workshop took on several good-looking fellows whose artistic skills were not the greatest, which might have been a factor in the community's eventual financial failure. But unlike all the characters we have been discussing so far, Ashbee decided to marry. In 1897, the thirty-five-year-old designer met seventeen-year-old Janet Forbes, and proposed to her very quickly (see Figure 17).

He wrote to her with surprising candour that 'Comradeship to me so far – an intensely close and all absorbing personal attachment, "love" if you prefer the word – for my men and boy friends, has been the one guiding principle in life.'[20] 'Comrade' and 'comradeship', words taken from Walt Whitman, were the common contemporary words to indicate homosexual attachment (which overlapped easily with political values in romantic socialism), but remained terms between homosexuals rather than common parlance. This was as explicit as he could be expected to be (and more so). As he added, 'These things are hard to write about.' He hoped she would understand when he says 'there are many comrade friends, there can be only one comrade wife'. It is pretty clear she had no idea of what he was talking about or what the consequences might be. In her diary she wrote:

FIGURE 17 Janet Ashbee in Arts and Crafts gear.

'Neither of us will, I firmly believe, ever be "violently in love" ... I expect we shall make the soberest, staidest, most gravely comic pair of lovers the sun ever looked on!'[21]

On the wedding night, he kissed her fondly and went off to write a letter to his mother about how he would always love her more than anyone else alive. After seven years of unconsummated marriage, though an excitingly transformative time for her in the Chipping Campden community, Janet fell in love with a married man, Gerald Bishop, who reciprocated her feelings; but both, committed to duty and morality, would not allow their relationship to reach any sexual fulfilment. The relationship dragged on painfully for three years. Perhaps unsurprisingly, Janet had a mental breakdown. The build-up is anguishing to read as the earlier excitements of marriage and her husband's artistic community collapse slowly into articulate despair at the lack of physicality in their relationship. In a long and tormented entry to her diary, she recognises his sexuality, her needs and the tension that her continuing but challenged love for him brings: 'With all his affection for me, and the lively and delicious understanding between us, he has I know not the slightest physical desire for me ever. It is like asking a horse to be a stag ... some price must be paid for marrying an abnormal man. And it is worth oh how much!' Her distraught pain at not being a full woman (as she herself puts it), along with her continuing powerful feelings for her husband, struggles against the possibility of sex with her lover, which is expressed shamefacedly as animality: 'The sacrifice of the animal to the spiritual, in me, *by myself*, alone, in silence, must be better and saner than the open sacrifice, for nothing, of the whole being, grovelingly begging for an impossible boon to be thrown to the animal part.' But she is agonisingly desperate for the physical experience: 'Oh how many years would I not give to know it even in its brutal completeness.'[22] Faced by his wife's misery, Charlie responded – at last – with understanding and sympathy, and, after Janet slowly recovered,

FIGURE 18 Janet Ashbee and her daughters, in Israel, posed for posterity and amusement.

they had four daughters in rapid succession (see Figure 18). (Charlie had wanted boys, his daughter recalled.)

The intimate dynamics of such a relationship are fascinatingly revealed in their diaries and letters – and show a shared personal honesty deeply at odds with the public morality that had led to the crisis. After Janet had had a child, Charlie described to his wife picking up a young guardsman on the Strand (he knows it is a cliché) – it was after a King's College celebration dinner – and taking him off on a walking holiday in France. She replied that she cannot deny shedding a tear over his letter, but concludes that because he had been so good to her over her difficulties previously, she gave his holiday romance her blessing: 'I confess I had a few tears this morning over the description of your lover. But I can never repay your understanding and generosity of 5 years ago, save "in kind", with counter-understanding when *you* want *your* romance. So bless you both.'[23]

This picture of an Edwardian marriage, finding some form of accommodation – 'counter-understanding' is a fine word for it – between a homosexual man and a woman coming to terms with her own needs and feelings is remarkable. Janet Ashbee kept a private journal from 1895 to 1908; there are commonplace books she kept, and a book of letters during the affair with Gerald Bishop; there are letters she wrote to her husband. There is even an unpublished novel, *Rachel*, which was written 'as a kind of healing after her love affair'.[24] What is more, there is a long account of the marriage by her daughter – which, like all children's accounts of their parents' marriage, is both profoundly intimate and deeply partial (not least as one of four daughters, with an eye constantly on her sisters in the family dynamics). The self-consciously provocative and experimental relationships of Vanessa Bell, Dora Carrington, Duncan Grant and other members of the Bloomsbury Group have been assiduously described and celebrated as transgressive exceptions to bourgeois norms, but such detailed portraits are far less common for the apparently traditional marriages which homosexual men increasingly conducted as a retreat from public scrutiny, especially as the legal machinery tightened after the Labouchère amendment, which criminalised 'gross indecency', and the Wilde trial. The marriage of Charlie and Janet Ashbee not only provides a lengthy, multi-perspectival narrative of how such a marriage could become over time a sympathetic and intimately shared partnership, but also gives us – for once in this history – a complex, sophisticated and insightful female perspective on such a family.

Ashbee's most influential book is *Where the Great City Stands* (I happen to have his personal copy, which I found, unvalued, in a second-hand book shop). It sums up his vision of a new urban future, which was deeply influenced by Edward Carpenter and by his conversations with Goldsworthy Lowes Dickinson. Unlike many idealists in this era, he worked to bring his vision about. The education of working-class men, the reduction of poverty and the integration of work into the fabric of a better life – material and social – were basic to this project. (William Morris is another obvious influence: already as an undergraduate Ashbee is promoting 'honour for the man, dignity for the work', and asking 'Would not this be a good basis for the art of our Democracy?' – all very Morris principles.)[25] He worked with boys and young men in the East End of London, while campaigning vigorously on architectural preservation and Garden City policy; after the failure of Chipping Campden, he moved to Egypt to a post in education, from where he took up his position in the administration in Jerusalem (his family followed him there and the perils of the journey, including using a potty on the railway platform, are beautifully recorded through a child's memory, eighty years later, by Felicity, his second daughter). In Jerusalem he both rebuilt the *suk*, the medieval market, and fitted it out with shops and small workrooms, because he wanted to enable a system of apprenticeships to revivify the arts and crafts of the city. He celebrated the success of the boys' training with a public ceremony (see Figure 19).

As with Lowes Dickinson, Ashbee's homosexuality was not merely a personal matter, but intimately tied into a political and social vision, a tempered version of

Weaving Apprentices' Ceremony of Indenturing.   No. 63.

FIGURE 19 The official, public transcript of the ceremony of indenture in the *suk*: the Westerners are on the right, the locals on the left, dramatising social difference all too clearly.

Carpenter's commitment to a 'human society defined by a shared sexual preference'.[26] Unlike Lowes Dickinson, Ashbee seems to have managed to link the romantic and the socialist with a degree of precarious harmony.

One man who visited Ashbee in Egypt was **E. M. Forster**, who had been an undergraduate at King's starting the year after Ashbee finished (1897), and who returned after the Second World War to a fellowship which lasted until his death in 1970.[27] Forster lived on A staircase, next to where Oscar Browning's rooms had been, for twenty-four years. Forster, as we have seen, was the executor of Lowes Dickinson's literary estate, and was close friends with him for many years. His novel *Maurice* was published posthumously, and academics have since researched Forster's life fully.

Consequently, the pattern of his sex life, and the details of his long chatty engagement with Ackerley and others, have been studiously set down, and his novels have been sedulously mined to see how his mantra of 'only connect' might have found a queer expressivity in his fiction – described most insightfully as a tension between Symonds' view of elite, Plato-inspired, Greek love and Carpenter's outdoor, socialist, Whitmanesque passion. He was not untypical in coming to a full sexual experience quite late in life, nor – as we have seen – in his middle-class taste both for working-class men and for foreigners, especially in the Middle East and India. (Christopher Isherwood claimed himself to be a typical homosexual of such a background in that he 'couldn't relax with a member of his own class or nation. He needed a working class foreigner.')[28] Forster's affairs with the dodgy police-man Harry Daley and then, over many years, with the reliable and married policeman Bob Buckingham, in whose house he died, ran through his life outside King's and gave him the emotional security from which to advise friends like Joe Ackerley (often uselessly) about his affairs with men from the London demi-monde. Where Lowes Dickinson and Ashbee turned to international relations, city planning and social activism as a political expression of their response to Carpenter and the world they saw around them, Forster for his part embodied an aesthetics of the personal in his fiction – which had a social thrust, for sure – but followed a public life that was withdrawn, notwithstanding his appearances in the press and on the radio. The politics of homosexuality took on a repressed but purposive form of public engagement around the value of personal relationships against social conventions and regulation. So his political essays collected in *Two Cheers for Democracy* were regarded as a significant enough manifesto for liberalism to be made a set book when I took my public English exams (A levels) in England in the 1970s, though, by the same token, his famous, provocative sentence, 'If I had to choose between betraying my country and betraying my friend, I hope I should have the guts to betray my country', is scarcely 'a kind of motto of the Cambridge spies for Stalin' – who may have betrayed their country, but had little truck with Forster's sense of *friendship*'s political claim.[29]

This sense of withdrawal is evident in the picture we have of Forster from the people around him, at least from those who were not in his immediate circle of gay men. It was not for nothing that Lytton Strachey nicknamed him 'Le taupe', 'The Mole'. The circle itself, despite his relationships with Buckingham and the artistic world of London, was also part of the long tradition I have been discussing: when Forster first met Henry James, latest novelist with the old master, they discussed Queen Victoria's letters, edited by Arthur Benson, Cambridge doyen and great friend of James. (Disconcertingly, though divertingly enough in the light of current debates about pronouns, James referred to Victoria with masculine pronouns throughout the conversation.)[30] Charles Sayle was delighted by Forster's first published short story which he summed up to Maynard Keynes in the bluntest of smutty descriptions – and as a sign of the direction the college was taking: 'Oh dear, oh dear is this Young King's? ... B[uggered] by a waiter at the Hotel, Eustace commits bestiality with a goat ... In the subsequent chapters, he tells the waiter how nice it has been and they try to b[ugger] each other again.'[31] So much for Forster's discretion. But the public Forster prompted innuendo to match his discretion. So, to the robust F. R. Leavis, a critic full of severe moralism, Forster's novels displayed 'a curious spinsterish inadequacy in the immediate presentation of love' – it's not hard to sense a nasty suggestiveness in such a judgement.[32] Even closer colleagues hummed and hawed. Martin Bernal (1937–2013), notorious now for his book *Black Athena*, who met Forster in King's when Bernal was a young fellow, states that 'He never "came out"', but adds, 'Everyone who thought about it, and certainly all his friends, knew his preferences' ... 'He was discreet ... He kept his homosexual books on a shelf above his bed in the bedroom which others seldom entered' (though Bernal clearly wants you to think he has). Yet, despite their daily meetings, 'Morgan ... never mentioned his homosexuality in front of me.'[33] Forster's discretion was specific to the company he kept. He spoke to those that knew. By contrast, Tim Leggatt, who was Senior Tutor of King's when I came up as an undergraduate – and died while I was writing this – travelled on holiday with Forster when he was a student (an echo of Oscar Browning's days), lived on A staircase at Forster's invitation, and spent long hours together with him, discussing both Forster's feelings and Leggatt's own messy relationships with several women.[34] At the end of the twentieth century, Noel Annan, former Provost of King's, could still write proudly of 'the King's ideal of dons and undergraduates treating each other as equals and learning from each other'.[35] To contemporary educational ideology, of course, that is likely to seem at best outmoded and at worst a self-deceiving and tarnished ideal. For Leggatt and Forster, it was friends of different generations sharing their stories from different perspectives and for different sorts of explorative learning.

In his diary, Forster was explicit about what happened to such young men if they left King's for National Service – they would come back 'coarsened, begirled, and lost, unless the feeling in me has struck a spark in him'. He could be scabrously ironic about his loneliness: 'This masturbational eroticism has had its conveniences. At all events I don't go hanging around urinals or showing my aged genitals to girls.' He was clear too about what he wanted, and its relation to his own writing: 'I want to love a strong young man of the lower classes and be loved by him and even hurt by him. That is my ticket, and then I have wanted to write respectable novels. No wonder they have worked out rather queer.' (That last phrase is a gift to contemporary criticism.) And explicit about what was at stake for him: 'In the best love-making I have known there has been a sort of laughter and the most violent embrace gets softened by it.'[36] To Leggatt, unlike Bernal, he was certainly explicit – and Leggatt's is rare in being a generous account of what it might be like as a young straight man to be the object of the affection and desire of a much older gay man. Leggatt quotes Forster summing up his discretion to others movingly: 'when I am nearly eighty-five how *annoyed* I am with society for wasting my time by making homosexuality criminal. The subterfuges, the self-consciousnesses that might have been avoided.'[37] It is so tellingly expressive of Forster's perspective, politics and style that he could encapsulate a lifetime of fear of prosecution and humiliation, along with the anguish of his consequent personal emotions, as *annoyance at a waste of time*.

Maynard Keynes came up from Eton to King's as an undergraduate in 1902, the year after Forster graduated.[38] His rooms as a fellow were first in F5 in the Gibbs Building but he eventually moved into the newly built Webb's Court, P staircase, a building which has Monty James' initials as a blazon on it, as it was completed during his provostship (even James was not above some self-memorialisation). As with Forster, Keynes' life has been anatomised at considerable length, including a celebrated three-volume biography, by scholars fascinated not by his discretion, for sure, but by the extraordinary range of his achievements and the connections between his seminal economic theory and his time as a student, fellow and Bursar in King's, as well as his artistic life in Cambridge and London. Keynes had recognised himself as a homosexual at school, where he had an intimate relationship first with Dillwyn Knox (who came up to King's before Keynes) and then with Gerald Balfour, the brother of the future prime minister. Lytton Strachey tells with shocked delight the story of how Keynes at school had been naked in an embrace with the naked Knox, when a younger boy called Young burst into the room, and immediately fled. Keynes was never sure what the boy had seen or made of it. All three – Keynes, Knox and Young – were now at King's, noted Strachey with a happy sense of others' social discomfort. Keynes was sexually rapacious, from his student days. From his early years in Cambridge, with an all-too-precise intimation of the economist he was to become, he kept careful records, two ledgers, one which itemised a list of his lovers, often anonymous hookups in London ('lift boy', 'young American near the British Museum'), and the other containing a list of each of the acts committed, carefully registered and counted (expressed in a code – c, a, w – that nobody is completely sure they understand); each list is carefully formulated in rows with dates, a dispassionate accounting of sex.

Keynes thought himself to be physically 'repulsive' – a view not challenged by Virginia Woolf's description of him as 'a gorged seal, double chin, ledge of red lip, little eyes, sensual, brutal, unimaginative'.[39] But Keynes was at least tall and could scan crowds for likely partners. Jack Sheppard, the future Provost of King's whom we will meet soon, was considerably more hagiographic – but he was one of Keynes' lovers: 'my memory is first of sensitive, expressive hands and of the beauty of his eyes. His mouth had not as yet, for me, the subtle charm, nor his pose the easy grace of later years.'[40] From pictures, it is easier to credit Woolf's nasty vision than Sheppard's tinted spectacles. Lytton Strachey, whose *Eminent Victorians* was a watershed in the dynamics of openness and (in)discretion in telling a life story, was bitterly cruel about Keynes' economist approach to sex: 'He brings off his copulations and speculations with the same calculating odiousness; he has a boy with the same mean pleasure with which he sells at the top of the market.'[41] But Strachey, 'sunk in the isolation of timid chastity', was not only a close friend of Keynes, with whom he fought with bouts of violent dismissal on Strachey's side – they spent so much time together at King's that Strachey was believed to be at King's – but also he was a rival with him for the affections of various young lovers.[42] Strachey could and did write excoriatingly about his friend: 'Looking back I see him, hideous and meaningless, at every turn and every crisis, a malignant goblin gibbering over decisions that are not his own.'[43] Keynes was happy to enrage Strachey by writing to tell him he had finally seduced Arthur Hobhouse, whose affections and body they both were competing for (his 'yellow hair was the brightest thing about him').[44] Virginia Woolf also spread the rumour that Hobhouse later slept with Rupert Brooke. Keynes and Strachey were both in the Apostles where 'It was obligatory to make the humorous assumption that all sexual relations were homosexual ones, so that even heterosexual love had to be treated as only a special case of the higher sodomy.'[45] The overlap between the Apostles and the incipient Bloomsbury Group was marked also in its shared values. 'The word bugger was never far from our lips', reminisced Virginia Woolf.[46] When Keynes came back from India to Cambridge he wrote with delighted and performative surprise to his most intimate and long-term lover, the artist Duncan Grant, that 'practically everyone in Cambridge ... is an open and avowed sodomite'.[47] Beyond the exaggeration, the student showing-off and the gestures of knowing transgression, recognising a gay community was a bold and desired aim; breaking the silence in shared disclosure a relief; challenging disavowal and secrecy a self-recognition of a modernity to set against Victorian demands.

One person who became a guru of open sexuality – and was prosecuted for it – was nonetheless performatively horrified by Keynes' openness, which has, in turn, prompted speculation by modern critics about whether his fervid protests were protesting too much. D. H. Lawrence, after a visit to Cambridge, wrote: 'I simply can't bear it. It is so wrong, it is unbearable. It makes a form of inward corruption which truly makes me scarce able to live ... Deep inward dirt – a sort of sewer – deep in

men like K[eynes]. and B[irrell]. and D[uncan]. G[rant] ...
I could sit and howl in the corner like a child. I feel so bad
about it all.'⁴⁸ The passion of Lawrence's denunciation –
howling like a child – is at very least testimony that
Keynes' willingness to provoke was successful.

At the same time that Lowes Dickinson (twenty-one
years older) and Forster (four years older) were struggling
with any possibility of indiscreet self-exposure, Keynes,
who was, of course, the most politically influential
Kingsman of his and pretty well any other generation,
both through his theories and through his work in
Whitehall, was happily and robustly breaking the law on
a regular basis and, to his friends at least, openly parading
his behaviour. Keynes later married the Russian ballerina
Lydia Lopokova, as Duncan Grant lived with Vanessa
Bell. These relationships, like Ashbee's with Janet
Forbes, were emotionally and socially complex, and not
just politically expedient conveniences. Angelica Garnett's
pithy summary – Grant was 'a homosexual with bi-sexual
leanings' – is trivialising of such dynamics (though she had
her reasons not to look too closely: Grant was her father,
and she married one of his lovers, Bunny Garnett, who,
shockingly, had been present at her birth, where he
declared his intention of marrying the newborn child).⁴⁹
The experience of sexuality over a lifetime is one of
transformation, not essence.

In contrast to Lowes Dickinson, Ashbee and, even in
his quiet way, Forster, there is little sign that Keynes, the
most instrumentally powerful politician of this quartet,
saw a politics in his homosexuality, except in his successfully displayed resistance to its criminality – a resistance
which was, in reality, a pursuit of satisfaction rather than a

reasoned position about social oppression or ethical norms. For Keynes, one suspects, it was more a case of making sure that his sexual demands created supply.

Keynes' academic career was articulated significantly against the work of his slightly older colleague at King's, **Arthur Pigou** (1877–1959).[50] Pigou came up to King's from Harrow in 1896 to read history with Oscar Browning – who was a mentor till they fell out over some trivial matter and barely spoke for decades – and then read Moral Sciences for Part II of his degree under the influence of Goldsworthy Lowes Dickinson. But his two greatest gurus were Arthur Marshall, who is still lauded as the founder of modern economics (he gave his name to the economics library in Cambridge), and Henry Sidgwick, the philosopher after whom the Cambridge Humanities campus is named. (Sidgwick was also the brother-in-law of Edward White Benson, and thus uncle to Arthur and Fred Benson – to keep the story in the family ...) Pigou was a brilliant young man who won a string of academic prizes both at Harrow and at Cambridge, including the Chancellor's Medal for English Poetry, and who was Marshall's chosen successor. He was elected as a fellow at King's in 1902 on the recommendation of Marshall – he moved into H staircase in H4 – and to the chair of Political Economy when he was only thirty years old in 1908, an election that Marshall engineered aggressively (to the dismay of some of his colleagues) – and part of the deal seems to have involved suggesting to Keynes' father, who was on the appointments committee, that a lectureship for Maynard – which duly followed – would be the payoff for electing Pigou. (It's a typical and unedifying story of academic gerrymandering.) Pigou is today returning into fashion as a founder not just of welfare economics but also of eco-economics; the idea that the damage of pollution, for example, should be controlled through aggressive taxation is associated with his name. But Keynes and the Keynesians argued fiercely and tellingly against Pigou's theory of unemployment, and he quickly found himself – bitterly – criticised and eventually marginalised as old-fashioned and methodologically weak, though his appointment had been made thanks to an insistence on precisely his empirical skills and methodological sophistication. Pigou became something of a recluse, grumpy, badly dressed, unsocial, writing fierce letters to *The Times* from his retreat in the Lake District, and '[h]e was addicted to an extraordinary burlesque jargon, part Victorian, part home-made, which was often accompanied by an indefinable foreign accent' – an exacerbation of the eccentricity that even his friends had noted from his schooldays onwards (see Figure 20).[51]

Pigou was one of those boys who knew well enough what the Harrow pupils got up to at school, but from a distance (he says, properly). In King's, Pigou fell in love repeatedly, and often hopelessly. 'P. always has a passion at hand', noted Benson in his diary with customary acid (as if he himself was not prone to the same infelicity). Keynes summed him up to Strachey as 'very nice but a little depressed and lovelorn'.[52] Over his fifty-seven years as a fellow of King's, Pigou went on holiday with Sheppard; climbed with Mallory – the beloved of Arthur Benson among others – and played chess with Alan Turing. He was renowned for his dislike of women, a distaste which, as with J. K. Stephen's views, went beyond

FIGURE 20 Pigou as a young man, on the cusp of great things.

even the difficult norms of the homosocial society he lived in. Even his laudatory obituary admitted 'He reveled in misogyny', and added that when, aged nearly seventy, he was kissed by Lydia Lopokova in thanks for his obituary of her husband Keynes, it was the first time he had been kissed by a woman other than his mother.[53] He praised his retreat in the Lake District, where he indulged his

127

obsession with mountaineering, for its 'fresh eggs and all-male' environment (the housekeeper, 'The Queen' – Miss Jackson – didn't count). A coach-tour driver pointed out this cottage as the home of 'the famous heconomist and woman-'ater'.[54] His affair with an undergraduate, Donald Corrie – Pigou was already a fellow – was one of those that prompted Keynes to write that Pigou's relationships with boys were becoming a scandal (even to Keynes, it seems). Benson was shocked that Pigou left a dinner party to walk Corrie home: 'Pigou is a fool; these romantic attachments may do great good both to the inspirer and the inspired, but they should be conducted with some seemliness and decorum.'[55] As always, Benson likes the idea of men and younger men having intense relation-ships, but only if nobody knows and the utmost public decency is preserved. Benson may not have been aware that Corrie and Pigou were living together in Pigou's rooms, with a single bedroom and a single bathroom. The economic historian Charles Fay describes them both fussing and giggling around the room, and notes with a raised eyebrow that they were known as 'Mr and Mrs Pigou' in college. By 1918, Corrie was Secretary to the London Office of the Imperial Munitions Board, and Pigou was trying to recover from the horrors he had witnessed in the First World War. Fay continues: 'World War I was a shock to him, and he was never the same afterwards.' His friend H. G. Johnson wrote: 'what he saw sickened him. There can be no doubt that this experience was responsible for transforming the gay, joke-loving, sociable, hospitable young bachelor of the Edwardian period into the eccentric recluse of more recent times.'[56]

FIGURE 21 Philip Noel-Baker, the British hope at the Olympics, and future politician and peace campaigner, beloved of Pigou.

Pigou also fell heavily for Philip Noel-Baker (see Figure 21), who went on to win the Nobel Prize for Peace, after an Olympic medal for athletics, and to become a noted politician in the post-war Labour Government, along with Hugh Dalton, another lovelorn man in the same circles of King's.

Pigou was devastated when Philip Baker (as he then was) became engaged to Irene Noel, one of Virginia Woolf's friends. He was terrified that she would not let them be friends any more and that he would be deserted and on his own. Pigou was thrown into an emotional crisis that reveals just how deeply his feelings for Noel-Baker ran. There is no suggestion that Noel-Baker reciprocated any of Pigou's erotic feelings, but they did remain friends throughout Pigou's life. Noel-Baker often went to Pigou's house in the Lakes (so, after the Second World War, many classicists, led by Patrick Wilkinson, continued the practice). It was there that Wilfrid Noyce, an undergraduate at King's, fell while climbing, and had life-threatening injuries, a disaster which traumatised Pigou. When Patrick

Wilkinson, who was there, told Pigou of the accident, Pigou had an immediate heart attack. Noyce survived his grim fall, and went on to be on the team that made the first ascent of Everest, a recovery thanks to the life-saving presence of a doctor and psychiatrist who was with Pigou in the Lakes, because he was in love with Noyce – the prophetically named John Menlove Edwards. Pigou may always have had a passion on the go, but, despite his reputation for increasing social withdrawal, he also surrounded himself with men with similar passions.

Pigou demanded that all his papers be burned at his death, and the few letters of others that talk of him are in general relentlessly discreet (even Strachey's). His friends in obituaries stress his uprightness (but they would, wouldn't they?). It is quite unclear what physical form his relationship even with Donald Corrie took. One biographer – who doesn't mention Corrie – declares him a life-long celibate; another a life-long homosexual who, like many we have already met, also had crushes on unreciprocating men, especially manly men like the strikingly handsome, athletic and intelligent Noel-Baker. It's not possible to fill in the gaps in the story with any certainty. Pigou believed passionately that 'Ethics and economics stand together' – the two strands of thought from Sidgwick and Marshall.[57] His welfare economics was prompted by a deep concern for the poor and for the good of society. He was prepared to link this to what he called love, and to see love as a force in economic thinking: 'Pigou – Keynes's "love-lorn" bachelor – treated ideals like love and good will with the same if not greater weight as that with which he treated pleasure or utility', those more usual economic categories. He also had strongly liberal views about social norms, though he was in many areas of economics quite traditional: Pigou decried '"the revival of Puritan influence in secular affairs" and … emphasised the "fall of all that was good" that arose from overly restrictive social mores'.[58] He was actively involved, like Keynes, in the politics of the country, both institutionally and as a commentator – though he engaged less enthusiastically with the administration of policy than Keynes. When asked why he would not go to college meetings, he replied, 'I have no public spirit – but I have quite a lot of private spirit', and he did indeed privately and quietly support many young men's careers with financial aid.[59]

Yet, just as his archive is discreetly silent about much of his personal life, he never wrote about sexual politics in society, as Goldsworthy Lowes Dickinson had done. He did link ethics, love, economics and social change, and had an instrumental effect on modern British politics, especially surrounding the foundation of the welfare state – but his writings were never turned in a way that led to any exposure about his own desires. Pigou strove to live in a world he called the 'all-male' (with fresh eggs), but the boundary between himself as a public and private figure became harder and faster as he lived through the two world wars and the changing world of Cambridge across the twentieth century. When he was young and obviously – performatively – smitten with passion, the undergraduates used to laugh at him. By the time he died, he had become to them and to the younger dons a rather baffling figure of a past age, tall, still strangely dressed, uncertain of his own intellectual prowess, sitting on a deckchair on the front lawn of King's by the Porters'

Lodge, in mute resistance to expectation, even and especially when the air raid sirens sounded to warn of a German attack, unmoved and unmoving while others ran to the shelters. Pigou stayed out when bombs threatened, but as he moved from his young brilliance to becoming an established professor and then to a much criticised figure for the new economics, he retreated from the sort of public display he once allowed himself. Falling becomes a recurring leitmotif: the 'fall of all that was good' thanks to overly restrictive social mores; the fall of Wilfrid Noyce; the fall of European values; his fallen friends in war; Pigou's own fall from esteem. There is a certain melancholia, laced with anger, as he retreats. Where so many gay histories are a story of 'coming out', Pigou's is a tale of retreating further and further inside his own self-enclosed spaces, the burying of the expression of desire.

If we know all too little about the physical details of Pigou's expression of desire, we know an excessive amount about the blow-by-blow details of Rupert Brooke's explorations of the body and desire. **Rupert Brooke** (1887–1915), who came up to King's as an undergraduate a couple of years after Keynes graduated, to live on A staircase next to O. B., was elected a fellow in 1913, and, with his death in 1915, became a national figure as a war poet, almost by accident.[60] Two of his melancholic and patriotic war poems were published in the *TLS* which helped his slim volume of verse to eleven reprintings, and his death (in reality thoroughly unromantic, though it was, like Byron's at least, on a Greek island) helped pushed the volume into the best-sellers list with twenty-four impressions immediately needed. His poem "The Soldier" was read out by Dean Inge, the Dean of St Paul's Cathedral, in a sermon on 5 April 1915, three weeks before Brooke died. Inge happened to have been a student at King's, a contemporary of Arthur Benson and the others. When Brooke died, Winston Churchill published in the London *Times* on 26 April an extraordinary tribute that made Brooke an icon. 'A voice had become audible, a note had been struck, more true, more thrilling, more able to do justice to the nobility of our youth in arms engaged in this present war, than any other – more able to express their thoughts of self-surrender ... He expected to die; he was willing to die for the dear England whose beauty and majesty he knew ...'. Churchill, seizing the opportunity to raise morale at a tough time in the war, ignored the fact of Brooke's death from a mosquito bite turned septic, to make the poet into the romantic voice of a generation, nobly and patriotically fighting and dying for his country. It is a remarkable piece of wartime rhetoric. Churchill had been instrumental in arranging Brooke's commission in the army, thanks to the intervention of his private secretary, Eddie Marsh. Eddie Marsh no doubt also drew the attention of Churchill to Brooke's death. Eddie Marsh was, like many, as we will see, in love with Brooke and saw himself as a close friend. (Brooke, self-obsessed in all he did, was quite capable of stringing along his friends for his personal gain.) Brooke's other friends were unimpressed to the point of rage by Churchill's rhetoric: Edward Dent, whom we will meet later in this book, wrote of 'the filthy romanticism of the business, and the bloody nonsense that the older people write about it', and saw it as an actual 'destruction of what we felt was our work'.[61] It was Eddie Marsh who in the year after Brooke's death wrote the first and extremely hagiographic biography of Brooke, published at the end of the war in 1918, which established Brooke's reputation of the sun-kissed, glorious youth, destroyed nobly in war while dreaming of his English landscape and honey for tea. Sir Edward, as he became after a distinguished civil service career, also edited the anthology *Georgian Poetry* which first made Brooke's name nationally as a poet – and he continued to act as a fixer for his homosexual friends in high places. Brooke's fame was carefully and knowingly curated by his friends in the corridors of power. Rupert Brooke is one of Winston Churchill's greatest propaganda hits. But it was a success facilitated by Eddie Marsh's erotic longing for a beautiful young man.

The myth of Rupert Brooke has been systematically dismantled – once Edward Marsh, Christopher Hassall (actor, lyricist and collaborator with Ivor Novello), and Geoffrey Keynes, Maynard's brother and friend of Brooke from prep school days onwards, all keepers of the flame as much as literary executors, died, and could no longer restrict access to the mass of papers that Brooke and his friends left behind, kept mainly in the King's College archive. In the case of Brooke, unlike J. K. Stephen, we can see clearly not only the conscious work undertaken to curate and maintain a very partial and whitewashed image of a young life, but also the rich and disturbing evidence that led to such an attempt. This whitewashing is evident at the major level of denying Brooke's unstable obsessive anxieties about his bisexual desires that led to his mental breakdown – 'overwork' was the offered explanation, where even Brooke himself gave 'sexual frustration' as its cause; but also at a less grand level. So where Eddie Marsh admiringly tells the story of Brooke's early brilliance at school where Brooke stood out for reading Walter Pater and Swinburne (the 'delicate' and 'flamboyant' anathemas of Chesterton), modern biographers gleefully add that he was given these books by a much older homosexual aesthete, St John Lucas, in whose grooming admiration the young Brooke basked.

The debunking of the Brooke myth has been enthusiastic and complete, at least in academic circles. One biographer lists Brooke's 'scorn, prejudice, paranoia and downright madness that can still shock', itemising his 'hatred of women, homosexuals, Jews, pacifists, promiscuity (except in himself)', concluding, 'The barefoot boy with the sun in his eyes and hair became a rabid ranter, obsessively raving about "dirt", "cleanliness", "foulness" and threatening to shoot himself or his enemies.'[62] Yet Brooke did glow in the admiration and love of many people. He was magnetically attractive to both men and women: 'he was sought out, admired, showered with adulation on every side', as one contemporary recalled, 'the handsomest young man in England', as W. B. Yeats called him. Strachey with characteristic bile tries to distance himself but fails in a single sentence: 'Rupert is a pseudo-beauty with yellow hair and a good complexion, but without any features of body to boast of. His mind from all I can see is merely washy and cultured ... On the hearthrug I found him rather nice in a queer way.' Brooke's modern biographers wonder, inevitably, about the damaging psychological effects of being 'the recipient of so much dumb worship, to be so inordinately praised for one's surface appearance'.[63] Two interrelated responses to his effect on

135

those around him are particularly telling. First, Brooke was intensely self-aware, manipulative and observant not just of the social dramas around him but of his role in them: he 'took with him, for all occasions, an invisible audience' – which he played up to, sometimes hilariously, sometimes cruelly, sometimes hysterically.[64] Like Arthur Benson, his constant self-observation is a sign and a symptom of his inability to locate himself securely on a map of desire. Second, although in his short life he had many affairs (at least in the light of the period's normative expectations), sexual consummation was repeatedly denied, by him or others, in an intense anxiety about the body.

These two strands come together in one of the most remarkable letters to have ended up in the archives. In 1909, when Brooke was twenty-two years old, his virginity was pressing on him. Until now, Brooke had maintained his chastity in a way which surprised his louche friends in Cambridge, especially the Bloomsbury chaps he met at King's. Brooke's crowd – which Virginia Woolf would go on to call 'the Neo-pagans' – were dominated by girls and boys who had been at Bedales, a trendy mixed boarding school influenced by principles stimulated by Edward Carpenter. The school allowed mixed nude bathing, at least for the younger children, encouraged long hikes together, insisted on the dignity of the body, but resolutely refused any sexuality to come with it. Sexual and misogynistic jokes were frowned upon, too. The women of Brooke's group – the four Olivier sisters were leaders – appeared to the outside world to be disturbingly 'fast' in their manners and dress, but were also fiercely and protectively chaste. Brooke was rarely not 'in love' with one or other or several of the Olivier girls (and the letters between him and Noel in particular form an intensely powerful and complex record of a disturbing relationship). But Brooke moved between the two groups, the so-called Neo-pagans and the Bloomsburyites, despite their different attitudes, not least to the sexual act. He did not like it that Maynard Keynes and Lytton Strachey held their 'knowledge' – knowledge of and from sex itself – over him.

So Brooke set out consciously and coldly to lose his virginity with a man for whom he felt nothing emotional (though he was briefly non-plussed by the news of his early death a little later: he had known him since their schooldays). Alone in a cottage for the weekend, Brooke carefully planned and executed his plan: he managed to get the man into bed, and to have sex, though it is less clear – to Brooke and to his readers – exactly what happened and even if his partner had an orgasm too. They do not speak afterwards or, it seems, ever again. The description of the plan and its consummation is described in a very long letter – in very full, distanced, physical detail – to James Strachey. James Strachey, who would be the translator and editor of the Standard Edition of Freud for Bloomsbury Publishing, was Lytton's brother, and had been in love hopelessly with Brooke for some time – as Brooke knew. The recipient of the letter is carefully chosen. But fascinatingly there is no mention of pleasure in the description of the sex. For Brooke, the act means Lytton and Maynard can no longer tease him for *not knowing*: 'At length, I thought, I shall know something of all that James and Harry and Maynard and Lytton know and hold over me.' Here is a brief extract, typical for its precise, self-conscious prose:

We kissed very little, as far as I can remember, face to face. And I only rarely handled his penis. Mine he touched once with his fingers; and that made me shiver so much that I think he was frightened. But with alternate stirrings, and still pressures, we mounted. My right hand got hold of the left half of his bottom, clutched it, and pressed his body into me. The smell of the sweat began to be noticeable. At length we took to rolling to and fro over each other, in the excitement. Quite calm things, I remember, were passing through my brain. "The Elizabethan joke 'The Dance of the Sheets' has, then, something in it." "I hope his erection is all right" – and so on. I thought of him entirely in the third person.[65]

The manipulativeness of writing such a letter to someone who could only receive it with bitterness (and then show it to his brother, to add to the humiliation) doubles the unpleasant manipulativeness of the scene of the calculated seduction of an old school chum, which Brooke dispassionately describes. His experience of losing his virginity with a woman is even less charming. He was having a long on-off relationship with Katherine Cox, where eroticism and arguments around desire and physicality reached a climax when she informed him that she had met a man she passionately wanted in a physical sense. In Munich, Brooke was violently jealous, and had a mental and physical collapse. When Cox came out to support him, he desperately demanded that they had sex, to end, as he put it, her 'extraordinarily randy state of virginity' (or, rather, his), and she acquiesced to his wild insistence.[66] He was unhinged, insistent, ill and afterwards still unsatisfied. While he could remember the beauty of her body a month after the event, he seems to have not responded with any sympathy to her exhaustion, pain and distress. Instead, again he wants to *know*:

The important thing I want to be quite clear about, is, about women 'coming off' . What it means objectively – What happens. And also, what *you* feel when it happens.[67]

Both Brooke and Cox wrote miserable revelatory letters to the long-suffering James Strachey. Apart from a relationship in Tahiti, on his travels, with a woman with whom he had an illegitimate daughter – again relationships are easier away from home territory – all Brooke's relationships seem to have foundered as much on his uneasy relation to his own body as on dealing with other people and their responses to him. He could not help looking at himself and acting out his persona as a fresh-faced, promising youth, even and especially when he met grandees like Henry James, who was smitten, or Bernard Shaw, who wasn't.

Despite all this nastiness, many of his letters bounce with amusement and engagement. His self-consciousness, even about his sexual difficulties, could produce theatrically poised prose: writing from New Zealand to Eddie Marsh, he describes eating strawberries in December: 'It feels curiously unnatural, perverse, like some frightful vice out of Havelock Ellis. I blush and eat secretively' – a sentence which hints and plays with more than fruit out of season for his absent friend.[68] He could flirt wittily and be the life and soul of a party, and was genuinely serious about being a poet. Virginia Woolf was persuaded to go swimming naked with him in Grantchester. He performed his party trick of leaping into the water and coming out instantly with an erection. Similar stories of his sexualised self-display abound. And yet, people remained smitten with him, and, in truth, the myth of Brooke lingers on, evocatively, beyond its academic dismemberment.

Yet my interest here is not so much in the deeply conflicted and acted-out anxiety of yet another young man – even such a cultural figure of poetry as Brooke – whose mother wanted a daughter and whose authoritarian father seemed not to understand his son. Rather, it is Brooke's politics that are especially salient here. His faithful friends, committed to his innocence, recognised his political concerns. J. T. Sheppard, the future Provost of King's who we will meet properly in the next chapter, saw an immediate link between his poetry and his politics: 'he never tired of teaching the importance of poets and artists in the good society which is to be built up by our children'.[69] Much as Brooke sought knowledge in and through erotics, so here too we can hear a Platonic lilt to the conversation, as Sheppard reverses Plato's censorship of poets and playwrights from his ideal republic. Poetry as a political act … Brooke had met Hugh Dalton outside M. R. James' door as they both paid the Provost a courtesy call. Dalton would go on to be the Chancellor in the first post-Second World War Labour Government, alongside Noel-Baker in the Cabinet. In another snapshot of the cross-generational links of the figures in this history, Dalton's father had been the long-suffering tutor of Prince Eddy before J. K. Stephen took over at Cambridge, and had been very fond of the young Arthur Benson; he had the job of tutor because Edward Carpenter had turned it down – Carpenter was not yet known as a socialist and supporter of homosexuality. Dalton père, despite his role with the royal family, was a close friend of Carpenter and shared many of his views. So perhaps it is no surprise that the young Hugh Dalton was already a Fabian. Brooke agreed to join Dalton's party, though he stressed, 'I'm not your sort of Socialist; I'm a William Morris sort of Socialist'[70] – a little like the tradition of Lowes Dickinson, or, perhaps better, that of H. G. Wells. (He wrote a scurrilous letter to Lytton Strachey about how Hugh Dalton had tried it on with James, Lytton's brother: Dalton 'conceived a light lust for James ... When James was in bed, D[alton] stood over him, waving an *immense* steaming penis in his face and chuckling softly. James was nearly sick' – another anecdote silenced in the 'honey for tea' image.)[71] Brooke rose to be the president of the Fabian Society, though his political philosophy was not deeply socialist: 'I don't know that "Progress" is certain', he said, 'All I know is that change is.'[72] But he did campaign actively for the reform of the Poor Act, stumping around Hampshire and Dorset in 1910 – a more committed political gesture than his other friends. The connection between the inheritance of Carpenter in sexual ethics and the commitment to a form of Utopian socialism is still present for Brooke, without the consistency of Lowes Dickinson or the instrumental work of Ashbee. In his illness and despair at the time of his trip to Munich, he imagines what he might have had in a more balanced and happy life with the hope that 'I'd still to "only connect" lust and immense comradeship.'[73] In 'only connect' we can hear Forster, of course, explicitly quoted – staying in a German *Pension*, the amused Brooke wrote 'they are all Forster characters', only to add, 'But to live among Forster characters is bewildering'; in 'comradeship', we can hear the language of Lowes Dickinson and Ashbee. When he was far from England, one of the things he missed was 'a speech of Lowes

Dickinson'.[74] Brooke, edging around a political commitment and testing ideological waters from which he would retreat later, while also testing his sexual ethics and preferences, was exactly the sort of young Fabian Beatrice Webb was right to worry about.

We started the first chapter with a young tormented man whose mental breakdown led to his young death, and we have finished this chapter with another young tortured man whose reputation for his 'sunny' disposition (which was often on display) was also darkened by a mental breakdown and violent emotions, before his early death. Both spent time with the highest levels of political life in the country; but Brooke, a full generation later, embodies a shift in the cultural horizons of his generation, as Britain moved towards the First World War. Even – perhaps especially – as a poet, Brooke was caught up in the move towards the struggle to make a better society, a struggle that linked his own attitudes towards his sexuality and the body to a wider political purpose. Brooke's fractured life ended before its conflicted trajectories could find any reconciliation. The older fellows and members of King's who led the way in the politics of homosexuality also struggled to reconcile their wish for political change with their own physical desires. For Goldsworthy Lowes Dickinson, the better society he fought quietly and instrumentally to bring about, even at an international level through the League of Nations, included a commitment to freedom, sexual and political, which he understood through an idealised ancient Greek politics of the self. But he could not live out his own sexual life except through frustration and longing, and reliving his own past responses to his misery. Like Lowes Dickinson, Forster tried to conceal his sexuality publicly, though both scarcely succeeded; but Forster also managed to maintain physical, sexual relationships, while promoting a politics of the personal, that aimed at a form of social change, though very much through the most local of interactions. Charlie Ashbee, in contrast, who was equally committed to a Carpenter-influenced romantic socialism, both actively laboured to build a civic infrastructure for men to work together in artisanal partnership and managed to transition – slowly and traumatically – to a marriage which somehow accommodated his and his wife's desires – and which could be celebrated by his daughter(s). When Lytton Strachey mocked Brooke's politics and in the same breath, tellingly, his sexuality for its 'Garden City-ishness', he was not only demonstrating Bloomsbury's lack of political interest with customary dismissiveness, but he was also accurately noting the lineage back to Ashbee in which Brooke's romantic socialism stood. Keynes, by contrast, the most politically influential of all of them, like so many politicians, saw no connection between his politics and his rapacious sexuality, though perhaps Wordsworth's extremely apposite language of 'getting and spending' from an earlier generation should have encouraged such thoughts.

Lowes Dickinson and Ashbee overlapped with Arthur Benson, Monty James and Oscar Browning, but are strikingly different in how their homosexual lives were lived, not just in the micro-calibrations of the physical expression of their desires, but rather in how the politics of the world might find a place for the politics of homosexuality. As the language and recognition of homosexuality are under construction, a key trajectory of its formulation is how and whether there *is* a politics of homosexuality. For Lowes Dickinson and Ashbee, and, differently, for Forster and even Brooke – in contrast to the economists and political figures, Keynes and Pigou – we can see the grounding of what will become by the 1960s – and beyond – a demand that the politics of (homo)sexuality is transformed not just for personal fulfilment but for the sake of society. We can recognise, if you will, a *politics* of homosexuality under construction.

3

The Art of Homosexuality

~

But we can also start elsewhere, again.

We have already met on several occasions in this history **John Tresidder Sheppard** (1881–1968) – known only to his closest intimates, Cecil Taylor and the Keyneses, as Jack. He was a dominant figure in King's College through the first half of the twentieth century up into the 1960s, when he haunted the college as a white-haired ghostly figure of its own past – shambling, untimely, like an old relative of whose long-ago wickedness and charisma you have heard tell. Back in 1909 in the college magazine, *Basileion*, Gerald Shove described its cliques like this:

The remainder of the College affect one of these three groups:

1. The Sheppard's flock.
2. The Dicken's sons.
3. They who keep Montem.[1]

Gerald Shove was another economist, and an Apostle, who went camping with Rupert Brooke (see Figure 22); he was part of the Bloomsbury Group, and a conscientious objector, who spent the First World War looking after the geese at Ottoline Morrell's house at Garsington (we all have our contributions).

At a party at the Bells' at Gordon Square in 1915, 'the evening ended with Gerald Shove enthroned in the centre of the room crowned with roses ...' – it was the year he

FIGURE 22 Rupert Brooke and Gerald Shove camping together. This picture was taken by Maynard Keynes, on the look-out as ever.

followed the trend of Bloomsbury men and married.[2] So he knew what he was writing about when it came to this sort of satire. He was living on G staircase in G2 when he wrote this piece – and it is very much an insider joke about the college for the college. He is referring to the three leading lights of college social life ('affect' indicates immediately the amused distance he is taking from such cliquey-ness, at least for the purposes of the article's satirical voice). The Dicken's sons are the students around Goldsworthy Lowes Dickinson, the group of fey Fabians that Beatrice Webb worried about. 'They who keep Montem' were Montague James' coterie, the less politically engaged, more churchy crowd. 'Keep Montem' is an Etonian joke. 'Montem' had been a ritual at Eton, which had originally involved a procession – a sort of initiation – and which later involved boys collecting money from townspeople to send one of the scholarship pupils to Cambridge. It had been discontinued already in the 1840s – sixty years before Shove is writing – and existed only in the folk memory of Etonians. It is a neat jibe against the old-fashioned James, the great lover of Eton and obscure history, to assimilate his name to this forgotten piece of Etoniana. The Sheppard's flock are the friends of Jack Sheppard. It is telling that while Dickinson and James were both born in 1862, Sheppard was nearly twenty years younger, and was only twenty-eight years old when this squib was written – but was already regarded as a social star.

There were other ways to divide the groups, of course, as is always the case with such small communities – students from public schools in particular found in King's the same infighting and contingent alliances as in their previous school life. Sheppard and Keynes together were known as the leaders of the Green Ties – the louche, sexually liberated and exuberant side of college – while John Clapham led the Black Ties, a rather more dour and self-consciously conservative coterie. (Clapham, who lived on F staircase in F2, was another of Marshall's students and, as Professor of Economic History, was also the Tutor and then Vice Provost of King's for many years: the sort of college man Pigou could never be.) Nathaniel Wedd, for his part, as we have already seen, divided the college between the 'scallywags' and 'the best set' – seeing class (the best set) as the crucial distinction, and everyone else as self-consciously misbehaving. But in all such distinctions it was clear which side Sheppard was on. Yet he rose to become one of the most praised Provosts of the college – the first non-Etonian in the role – a figurehead of the institution which often seemed to be formed in his own image.

Sheppard came to King's from Dulwich College School in South London where he had been taught by Arthur Gilkes. Gilkes, like Sheppard, was a middle-class boy who made a career in education through brilliance and hard work, and who maintained a commitment to social improvement through his contribution to mission schools in working-class districts while teaching in the elite public school system – a classic career path for Victorian liberal achievement. But Gilkes was particularly well known and beloved by his pupils both for his rare love of literature – he read and expounded a piece of poetry with them every week – and for his inspirational sense of performance: it was drama above all that he loved and acted out with his pupils. Sheppard was deeply influenced by Gilkes, and his whole career became known too for its passionate commitment to enthusing young men with a love of literature and for his equally deep devotion to theatre and his own theatrical life. One student recalled a first meeting with Sheppard lasting three hours while Sheppard paraded around his rooms, reading, declaiming, questioning, demanding responses from the young man – until, enthused but desperate for a pause, the young man pleaded hunger to end the performance. He called it a transformative moment in his intellectual life.

It is impossible to get much sense of Sheppard from his rather thin and dull academic writing. Despite much early success in the exams and prizes of student life, and an apparent commitment to learning as he prepared to apply for his fellowship, when he actually became an established academic he showed little aptitude for advanced scholarship or interest in his own or anyone else's research. Insouciance was his preferred mode. The one existing film clip of Sheppard comes from a British Council Film about Cambridge, which lauds the university town as an 'essentially English' place 'where men work for the future but do not forget the past', 'a privilege that will always last'. It was made with an obvious, patriotic political agenda in 1945. It provides a modern viewer with a bizarre scene of a posh and over-exaggeratedly enthusiastic Sheppard lecturing to baffled American servicemen about the wonders of Homer, 'the poetry of freedom and friendship': it is very open to parody.[3] Sir Geoffrey Lloyd, mind you, no mug, even as a student, remembered Sheppard's lectures as 'mesmerizing' though 'not at all scholarly', and 'packed' with students: Sheppard was 'on a high', performing. Patrick Wilkinson, the classicist who was enthused as a youth by Sheppard and who wrote so much of the official history of King's from his own liberal and decent love of the place he made his home, tried to capture the power of Sheppard in his loving but robust obituary. Wilkinson himself was another fellow who married, despite living for many earlier years fully in the queer environment of King's. The joke that circulated, I was told, was that he chose Sydney – his wife with whom he had a long loving life – because she was 'two choir boys, one on top of the other': she was very tall. How, Wilkinson wondered, could one sum up

the attraction of his personality; the almost hypnotic power of those slightly protruding eyes, which could have been sinister, had it not been so patently benevolent; the dignity willfully varied with clowning; the histrionics and rhetoric; the splendid sense of humour and fun; the shrewdness streaked with naïveté; the constitutional toughness masquerading as senile debility; the inexhaustible interest in people and desire to help them; the egotism which yet did good by stealth; the total devotion to the College. Which was yet an extension of the ego; and the paternal hold established on it, such that after nineteen years the Fellows unanimously prolonged his tenure of the Provostship for two years beyond the normal retiring age.[4]

I can't help noticing how the balanced and opposed clauses of this description reveal Wilkinson's long and fully embodied reading of Latin prose and verse. It is a very *composed* portrait. (Elsewhere, Wilkinson coined the marvellous phrase for Sheppard of '*enfant-terrible* of father figures'.)[5] The photographs of Sheppard as a young man show a smug, self-confident man about town (see Figure 23), about to be the leader of the Green Ties (as do his letters home in these early days).

As he grew into his life he became prematurely white-haired and affected a style of a man much older than he actually was (see Figure 24).

He addressed almost everyone he met as 'dear boy', 'my dear boy' – a habit he seems to have picked up from Oscar

PLATE I The Gibbs Building on a glorious February morning, with a rainbow flag flying.

PLATE 2 Provost Sheppard, presiding over the room.

PLATE 3 J. K. Stephen.

PLATE 4 Provost Annan, instiutional grandee, by Renato Guttuso.

PLATE 3 J. K. Stephen.

PLATE 4 Provost Annan, instiutional grandee, by Renato Guttuso.

PLATE 5 Rupert Brooke, the very carefully curated image of carefree youth.

PLATE 6 Arthur Cole, by Duncan Grant.

PLATE 7 Roger Fry, arbiter of taste, the art critic satirised by the artist.

PLATE 8 *Pouring Tea* by Vanessa Bell.

FIGURE 23 John Sheppard as a student, dressed to kill.

FIGURE 24 Sheppard, posing as an intellectual.

Browning's baroque social manner. When, after the Second World War, the first woman dined on High Table – Janet Lloyd, the strikingly beautiful half-French wife of the classical philosopher Sir Geoffrey Lloyd – the disconcerted Sheppard greeted her with a failed handshake and a mumbled 'my dear boy'. His close friend Cecil Taylor in return wrote to him over the many years of their relationship as 'my dear boy'. The age difference that grounded so many male erotic relationships in college became institutionalised in a vocal tic that worked to ironise and deflect but allow the continuation of such relationships. When a student from Selwyn replied to Sheppard's greeting of 'my dear boy' with 'I am not your dear boy', he may not have been merely referring to the fact that he was from another college ('I'm from Selwyn'). He was also from a different world of relationships – the austerely low Protestant Selwyn College, not H staircase in King's.

Sheppard was indeed living in H staircase in H3 when Shove wrote his article. (H3 was the room in which the famous argument between Karl Popper and Ludwig Wittgenstein would take place, the subject of the documentary and book, *Wittgenstein's Poker*.)[6] Sheppard later moved into Oscar Browning's old rooms on A, and then, of course, the Provost's Lodge. And he was surprisingly open – dramatically so – about the boys he found attractive. He was happily capable of public indiscretion, so wilfully performed that, as with Browning, it became its own defence. The case of Dadie Rylands we will come to later. But if Wilkinson gives a carefully laudatory portrait, Lytton Strachey – whom Wilkinson calls 'devoted' to Sheppard – records a far more ambivalent response to Sheppard's attentions. They were elected to the Apostles on the same day, went to plays together in London (Oscar Wilde's *Lady Windermere's Fan*), socialised intimately, but Strachey, whatever the initial attraction, became disenchanted. He wrote in a letter to Keynes in 1904: 'Sh[eppard] is a wretched spectacle, whom I alternately despise and pity. His bad parts have swelled terribly, but sometimes – I don't know how often – perhaps most when he's alone – he's utterly aware of his abasement. He's genuinely anxious to show his feelings for me – and does so by asking me to be his guest at the Union Presidential Dinner. Isn't this rather pitiful? He knows I hardly like him. And I have cause.'[7] But a year later Strachey recalibrated this cruel outburst. '[I] took down the letters from Sheppard. As I read them, I nearly expired from horror – they were echoes of such a remote and agonizing past. Do you know that there is no doubt that he was in love with me quite as he ought to have been at the beginning of the incident? His letters show this plainly though I hadn't realised it before.'[8] Strachey has just realised on rereading Sheppard's letters to him – now lost – that far from being just a wretched spectacle, abased, Sheppard was genuinely and properly – whatever 'as he ought to have been' means – in love, and that their relationship, remembered as a 'remote and agonizing past' (though it seems to have been no more than a year ago), was actually a scene of pain for Sheppard and of misrecognition by himself. Strachey's language is characteristically hyper-emotional and exaggerated about 'the incident', but it does open a brief portal onto a strained and difficult erotic encounter between young men, trying to find the language to express their feelings, and testing the boundaries of behaviour, with a self-conscious awareness of its own performativity. These descriptions come from letters between friends – strategies of self-presentation as much as records of events.

In 1915, however, we find Sheppard having sex with Keynes (as so often, Strachey and Keynes are locked in triangulated relationships, which Strachey anatomises with exuberant and vitriolic prose, while Keynes does the business). In his ledger for the year, Keynes records 'Tresidder' – using Jack Sheppard's distinctive middle name. Sheppard lived for a while in Keynes' place in Gordon Square, along with Shove, and they remained friends throughout Keynes' life, and both Keynes and Keynes with his wife, Lydia Lopokova, went with Sheppard to Monte Carlo to gamble. (Keynes ended up lending Sheppard money more than once.) Strachey continued to observe Sheppard's relationships. After a party in London just before the end of the war in 1918, Strachey recorded, 'I suppose we all wanted to kiss Duncan, though Sheppard alone did so – while I was there – after that ...'.[9] In 1920 he wrote, 'The Sheppard-Doggart affair has completely fizzled out, they say, with the result that Sheppard's spirits have risen and he's no longer a bore, spending his days flitting from flower to flower.'[10] Once his particular passion for Doggart has passed – Doggart was a 'pretty surgeon ... who preferred rugby to philosophy' whose election to the Apostles Sheppard engineered – Sheppard is back flitting from attractive young man to attractive young man rather than obsessing annoyingly over one.[11] One of Sheppard's longest relationships, however, was with Cecil Taylor, who had been an undergraduate at King's and from 1912 became a schoolmaster at Clifton College in Bristol in the west of England. They holidayed together – Sheppard loved to go to Monte Carlo and gamble in the casino – and they visited each other , and other friends together, repeatedly. Keynes arranged the finances for Taylor to come back to Cambridge for a while before the war, to help out his friend: 'You are really awfully like God', gushed Taylor.[12] Taylor and Sheppard maintained a correspondence over decades. The surviving correspondence is largely mundane, although Taylor regularly signs off with 'much love, dear boy', or 'my best love, dear boy, your loving Cecil'. Only occasionally do we come across more heated traces of the intimacy that they shared. In one letter, which is not possible to date, Taylor lets us see a more intricate set of circumstances: 'I feel a fraud when you talk of my "loving kindness" but like you to do it all the same – anyway *I* don't think that there needs to be (whatever happens to you and him) any pain between you and me. I confirmed to Lucas that I had been deliberate in preventing him travelling with you: and he told me that he had been aware of that – he bears no resentment!'[13] The story is not easy to unpick, but Taylor seems to be responding to Sheppard's thankfulness that Taylor has not been angry or hurt by his relationship with another man, and confesses – and this may be another story – that he has been complicit in stopping one Lucas (a schoolboy maybe? Or, more likely, F. L. Lucas who later joined Sheppard as a fellow at King's) from going on a trip with Sheppard – perhaps the sort of continental journey that plays such an important part in the histories I have been recounting, from J. K. Stephen's journeys with Browning onwards. But Taylor is also keen to maintain that their relationship, Sheppard's and Taylor's, need not be damaged by Sheppard's other actions. Taylor was known as 'Madame' to Sheppard's friends, and James Strachey calls Sheppard and Taylor a 'married couple'. This remark was made as Strachey, a gooseberry at the house party, tells his brother Lytton how 'Sheppard was edgy at the prospect of Madame's impending departure for a year in Germany and suspected Duncan [Grant] was flirting with "her".'[14] Duncan Grant was at the time painting a portrait of Taylor. There is a single much faded photograph of Taylor and Sheppard together at a (different) house party at Garsington, Ottoline Morrell's house, where the two men stand relaxed and smiling in matching tweed suits, waistcoats and ties, guests together as a couple at the house of one of the great hostesses of the era. (It is too faded to print here but can be found online.) It is fascinating that the National Portrait Gallery, which houses the photograph, does not know who Taylor is. The picture has scrawled on it the names 'Taylor and Sheppard', presumably by Ottoline Morrell, which the curators gloss as 'Sir John Tresidder Sheppard' and '"Taylor"'. There is one other, better preserved but unlabelled picture of the men together, now in the archive at King's, which shows them in similar clothes and relaxed companionship. Not much to show for years of an intimate relationship. For all his flamboyance, there is still a real reticence in the Sheppard archive (see Figure 25).

Sheppard was responsible for George 'Dadie' Rylands coming to Cambridge. The story is as counter a version of contemporary arguments about access to elite institutions as it is possible to imagine. Rylands came from Eton (proudly the most privileged school in Britain) to take the scholarship exams at King's. Sheppard caught sight of him and was smitten by the boy's beauty. He immediately wanted to bring him to Cambridge, in the first place to appear in the Greek play that Sheppard was about to direct. Sheppard's love of theatre, nourished as a boy by Gilkes at Dulwich College, was enacted by a series of productions, especially of plays in ancient Greek, which started a tradition for theatrical excellence which would – under Rylands' care later – flourish and produce some of Britain's very finest actors. Sheppard's

FIGURE 25 Sheppard, on the right, with his familiar wing collar and pipe; Taylor, more shy, with a cigarette.

correspondence is full of his friends' writing to congratulate him on one stage show or another. Sheppard, however, seems simply to have offered Rylands the opportunity to come to King's immediately, based mainly – or totally – on the boy's looks. The fact that Rylands would win a scholarship and eventually become a distinguished fellow of the college does not retrospectively validate Sheppard's behaviour, beyond the pale even for the period. What is even more surprising and revelatory, however, is the flirtatious relationship that started up immediately between them. Dadie's first letter to Sheppard begins, 'Dearest tutor-to-be, both your letters

were the greatest joy ...'.[15] Sheppard sends Dadie a book,
and he writes back: 'You shouldn't have sent me anything – and that book is one I have coveted and coveted.'
He signs off 'Much love, always yours George Rylands' –
this is a schoolboy writing to an established academic,
remember. He affects a knowledge of Sheppard's circle –
'I have been enchanted by a piece of Lytton's ...' (first
name, note: he went on to have a long flirtatious relationship with Strachey throughout the 1920s) – and starts to
sign his letters 'Love from Dadie', 'Love and happiness to
you, Dadie'. As he spends more time in King's, Dadie
writes, 'Thank you ten thousand times for all your affection and kindness – I mean love.' And when he is elected a
fellow – aged twenty-five – he writes in loving retrospect,
'I love King's and I believe I love it somewhat in the way in
which you do and which you first instilled in me.' Dadie as a
young man was happy to bask in the company of older men
who he knew wanted him, and to play up to and indulge
such feelings. ('Grooming' is consequently too simple a
term for this sort of relationship, uncomfortable though it
will make many a modern reader feel.) It was with Dadie
that Virginia Woolf had the beautiful lunch 'with a Fellow
of King's' that she describes in her famous essay 'A Room of
One's Own', though she does not confess in that essay how
good-looking her host was. She worried too about Dadie's
heart and heartlessness: 'but at heart he is uncorrupted, (so
I think – others disagree) and all young and oldish men, like
Eddie Marsh and so on, fall in love with him, and he dines
out every night, and treats his lovers abominably'.[16] Cecil
Taylor was also well aware of Dadie's arrival and counsels
Sheppard: 'Don't try him too much with your depressions.
He isn't age-steeled like me nor so Olympian as Jimmy, and

takes things a little hardly. He is brimful of affection for you and it would be a pity if he felt it was his difficult duty in life to keep you cheerful!'[17] Arthur Benson, then only two years from his death and still Master of Magdalen College, was one of the very oldest men who fell for Dadie, and there is a fine picture of them in front of Lamb House, which Benson had bought from Henry James, striding out together, arm in arm, both in their natty double-breasted suits, Benson with his characteristic walrus down-turn of mouth, Dadie with an assured smile, like a cat who has got the cream – see Figures 26(a) and 26(b).

The turn of Dadie's head and his smile make all the difference between these pictures and catch something of Dadie's charm. Benson's diary tells the story of his infatuation. He met Rylands at the end of April 1923, when he was sixty-one, and noted immediately that the twenty-one-year-old Rylands was 'a most charming, handsome, eager unaffected boy … gracefully puritanical. A loveable creature altogether.' Prophetic words. Dinners and meetings followed. His judgement of Dadie's character – 'He has a fine beautiful rather austere character, I think. His shyness makes him formidable' – quickly becomes a more physical appreciation – 'He is not handsome exactly, but very charming and attractive. Features dull even heavy – but a childish look, and his eyes have a dancing smile when he is amused – his hair thick and wavy, like pale gold', 'a charming creature with his thick golden hair …'. Benson revelled in their intimacy, especially when they talked precisely of intimacy: 'We had a strange intimate talk – about being in trouble, and speaking to other people about troubles, whether it helped or not.' As ever, to find the language to discuss desire and its travails vexes Benson

FIGURE 26(a) Arthur Benson and Dadie Rylands at Lamb House,
Henry James' former home.

above all, and his perception of the 'strangeness' of their intimate chat is a sign of his discomfort rather than the conversation's oddity: the talk is absolutely typical of the exchanges he regularly records between himself and younger men. He walks Rylands back to King's. Benson finds himself falling in love: 'Am I foolish about this boy? He is an impulsive creature ... But what is irresistible to me

161

FIGURE 26(b) Arthur and Dadie more formally posed, same day.

is that he likes and seeks my company.'[18] Dadie was comfortable with the old man's attentions and sought them out. Other men too, like Denys Winstanley and Dennis Robertson, were chasing him, Rylands confessed to Benson, and how much he felt the strain of such attentions. The same year, and, by chance, the day before he was due to have dinner with Benson, Denys Winstanley, seeing the story differently, wrote to Dadie: 'I cannot hope that I am sufficiently grateful, but I am content if you understand how much I prize your love and friendship and how much they mean to me. You have thrown a bridge across the gulf of years that separate us, and in this, and for so much more, I shall ever be your debtor.'[19] (Winstanley, unlike Benson, will come back to haunt Dadie's later relationships, especially with Dennis Robertson.) As Dadie entered the circle of Bloomsbury, Benson – another generation – was mortified by their promiscuity and social licentiousness. Benson was moved finally to tell Dadie how he felt, a scene recorded with the dewy-eyed language of a romantic novel: 'I told him very simply how much I thought of him and how happy he made me. He took it very sedately, but was surprised ... As he stood in is blue clothes, pearly stockings, slouched hat, with his scarf blowing – with his blue eyes looking out to sea and a touch of gold in his hair I thought I had never seen so beautiful and gracious a youth.'[20] They walked home arm in arm. As in the photograph, arm in arm is how they spent much of the next months, Benson 'completely bewitched'. As they walked through King's together, John Clapham, the leader of the 'black ties', of course, 'looked sternly' at them.[21] For once, Benson was not worried by the public recognition of his own longing. When Dadie graduated in the summer, however, he left Cambridge for a short while, and Benson's *grande passion* settled into a more gentle friendship, which repeatedly lifted his spirits until his death in 1925.

At one level, their relationship marks a historical transition of the generations. Benson was formed in a world where family prayers were normal, where the church was a dominant force in his life – especially as his father was Archbishop of Canterbury; he had edited the letters of Queen Victoria whom he had met, and, like his brother, Fred Benson, epitomised for a general public a lost Edwardian world, a Cambridge of 'books, music and beautiful young men'.[22] The latter years of his life – as for so many – were scarred by the losses of the First

World War: British society was radically altered in the decades after the conflict, and Benson was one of many who did not, could not embrace that change. Dadie Rylands, young in the 1920s, had his photograph on the side of buses advertising cigarettes. From his rooms in King's, in the years before and after the Second World War, he transformed how great actors spoke Shakespearian verse – John Gielgud, Peggy Ashcroft, Laurence Olivier, Corin Redgrave, Derek Jacobi and Ian McKellen all record how he made them study the verse form, the punctuation, the sense of flow of the lines – as did John Barton and Trevor Nunn, directors crucial to the history of the Royal Shakespeare Company. (I have a little silver Roman coin that Dadie gave to Pat Easterling when she took over the Greek play, which she gave to me when I became chair of the Greek Play Committee. I will pass it on soon.) Rylands lived on through the 1960s into the time of legalisation of homosexuality – and the changes that preceded it and followed it – still in the same rooms. He died at the end of the twentieth century, aged ninety-six – another white-haired figure, like Sheppard, who haunted the college as a figure of its lost past, gently jogging along the path by the Gibbs Building back towards his rooms for his evening glass of whisky.

At another level, the picture which the elderly Benson gives us of his last romantic stirring is paradigmatic of the particular dynamics of age that I have been discussing. Dadie Rylands' letters to Sheppard from their earliest stage are flirtatious and inviting. He sought out Benson and chose to spend time with him, as he did with the other men, like Winstanley, about whom he complained to Benson. For Dadie Rylands these relationships opened a world he wished to inhabit; Sheppard and Benson knew the great and the good; they knew *how* to be with the great and good, and were arbiters of form; they told the stories of the past glories, a narrative whose next chapter Rylands was keen to enact. They were intellectual forces. It is not by chance that in the photograph of the two arm in arm, Rylands' clothes mirror the older man's. Oddly enough, the best description I know of how *empowered* a young person can feel by their own mix of sexual and intellectual becoming is to be found in Jane Gallop's bitter but brilliantly analytical book *Feminist Accused of Sexual Harassment*, a book written in a place and time far away from 1920s Cambridge (see Figure 27).

Jane Gallop contrasts her own sexual past with university policies in America and elsewhere in the West which now regularly criminalise even consensual sexual relationships between professors and students – even, indeed, consensual relationships that do not involve any sex acts, if they are deemed nonetheless 'amorous', a word Benson would have appreciated for its sly and destructive proclamation of unregulatable virtue. She recalls how, as a

FIGURE 27 Jane Gallop, brilliant critic, back in the day, as posed and poised as Sheppard.

165

young single woman, she had wanted to get two members of her dissertation committee into bed (severally, she immediately adds, not at the same time). 'Their opinion of me already mattered profoundly; their teaching had forever changed the way I understood the world.'[23] The power they had over her, she continues, was not expressed institutionally, but intellectually: 'I was bowled over by their brilliance: they seemed to me superior.' She concludes that '[s]educing them made me feel kind of cocky and allowed me to presume I had something worth saying'. What was important, looking back for her now, was how these events left her 'feeling powerful and sexy, smart and successful'.[24] Which is exactly how Dadie Rylands looks in Figure 26(a), stepping out on the arm of Arthur Benson, at the very least 'kind of cocky'. None of what I (or Gallop) have said should be taken to justify predatory sexual abuses of institutional power, which are unacceptable, as are the self-delusional ruses by which such institutional power can be enacted through self-serving strategies of denial. Rather, it is to underline how this history of H staircase cannot be written without recognising the sort of complex motivations and personal agency that run through such relationships between the beautiful young student and the older established figure of authority. It may well dismay the current regimes of heavily policed desire to recognise and acknowledge this dynamic, but many of these young men wilfully, knowingly and with joy entered into relationships that were largely amorous and sometimes sexual with older men because it made them feel 'powerful and sexy, smart and successful' and because they actually liked and learned from the older men. These older men had often been the younger beauties in their day, and now had a complex and difficult sense of their own aging desires, marked by nostalgia, the potential for humiliation and the thrill of reimagining their own stories. There were, too, as we will see, more unpleasant and threatening encounters, as well as patterns of shame and despair. But it is impossible to understand a man like Jack Sheppard without the acknowledgement that his 'dear boys' were an integral part not just of his real and fantasy-filled relationships with Strachey, Keynes or Taylor, say, men of his own age, but also of how his life in this educational institution played out over many years. Sheppard and Rylands both aged in King's, spent their adult life in King's – in the same building – and their intertwined stories run across nearly the whole of the twentieth century, as they each turn from young men on the threshold, to middle-aged dons, to white-haired figures on whom the next generations project a lost and faded past, and calibrate their own present. The community finds its self-representation in the continuity which is these men's transformations. The stories about them, told by themselves and others, become a collective memory of the institution and its *space* for relationships, its topography of desire, inhabited over time. The fading pictures of the era are part of this constructed memory. Here, typically, we see a picnic in King's Fellows Garden. The whisky, Bath Oliver biscuits and cheese are exactly what you might expect for such a picnic. Dadie is lounging with relaxed sexuality against Lytton Strachey, while Rosamond Lehmann looks on rather grimly. There are many recorded memories of beautiful young heads resting on old knees, while books are read aloud (see Figure 28).

167

FIGURE 28 Lytton Strachey, Dadie Rylands and Rosamond Lehmann
lounging in King's Fellows Garden.

One value of the history of H staircase is that it lets us
see a community of gay men not just as a snapshot in time
but as a group transforming – and telling its own
story – over time.

Sheppard not only lived in King's for nigh on seventy
years and dedicated his working life to it, but he also
theorised about it in the smug way that outsiders can find
so annoying when the obsessive display of the narcissism
of small differences between colleges is on display.
He gave a paper to the Apostles – he was also well known
for failing to give papers when expected – in which he
compared Trinity and King's at length. Trinity and
King's provided the vast majority of the society's
members, and it might be supposed that the paper would
have interested the audience, or at least appealed to their
narcissism. It is not a talk to support the belief that the
Apostles represented the cream of Cambridge intellects,
but it does give a telling insight into Sheppard. 'King's has

an unconquerable faith in the value and interest of human beings', he orated, 'and finds an interest in the average man – as most people call him; the stupid man – as Trinity calls him.' That is, he compared Trinity's restricted focus on a narrowly conceived academic excellence with a broader fascination for the quirks and differences of humans at King's: 'We care for what we call "character"; I think we care for it more than intellect.' He quotes Shelley – 'I never was attached to that great sect ...' – to justify his refusal to ascribe to any intellectual creed.[25] Sheppard epitomised the idea that a college was a place where people lived, met, talked, learnt and developed as human beings (as opposed to a hall of residence where the instrumental necessity of education might take place). Eddie Marsh wrote appreciatively of Sheppard that he 'never tired of teaching the importance of poets and artists in the good society which is to be built up by our children'.[26] It may be generous to see any profound political theory in Sheppard's insistence on the value of poetry. But, for him, living in and through the arts was a necessary and demanding commitment to the art of living. The question of Socrates was 'How should one live?' Sheppard found his place in King's to answer this question, to his own satisfaction.

To his own satisfaction ... Sheppard's life was elite, privileged and self-satisfying. He was proudly elitist even and especially in his proclaimed 'faith in the value and interest of human beings'. In 1946, he railed against what he saw as the current democratic fashion of ignoring differences between the best and less good, which was 'sapping this country in every direction'. 'If we go down to perdition', he pontificated to Keynes, 'it will ... be in foam of slop and soap'.[27] Even his depressions were causes for the earnest exchange of letters and the search for the warm comforts his friends provided. He promoted an *art of living* – a style, to make the man. But it would be misleading to compare this art of living too purposively with Foucault's promotion of a stylistics of living, let alone later queer writers' claims about alternative ways to inhabit time in order to challenge the commitments of normative sociality. Style is not the same thing as biopolitics, though they can both be masks for each other. For Sheppard, style did make the man (see Figure 29).

What remains surprising is that he was elected Provost – the institutional head of the college – and was largely regarded as an excellent choice. He made his interventions on appointments, on how college was organised and what the atmosphere of its social scene was. As many outsiders noted with either awe or consternation or pleasure, under Sheppard King's was a rather queer place.

The image of **Dadie Rylands** as a sunny youth of shyly austere character that the elderly Benson constructed for himself, and the picture of the exploitative beauty of uncertain heartlessness that Virginia Woolf drew, are themselves framed by a remarkable portrait produced in the year of Rylands' death by Noel Annan, who was the Provost of King's, and later, now as Lord Annan, Vice-Chancellor of the University of London. Annan was fascinated by the networks of intellectuals who dominated not just the university life of the twentieth century but also the higher reaches of the arts and of government – an integral thread of the establishment which Annan influentially called 'the intellectual aristocracy'. He himself, as we

FIGURE 29 Sheppard in full lecturing flow, on the desk. This picture
captures his charisma most.

will see, was one of those who inhabited the fertile terrain
between university and Whitehall, not least with the
Annan Report on the Future of Broadcasting. Annan also
declares himself to be 'platonically devoted' to Dadie
since his undergraduate days.[28] The cache of letters that

survive from that early period certainly show him relentlessly enthusiastic, grateful and keen to please the charismatic Rylands – and he also records that Rylands, who had
won the most votes in the first round of the election for
Provost in 1955, stood aside and asked his supporters to
back Annan himself for the job. Annan has insider knowledge, gained over many decades, to put Rylands in his
context both in King's and as a national figure.

The portrait he offers is cruelly frank and lovingly
hagiographic. The praise is unstinting. Rylands was, he
records, a fine administrator – although he turned down
the chance to become Provost in order to avoid endlessly
chairing meetings – showing his skills especially during
the war when he and Sheppard kept King's going under
extraordinary pressures (not just the war: he was terrified
of the acerbic Keynes' judgement of his work). He duly
describes Rylands' extraordinary influence on modern
theatre and especially Shakespearian performance, for
which he was awarded a CBE in 1961, an influence that
took material form when he raised the money to keep the
Cambridge Arts Theatre, Keynes' project, afloat. He was
chairman of the theatre's trust for more than thirty years,
after Keynes. Annan wonders at Rylands' inexhaustible
'vitality and stamina' that 'made any party, any dinner,
any gathering where he was not present, seem devitalised'.
But above all, Annan emphasises Rylands' 'power'. 'As a
moral influence', he declares, Rylands 'was formidable.'
Time and again, he recalls, Rylands would intervene in a
meeting 'with an argument that cut through scruples and
hesitations and convinced the fellows that there was a
right course of action and any other was wrong'. The
portrait ends passionately – it was written just after

Dadie died – 'His friends thought of him as Plato did of Socrates: "a man of whom we may say that of all we met at that time, he was the wisest, justest and best".'[29] The reference to Plato is layered with a poised sense of history. Annan was indeed devoted.

But this praise comes after the most brutal analysis of Dadie as an object of devotion. After he first left Cambridge for London and the Bloomsbury Group, Dadie soon 'acquired a reputation of being tricky, ill-behaved and demanding'. Annan put this down to the combination of 'a volatile temper with physical beauty', and the anxieties of being 'violently desired'. But Annan goes on to analyse deeper causes. Rylands' father had died when he was young, and his relationship with his mother was tempestuous. She 'possessed his soul', writes Annan, trying to capture her lasting influence on his life. There were between them 'strong emotions of love and hate'. She both disciplined him fiercely and encouraged his waywardness; they had 'furious quarrels ... followed by intense reconciliations'. His mother, Annan insists, ruined his sex life. 'Between him and his desires came the curse of his mother.'[30] The description of Dadie and his relation-ships becomes more garish:

Dark and hideous neuroses pursued him and, like the Harpies, snatched the food from his mouth before he could eat. His life was tragic. Guilt denied him any happiness or love he might have found in his sexual encounters. Drink alone released him from this sense of guilt, but when it operated it released other evil potencies which ran like rats among his guests. He became quarrelsome, pettish and jealous; he would declare himself deserted and betrayed by his friends ... When his sexual pas-sions were aroused he became a travesty of himself and behaved so outrageously that his friends would cap each other's stories of the devastating evenings they had endured with him.[31]

This of a man whose 'moral influence' Annan declared 'formidable'. There is little attempt to bridge the profound contradictions or tensions of this portrait. Annan duly progresses, with his Platonic credentials assured, into the bedroom. Dadie 'did not believe that sex and love were compatible … He fell in love only three times and suffered much; and he was so racked with guilt and a sense of physical shame that he sometimes became impotent.' Like James Froude, who shocked his Victorian readership by hinting at Carlyle's impotence, or Lytton Strachey who outraged and delighted his audience by his debunking of eminent Victorians, Annan knows full well that he is pulling back a veil. He explains Dadie's problem: 'He identified sex with lust, not love, with danger and with frenzy.' But he immediately sticks in the dagger. 'Someone who went to bed with him described it as like being in a rugger scrum' – a description most likely to be evocative to someone who has not been in a rugger/rugby scrum rather than a serious sportsman. But Annan's account has a real edge to it. He adds how Dadie 'used his tongue as his mother had taught him, to sting those about him', and how 'when nervous a couple of cocktails turned him into a staggering sot';[32] Dadie did nothing to stop F. L. Lucas' wife, Topsy, from leaving her husband because of an unrequited passion for him, but rather continued to encourage her friendship (see Figure 30).

Being friends with Dadie was hard work: 'He was an exacting friend: if you made a remark he considered silly,

Dadie & Topsy Lucas

FIGURE 30 Dadie Rylands and Topsy Lucas: the contrast with his younger picture with Benson is marked: no swagger here, no smiles, both turned away from each other.

insensitive or devoid of moral insight you would be devastated by a satirical or wounding remark'; yet he was 'defenceless himself before any attack, so thin-skinned and vulnerable'.[33] It is hard not to suspect that there was some deep hurt behind this conflicted portrait, a spurned devotion, that leads both to the brutal candidness and to the heightened eulogy.

Annan published this portrait in his last book, *The Dons*. He too died the next year, the end of the century, 2000. His book is self-consciously about tradition and its construction. The story of Rylands as theatrical artist (Annan's chapter title is 'The Don as Performer') is also the story of Dadie's histrionics as a lover. The conflicted doubleness that is so striking in this account of Dadie is also another narrative to add to the understanding of the community, a narrative that strives to understand the role of *acting out*. As with Sheppard, who brought Dadie to King's, the theatre became an extension of a life-style, as much as an expression of it. Telling such stories is integral to the community's understanding of itself and to the performance of its continuity, part of what is passed on. This sort of story-telling, both in private and in public, is the means and the matter of how a community is formulated: whether you call it anecdote, gossip, myth or history, the power is located in the retelling and in the circles, like the students gathered around Monty James to hear his ghost stories read by a single candle-light, which these tellings and retellings form.

Annan's account of Dadie Ryland's emotionally buffeting dramas of desire is borne out by a set of letters that are preserved from his long-term lover, Dennis Robertson. Dennis Robertson was at Trinity, and an economist of real distinction – he was knighted for his services to the government on economic policy, and he also worked closely and cantankerously with Keynes.[34] He and Dadie were intimately connected over many years, and the letters that tell of their attempt to live together and their subsequent break-up in 1930 are detailed in their misery and intensity. Robertson was one of those men who walked down the road from Trinity to King's, compulsively.

The terrible rows that rocked their relationship are evident already in 1926. Robertson writes back to Dadie in December, a six-page letter, after waiting six weeks to reflect on his response. 'This is the third year running, to go no further back, that in spite of very great efforts at self-mastery a row with you has made great havoc for weeks on end with my powers of reading and of general receptivity and of give-and-take of happiness with my family and friends.' Bitter, distressing rows, it seems, rock their relationship repeatedly. Robertson knows he is partly to blame, though this recognition veers immediately into recrimination: 'Don't think I'm trying to land all the responsibility on you: I know very well that my physical hunger, and my obstinacy in refusing to part, and my moody and melancholy temperament must bear their full share. You taunted me ...'[35] But, he also recognises, the arguments affect him in an all-embracing way that is simply not the same for Dadie: 'These rows and their sequels are deadly and devastating for me, utterly boring, as I realise, for you. To me at least it's absolutely vital, if I'm to be a bearable person or even earn my salary honestly, that they should be prevented in future. How, how, how can we prevent them?'[36] His answer to this passionate question, rather unconvincingly, is that they should try not to talk about the past, the dangers of which he exemplifies by ... talking about the past. In particular, the bone of contention is Dadie's relationship with Denys Winstanley (a historian who wrote a history of the University of Cambridge and who became Vice-Master at Trinity, and whose letter about age difference I have already quoted):

You felt that I had done you a great wrong in destroying his affection for you. *I* felt that your view of the *effects* of my action was chronologically impossible, a fiction, to put it bluntly, of vanity and irritation to erode more natural explanations. And that your view of the *blameworthiness* of my action needed very great modification, because you had left out of account the most important factor, the unfair strain which you had put, week after week, on my loyalty by complaining to W. of my fault-finding without being prepared to be candid with him.[37]

You said, he said, we said ... and on and on, with increasingly desperate self-justification and anger. Although we can hear only one side of this triangle, the pain and the twisted feelings of need and upset come through very stridently.

In 1927, things are looking up again. 'Darling Dadie', writes Robertson, 'My dear, I can't write you pretty and gallant letters – it's too late to begin to try: but you know what a precious memory that month is, and will remain for me',[38] and in 1929 Dadie and Robertson are contemplating living together in Heathcote Street in Bloomsbury – what Robertson calls (using Greek letters for their Greek love) *sumbiôsis*. Soon after, Robertson is blaming himself for not helping enough with Dadie's attitude to sexuality and physical desire – tellingly using Plato as the model to aspire towards, as he discusses their feelings obsessively:

You see, with my ex-nonconformist soul, it's terribly bitter to me to know that I haven't helped you at all directly in your growing up, as Plato helped his young men in spite of/with the aid of his desire for their bodies. But it is true, and I would rather know it. The only thing that would make this bitterness less would be to be able to feel that at that particular period I did fill a sort of gap in that respect (not a very large one, it is true because Topsy was in it!). But I am not going to ask you whether it is true, because I don't want to tempt you away from the courageous truthfulness which you've given me the last two days.[39]

Topsy is the wife of F. L. Lucas, who, as obsessed with Dadie as Robertson is, was another force with which Robertson contended. He signs this letter 'Your (?evil) Fortune' – ironically, marking both what he hopes is his fate – namely, to be Dadie's fortune – and his anxiety that this fortune might not all be good. The question mark acts like a complicit raised eyebrow between partners.

By August of 1930, things are breaking down. Dadie has accused him of only wanting his body, and complaining too much about his faults (the sort of narcissistic recrimination Annan regrets in Dadie's behaviour). Robertson replies:

I think you misjudge it if you think I could have remained in thrall all these years if I hadn't been drawn to you by your character as well as by your charm and your beauty, and dreaded losing contact with it. What seems to be true is that your faults are (though far less than they used to be) just those which become specially prominent in a person who is the object of unreturned love, and just those which dovetail worst with my own.[40]

And from a distance, Robertson appeals to their shared and long history together: 'I send you two of your old letters to show you what I mean – **please** return them to me, for you meant them at the time, even if they now seem faded.'[41] But it seems that he hadn't fully realised that Dadie was actually breaking up with him, and then couldn't face the thought: 'I realised that you had begun our conversation in Cambridge by suggesting separation, that I hadn't then been contemplating it, that my letters though written in a state very near despair, didn't mention it: and that therefore (unless my letters so put you off as to make you take it) fresh action if any must come from me.'[42] The narrative grammar is an expression of tortured recollection and recalibration (and the sentence itself is written over with additions and crossings-out as he struggles with what is happening). He suddenly realises it is all over – the letter is full of his anguish – and he does take action, with a histrionic turn: 'I've thought about various compromises about Heathcote Street, with a view to minimizing theatricality or gossip. But I am afraid that none of them is sensible or tolerable, and I don't propose to go there again.'[43] As ever, this grand gesture leads both to the analysis of emotion, the display of emotion – and the analysis of emotion *as* the display of emotion – ending with a dramatic and even histrionic promise to disappear:

I hadn't realised how little you'd been able to accept what seemed to me a new modus vivendi, how utterly unsuccessful my efforts to keep jealousy in bounds had seemed to you, how big a gulf you still felt to exist between your friendship with me and your other intimate friendships, how deeply rooted in your mind was this feeling of my being unappreciative, how little you felt there was to get on the credit side.
Now that I do realise all these things, I don't see what else I can do but vanish.[44]

Living together has collapsed; jealousy has been thought unbounded; there are gulfs; others are involved, who cared more and how ... the story is no less painful for being a mess of clichés, concluding in the desperate prom-ise to vanish, made in the full but unlikely hope of being called back. The final, conclusive letter, however, not long later, is brief, scribbled on a small page, and rather beautifully moving in contrast:

And make allowances in your heart – I know you do – for all in the history of 39 years that makes me inarticulate in asking and gauche in taking.[45]

After which, the archive is silent. Back in 1910, Dennis Robertson, then aged only twenty, had written a letter to Arthur Benson – 'a most intimate letter, revealing the devastating emotions of his heart and soul'. Benson had written back ('as kindly and as straightforwardly' as he could) and they had met and had a desultory and unsatisfactory conversation.[46] Keynes found talking to Robertson at times, on economic questions, deeply annoying because of his passion, which disturbed Keynes' sense of cold truth (that is, they violently disagreed, to Keynes' vexation). Robertson was undoubtedly a man of feeling. Nonetheless this exchange of letters with Dadie Rylands is strikingly intense and emotionally overwrought and desperate both in love and despair. It gives a few, distressing glimpses of a sexualised relationship between men that is neither mercenary, nor brief, nor ironically manipulative, nor determinedly chaste, but riven with anxieties of the flesh mingled with love, recrimination mixed with care, articulacy with emotional confusion – over time. It was precisely *sumbiôsis*, living with each other and living with their own conflicted feelings, that proved ultimately impossible.

In 1924, Rylands, then aged twenty-two, played the part of the Duchess in John Webster's *Duchess of Malfi* – theatrical shows in Cambridge were usually single-sex events at this time. Although Arthur Benson found the

play and the part deeply unpleasant – as T. S. Eliot
memorably wrote, 'Webster ... saw the skull beneath
the skin' – Rylands' other friends marvelled at his performance, and the play and his acting went down in local
folklore as a great moment in the history of Cambridge
theatre, and a founding moment of what would be Dadie's
starry dramatic career.[47] Another person who had audi-
tioned for the role was Cecil Beaton, later the celebrated
fashion photographer and designer who created, for
example, the stunning costumes for the film *My Fair
Lady*. Beaton was miffed not to get the part and consequently was prepared to dislike Rylands (though much
later he would photograph the masque Dadie staged
with Lydia Lopokova in the starring role). His record
of the cast party might be a little jaundiced therefore,
but in his diary he described Dadie drunk, 'in a blue
dressing gown – his face covered with dry blood',
rushing around kissing everyone, and then declaring
to Wase, who had played the Second Executioner, that
he was very beautiful; and then proceeded to snog
him for a 'quarter of an hour' in front of everyone – to
Beaton's disgust. Rylands had tried it on with Boy,
Beaton's closest friend: 'I was very surprised and jealous', records Beaton, only to add, 'I should have liked
him to be all over me' – which does rather undermine
his outrage with a certain irony. He was doubly surprised at the snogging, however, because Wase was 'un
homo' – that is, straight – and 'so quiet and the straight-
forward Britisher having no nonsense'. 'I do think
its extraordinary the most un homo people behaving
in this manner', he reflected.[48]

FIGURE 31 Dadie Rylands as the Duchess of Malfi, sketched by Cecil Beaton.

Beaton also made a bitchy, satirical sketch of Dadie dressed as the Duchess (see Figure 31) which he published that Christmas in *Granta*, the student magazine (which has since been revived and has grown into a major literary publication).

The portrait, cruel as it is, is surrounded with pronouncements, which appear to be the demands of the actor: 'No blatant truths', 'Please don't hurry', 'No large pearls', 'No self-advertisement' (all of which, it might be said, Beaton himself would be happy to transgress).[49] 'No radiators', like many a pop-star's hospitality rider, seems a deliberately perverse flaunting of ego. The sketch is rather brilliant, evocative both of the moment and of the young Rylands. The portrait can be nicely compared with Beaton's own remarkable photographic portrait the next year, also published in *Granta*.

On the left, in perfect mimicry of the sort of society photo of which Beaton would himself become master, Beaton in half profile, swathed in pearls, unsmiling, is uncannily convincing. On the right, he leans on a classical pillar, but in a thoroughly unclassical pose, the long dress and bustle, high hair-do, heels and emphatically 'large pearls', go beyond camp or burlesque into a full-scale embodiment. Think Jane Harrison, the redoubtable don of Newnham College, posing as a flapper. Beaton at Cambridge wore full-make up – more attractively and subtly, he insisted, than his friend Norman Hartnell, who also went on to be a famous fashion designer. Dressing up and acting out overlapped the performance on the theatrical stage and the performance of consciously anti-normative sexuality in the Cambridge scene.

A couple of days after the cast party, Beaton discovered by chance that one of his friends, Collier, had had sex with Arthur Jeffress at a party. (Collier went a 'dull mauve' and mumbled 'Oh God, does everyone know?'")[50] Beaton was

The examiner examineth.
Your pains are registered, where I turn the leaf
To read them.
    .   .   .   .
They have more in them than mortal knowledge.
    .   .   .   .
Poor prattler, how thou talk'st.
    .   .   .   .
Say from whence you owe this strange intelligence.
    .   .   .   .
Art thou but a false creation proceeding from
The heat oppressed brain ?
    .   .   .   .
What you have spoke it may be so perchance.
    .   .   .   .
Question this most bloody piece of work
To know it further.
    .   .   .   .
Little is the wisdom where the flight
So runs against all reason.

It is a tale told by an idiot full of sound and fury,
Signifying nothing.
                  You'll rue the time
That clogs me with this answer.
    .   .   .   .
Oh, well done ! I commend your pains.
    .   .   .   .
He hath a wisdom that doth guide his valour
To act in safety.
    .   .   .   .
Such welcome and unwelcome things at once
'Tis hard to reconcile.
    .   .   .   .
The Happy Ending.
To conclude, the victory fell on us.
    .   .   .   .
                I have bought
Golden opinions from all sorts of people.
    .   .   .   .
New honours come upon him.
    .   .   .   .
You know your own degrees.   F. G. E. F.

Cecil Unbeaten

Photos by Scott & Wilkinson.   MR. CECIL BEATON IN *ALL THE VOGUE.*

FIGURE 32 Cecil Beaton in costume.

amazed at the scene: 'It's the most extraordinary thing,
Collier is so hearty and the all-time woman worshipper! …
Acting does seem to have a curious effect on people.'
Beaton, who was very chary of actual physical relation-
ships at this point in his life, was told the story of the party
the next day (like a latter-day version of Plato's
Symposium). The events, he thought, were 'nearly too

terrible to be funny'. At the party, 'everyone behaved very badly', and only two men there 'did not lie with people'. One confessed he took part to experiment: 'he only did it to see if he was homo sexual or not' (the further decision is not recorded). Somewhat out of joint, Beaton concluded, 'I think its a good thing that term is only two months long. Everyone seems to be falling in love with someone.' So, he reflects finally, 'nearly all [the cast of the *Duchess of*] *Malfi* have been completely turned over the last few days'. Theatre, it seems – or seemed to Beaton – was a place where the usual restrictions of sexual identity slipped and slid. Acting had a curious – one might say, queer – effect on people: the theatre was a place where the gap between 'un' and 'homo' was precariously articulated.

It is perhaps no surprise, then, that the national press, fascinated as ever with the elite world of Oxford and Cambridge, the training ground of the future leaders of the country, ran a story about the dangers of student theatricals to the development of a solid national masculinity. In 1925, the year after the staging of the *Duchess of Malfi*, the *Daily Sketch* printed a trivial, sensationalist piece based on the view of one of its 'expert' commentators, who is quoted as saying:

I have seen youths lounging down the street in bunches of half a dozen … with powder on their cheeks, paint on their lips and bistre on their eye-lids. I know the secrets of theatrical make-up, and it cannot deceive me. The vast majority of these 'girl-men' are University students … In my day at the University, they would have been thrown into the river, but now nobody seems to mind. People just accept them as an expression of modern life.[51]

This perceived degeneracy (the paranoia of 'it cannot deceive me' is particularly striking) is linked to the theatre: 'some of these youths have played women's parts in University theatricals, and I think that has encouraged their loathly effeminacy … games do not appeal to them. They seem to have no normal healthy tastes … Sometimes one longs for a gun.' The rot runs beyond the university in his imagination: 'They take their cue from decadent playwrights and I imagine they will be thought as clever as those advertised young dramatists if they dress and act as women.' The lack of coherent grammar no doubt marks the overflow of feeling. *Granta*, the student magazine, duly picked up the story and delightedly mocked it under the headline 'Girl-Men of Cambridge'. The anxiety and prurience of such rhetoric is familiar enough – but it would be hard to declare it baseless. Dadie Rylands, however his lovers described sex with him, certainly did not find sport – 'games' – appealing. Philip Radcliffe (1905–86), the musicologist, who read plays with E. M. Forster and Noel Annan in the Ten Club and lived as a bachelor in college for over sixty years, told me on the sixtieth anniversary of his coming to King's that he still recalled the joy of knowing on that day he would 'never have to do games again'.

Keynes, Sheppard and Rylands were linked by their love of theatre and the arts, and each made important contributions in Cambridge and more widely. Together they form a not insignificant chapter in the history of British theatre. But it was also the lure of dressing up and acting out, on the one hand, and the social pressure to wear a mask, on the other, that made the men who desired men find a space for themselves in the theatre. As theatre provided a space where the demanding strictures of social conformity were less stridently enforced, so too the acting of the theatre spread into the dramas of life, as the emotions and performances of daily existence fed the performances on stage. The flamboyance that so many noted in the public personas of Rylands and Sheppard is code for the theatricality of their queerness.

Music was perhaps less worrying than dressing up as a woman on stage, but nonetheless it also attracted the anxiety of the public policeman of sexual propriety. The *Musical Times* back in 1889 captured and generalised the worry:

All musicians are as a class wanting in the manlier qualities. In a country like England, where devotion to athletics forms a cardinal tenet in the national creed, such an impression cannot fail to have operated greatly to the prejudice of the art – indeed, of all arts, for there are many excellent people with whom the term 'artist' is simply a synonym for 'Bohemian' or 'black sheep.' They are so firmly persuaded that exclusive devotion to the study of music is inevitably attended by a weakening of moral and physical fibre that they avoid all personal contact or association with such persons.[52]

As in the 1920s, sport provides the criterion of manliness; and, typically for this earlier period, sexual denigration appears veiled in the judgements 'Bohemian', or 'black sheep', glossed as a 'weakening of moral and physical fibre'. Artists, and musicians in particular, are degenerate and to be avoided socially. Bizarrely enough, the same journal as late as 1994 writes once more with a certain despair, tempered now by a willing embrace of the queer, that '*All* musicians, we must remember, are faggots, in the parlance of the male locker room.'[53] In 1889, the article goes on, with a rather shuffling eyes-to-the-floor apologia, to question such a view as applicable only to some musicians and not musicians in general – this is the *Musical Times*, after all – and Beethoven is held up as an exemplum of untrammelled masculinity. (You can almost hear the sigh of relief at the memory of Beethoven's manly scowl.) But the association of artists with effeminacy or degeneracy continued, and was part of the fixing of the public image of the homosexual that was effected by the Oscar Wilde trial. So, in 1914 the German sexologist Magnus Hirschfeld theorised that typical male homosexual listeners 'experience music only as an aspect of mood, a purely sensory impression'.[54] Lacking the 'intellectual engagement' to follow the complex formal structure of 'older, classical music', they naturally prefer the 'more colourful or sensual music' of nineteenth-century musical Romanticism. 'As to music', wrote Edward Carpenter in 1908, 'this is certainly the art which in its subtlety and tenderness – and perhaps in a certain inclination to indulge in emotion – lies nearest to the Urning nature. There are few in fact of this nature who have not some gift in the direction of music.'[55] Indeed, '[t]he association between music, male homosexuality and the emotionally receptive body [is] insistently drawn in sexological texts'. And in the burgeoning small ads that spread during and after the First World War, where 'musical' was a regular code word.[56] Amusingly, in E. M. Forster's *Maurice*, his posthumously published novel of homosexual desire, Tchaikovsky's 6th symphony, usually known as 'the Pathétique' for its swirling emotion, is called a 'symphonie incestueuse et pathic' – that is, incestuous and gay ('pathic' is a word used regularly in the study of ancient Greece, and adopted by some sexologists, to refer to the negative idea of a passive homosexual partner, one who receives rather than penetrates).[57] Edward Prime-Stevenson, who wrote a defence of homosexuality published under the name of Xavier Mayne, *The Intersexes* (1908), saw many a sign of homosexuality in music itself; he commented: 'Some homosexual hearers of Tschaikowsky's last (and most elegiac) symphony, known as the "Pathetic" claim to find in it such revelations of a sentimental-sexual kind that they have nicknamed the work the "Pathic" Symphony.'[58] Forster's inconsequential joke is rather more knowing than it might at first seem.

H staircase is next door to King's Chapel, and while daily services there were part of the routine for college life, over the course of the twentieth century music and the choir became more and more a celebrated part of King's College. The Christmas Eve carol service of Nine Lessons and Carols, first devised by Edward White Benson, Arthur Benson's father, is now watched by millions on television, a world-wide audience. The strength of the choir was built up in particular by **Boris Ord**, who moved into G4 in 1923. He took control of the choir in 1929.[59] Ord – born Bernhard Ord but always known as Boris – was educated at Clifton College in Bristol where Cecil Taylor was a housemaster, but there are few detailed records of his life that I have been able to find. The one fact that is agreed is that it was widely known in the music profession that he was homosexual (though apparently his right-hand man, David Willcocks, remained largely in the dark about his boss's proclivities). He did go on holiday to Venice in the 1920s with men who were acknowledged couples, invited by Edward Dent. The one story I was told about Ord was that he was arrested for cottaging – for trying to pick up a young man in a public toilet in Bristol. It appears that he escaped prosecution, as many upper-class and well-connected men did. But it was nonetheless a humiliating event. When he returned to King's and sat down to his first High Table dinner there was total and embarrassed silence, which was broken by a fellow saying loudly: 'Don't worry, Boris old chap, could have happened to any one of us.' The noise of dinner broke out unrestrainedly. The story may be a college myth, of course. But it was told to demonstrate the embrace of community.

Edward Dent (1876–1957), who invited Ord to Venice, was the presiding genius of musical life in King's, an academic and composer who transformed the study of music at Cambridge and internationally (see Figure 33).

He has a strong claim to be the first modern musicologist in this country, a scholar fluent in German, Italian and Spanish, and expert in the manuscript and performance traditions of more than one musical genre, based on painstaking philological work across the libraries of Europe. He came from landed gentry in Yorkshire, went to Eton and then King's in 1895, and became a fellow in 1902, the first musicologist to be elected, and the question of whether composition could even be considered as part of his application much vexed the committee of appointment. He was a great authority on the

FIGURE 33 Edward Dent – his official portrait as a young man.

manuscript scores of early music – especially Scarlatti, on whom his fellowship dissertation was focused – and on opera in all its forms: he insisted on the academic study of music, and his insistence led to the formation of the music tripos and a change in how music was discussed from popular journals and newspapers through to the expectations of academic publication. He was passionate about contemporary music too and a force in modernisation of the habits and understanding of listening and performance through Cambridge-based, national and international organisations. He helped set up the International Society for Contemporary Music and acted as its president for many years – which was also an expression of the profound internationalism that he had developed in his relationship with Goldsworthy Lowes Dickinson: Dent sat on the committee for the arts at the fledgling League of Nations (though when he left, he sniffed, 'it was a great waste of time, and on the whole, a bore').[60] Dent travelled regularly to Italy and Germany for his research, and had a huge network among modern composers, performers and academics. He could easily have appeared in my chapter on the politics of homosexuality, although how he related his homosexuality to his activities in the politics of culture was, as we will see, less systematic or purposive than Lowes Dickinson. As a governor of Sadler's Wells Opera and the Old Vic Theatre, along with the many festivals he organised for the International Society for Contemporary Music across Europe, he changed the shape of the modern British arts scene. It is typical of his response to recognition for this starry career that he not only turned down a knighthood from the Attlee Government, but also never wrote a word about his refusal to even his closest friends.

Dent is a figure who links many vectors of the history of H staircase, and his story can be told now thanks to the painstaking biography, researched over many years, by Karen Arrandale, the proofs of which I was delighted to be able to read: Arrandale shows in great detail how extensive Dent's musical, intellectual and personal networks were, and how they were formed and maintained over time. Although Dent comes from an established family with a large house and property in Yorkshire, and attended Eton and King's, and is central, if anyone is, in the cultural establishment of the country, he never felt that he fitted in, and repeatedly resisted the expectations placed on him by his class and family. There is a lovely description by him of going home as a young man to his fearsome mother: 'after lunch received a lengthy oration from mother – in which she abused the two dearest objects of my affections – music & Cambridge – however she was too much out of temper to be open to conviction by argument – so I could only sit & blink at her in silence ...'. Needless to say, his sense of alienation was fostered by his awareness of his own sexuality. Like so many, it was coming to King's that transformed his self-understanding, and he was fond of quoting Bismarck afterwards that 'life only really begins at university'.[61]

He met Oscar Browning quickly – his description of O. B.'s contradictions was quoted in the first chapter – and became friends with Goldsworthy Lowes Dickinson, and with many other men in Cambridge: with Keynes, with Sayle, with Lubbock and Sheppard, many of the heroes of this history. He describes in his diary on a single day having Forster, Sheppard and Lubbock to lunch, calling on Sayle, and having dinner later with Lytton Strachey and his brother. Dent was fully embedded in the community. He knew that he was the model – or a major part of the model – for Forster's conflicted and ineffectual character Philip Heriton in *Where Angels Fear to Tread*, and, more worryingly for Dent, Cecil Vyse in *A Room with a View*. When Forster took his trips to Italy that form the plot of *A Room with a View*, he followed an itinerary organised for him by Dent, already an expert on the country – his Italy was viewed through Dent's lens. His friend Francis Toye captures something of why Dent could have evoked Vyse: 'Dent's was a curious personality. A bachelor from passionate conviction, he gave the impression rather of prim old-maidishness; by nature the kindest of men, he was often at pains to indulge in acid comments on people and their motives calculated to wound deeply; in practice exceptionally beneficent and unselfish, he proclaimed with vigour his detestation of the Christian virtues – indeed, of Christians in general.'[62] Rupert Brooke was characteristically funnier and bitchier: 'I always imagine Dent as the Serpent telling Eve about the Apples. "My dear Eve …" pointing out all the blemishes on them, with back-hits at God and Adam, and a rumour that the Holy ghost was *enceinte* [pregnant]. But so kindly.'[63] He could be the model for the learned, prim and frustrated Vyse also because, thanks to his home life, he 'suffered from residual prudery all his life',[64] and took a while to overcome the ignorance and inexperience of his upbringing. Yet, like Forster, he moved from his early hesitations and frustrations to a much fuller sexual life, not least thanks to his experiences in the other world of Italy and Germany. He begins nervously testing for reciprocated feelings, before slipping into self-consciously marking his own lack of articulacy: 'I think – in fact I feel almost certain – from the way he looked at me sometimes – when I looked at him in almost the same way – that my affection for him is in an appreciable degree reciprocated – What a lucid sentence!' In Italy, he found more physical pleasures with military men, especially one Emilio Bacchia, who 'became for years a regular uncomplicated companion and lover', though he resisted the more commercial opportunities on offer.[65] He described his relationships as the search for young plants for his garden: 'I consider my Bologna gardens well planted', he writes with calm satisfaction. But he also – for a while at least – was expressive in Cambridge.[66] He was great friends with Sayle and went to his salon to view what Sayle called his 'swans' – the beautiful young men he invited – until he moved out of college to his own salon on Panton Street which caused frictions of jealousy and fussing between the two men. He was close to Clive Carey, and furious when Percy Lubbock made a play for him. Denis Browne, the close friend of Rupert Brooke, who was also, like Brooke, destined to die young in the First World War, was Dent's passion of the moment when Clive Carey took him to visit Monty James in the Provost's Lodge. This produces an outburst from Dent:

But it is too bad: as you know, Denis is my very particular swan just at present, mainly because of his extraordinary musical capacity (at present he is only the prospective favourite disciple & no more) – and I was keeping him even from Sayle. And now Clive comes & hands him over to the Lodge! ... you may say I ought to have personality enough to hold my friends myself – I lost Clive when Percy handed him over to James. I did not lose his friendship, but I lost him as a disciple ... And though people say Sayle spoils his undergraduate friends & makes them prigs – he does make them see that they have got to be leaders. He made me see it, I think more than anybody, except perhaps Allen – and naturally I don't bring you into these comparisons. James hates leaders as he hates philosophers ... I want to combine the two, and bring it about that the leaders shd be civilised people, but leaders none the less.[67]

This is an extraordinary portal into the complexities of Cambridge life and Dent's personality. There is a tiff of jealousy, of course, that Denis is someone Dent wants just for himself, at present as a disciple in music, though this leaves the future open for a further, more physical relationship: he is one of Dent's 'swans'. What upsets Dent is not just that Browne is meeting other people but specifically Monty James, a different circle, a different charismatic social force. This hostility is expressed against James' resistance to leaders and philosophers. We have already seen how James seemed to his contemporaries to embody an antipathy to thought; here the concept of leadership is added. Dent wants his 'swans' – and he is, of course, talking about the ideals he sets for himself too – to be leaders. Surprisingly he acknowledges that this principle is something he has learnt from the fussy and ineffectual Sayle. But it is a principle that Dent would go on to exercise throughout his career. He repeatedly took control – of institutions, of people, of plans – and was indeed a real leader. This idea of leadership he sums up as a combination of 'philosophy' and 'leadership', where 'philosophy' – a term Wilde used to announce and veil his homosexual tendencies – is immediately explained as 'civilised people'. Here we see the politics of culture that Dent epitomises, a fight for civilisation. Like Carpenter, who both saw musicality as a possibly integral attribute of men who desired men and insisted that an integrated, civilised culture would include a community of men who desired men, Dent is moving – in his rage and jealousy – towards at least an echo of such systematic thinking. It is not by chance that Dent, when he was asked directly in 1916 if he was Uranian, replied that he was rather a disciple of Edward Carpenter. He was denying that he was no more than an aesthetic or sentimental lover of young men, and insisting rather that he had a social vision. As Karen Arrandale summarises, it is striking to observe '[i]n these years, Dent's constant experimenting with ways in which he could draw together the complicated strands of his life – his music, his sexuality, his internationalist leanings, his hopes for Cambridge'.[68]

Unlike so many of the figures whose lives I have been tracing, Dent is strikingly different in forming a long-term relationship. J. B. Trend (1887–1958) was one of his swans – he was eleven years younger than Dent – and for many years after they first met, although they clearly enjoyed each other's company greatly, Trend was overshadowed in Dent's mind by his other passions. But they gradually grew to depend more and more on each other, intellectually and emotionally. In 1916, Dent suggested that they took rooms together; typically, Trend had to find the rooms, in New Quebec Street in Mayfair in London. They lived together for more than twenty-five years. Both travelled regularly and they wrote voluminously and often. Their relationship seems to have been open, kind and without violent disagreements or jealousy. Dent could write of his flirtations and even affairs with Germans and Italians; Trend spent time in Tangiers where his dalliances made it into his dispatches home too. Trend became Professor of Spanish at Cambridge, and introduced Dent to Spanish culture – and to his long-lasting engagement with Falla and his music. Unlike the temperamental and destructive rows of Rylands and

Robertson, *sumbiôsis* was easy and mutually enriching. Dent seems to have managed to link his sexual and professional life into a distinctive compatibility, where his sharpness of tongue, scholarly and institutional demands and intellectual ambition did not destroy the potential of his personal relationship at a more domestic level. He transcended the Cecil Vyse that Forster saw in him.

In 1906, when he was thirty, Dent spent a sabbatical in Berlin, which had a flourishing homosexual scene. In particular he met there Magnus Hirschfeld, the sexologist who ran the *Wissenschaftlich–humanitäres Komittee*, a research centre which, despite its title, was focused primarily on male desire for males. They had several meetings that year, and later Hirschfeld came to Cambridge, where, through Dent, he had dinner with Keynes and Lowes Dickinson, who also visited Hirschfeld in Germany with Dent; Hirschfeld had sessions with Hugh Dalton and Gerald Shove too. He went to a service at King's Chapel at Dent's invitation where he scandalised the congregation by rustling a newspaper during the proceedings. What is fascinating, however, is to see how Dent is struggling to understand himself through contemporary academic research. Unlike Havelock Ellis in Britain, whose work was regarded as dangerous – something to be kept in locked cabinets and used only by professionals – Hirschfeld in Berlin was a public personage whose work was known and broadly circulated. His 'public visibility' led him also to being hospitalised after an attack, and his institute was destroyed by Nazis in 1933. Although Dent remained profoundly reticent about himself, openness of research and a commitment to the highest levels of informed understanding based on such academic enquiry were principles that followed from his musicology into his views on sexuality. The fruits of his invitation to Hirschfeld were seen when, thanks to Hirschfeld – along with Havelock Ellis – the British Society for the Study of Sexual Psychology (BSSSP) was formed in 1914, primarily to research and discuss homosexuality. The BSSSP published a short series of pamphlets but fizzled out, unmissed, in the 1940s. The translation of sexology from Germany to England is part of the history of British awareness of sexuality, but the study of it has not adequately registered the role of Dent and others like him, who actively facilitated the transfer of continental theory to a British context. John Forrester and Laura Cameron's brilliant, detailed history of the development of the subject of psychology at Cambridge, *Freud in Cambridge*, has demonstrated both how many Cambridge figures visited and were treated by Freud, and how experimental psychology was precariously shaped against competing disciplinary models, such as psychoanalysis.[69] Yet the figures I have been discussing only gradually approach psychology: they do not, it seems, know of Freud, for example, but they do engage intently with Havelock Ellis, with Krafft-Ebing and, through Dent, with Hirschfeld. That is, the sexologists whom they read are those who work most committedly on male desire for men as a pathology. There is a particular dynamic here that is central to the history of homosexuality. At one level, the legal and medical professions, with the ideological support of the church, both Anglican and Catholic, were committing to a diagnosis of homosexuality as a pathology: across the life-time of Dent, public discourse shifted from the language of Uranian, Urning,

Invert, Sodomite, to the fixed category of homosexual (with its buttressing of slang insults), and the term homosexual defines what is to be the identity of a person: you could now be 'one of those' – inscribed and proscribed in a language of alienation. At another level, for men who desired men and did not have an established vocabulary of self-expression and were searching for a way to describe themselves to themselves and to others, within this increasingly frightening and aggressive social environment, the turn to sexologists like Hirschfeld was a salvific gesture. This sexology gave a mirror in which they could see themselves and find themselves and others like them: one of us, rather than one of those. One consequence, however, was also an internalisation of the structures and strictures of shame. The desire to escape self-alienation became a necessary trajectory in the narrative of a pathologised homosexuality. Sexology also helped to make men complicit with their own social denigration.

Despite his desire to bring together leadership and philosophy, when the Second World War broke out, Dent was found wanting. He saw what was happening first-hand in Berlin: 'Göring ordered a raid on the queer places … I think myself that the most horrible part of the whole thing is the utter indifference with which the public seems to regard these political assassinations en masse.'[70] He saw the threats to his friends, but responded to them largely as moments of discomfort for them. He tried to change the course of things by civilised concerts, and his tolerant appeasement was wholly bypassed by more powerful and horrible forces: his internationalism had no impact. After the war, helped by his friend Hugh Dalton who was now the Chancellor of the Exchequer, he was instrumental in changing the cultural institutions of England, and keeping modern music and theatre a central cultural strand of society; but this success was raising something from the ashes of an ideal that had been severely challenged. He maintained his relationship with J. B. Trend, but he had also noted much earlier that 'I must be growing very old – for I no longer fall in love with every other person I meet. The standard of beauty seems to me to be much lower.'[71] His last years were spent in pain from an ulcer, increasing deafness and a certain loneliness in his apartment in Panton Street. He had come to King's because it 'cared for poetry, music and drama'.[72] He followed those sirens all his life. Like Sheppard, Rylands and Forster – to take the most evident paradigms – Dent's commitment to the arts was also a commitment to what he saw as the struggle for a better society, which he located in personal values of friendship and decency and the values of what he termed, typically for the era, civilisation. He added a robust sense of the importance of scholarship. His homosexuality was imbricated with these principles: he saw himself as an outsider who happened to be on the inside, a position which required observation and concealment. Lytton Strachey tellingly wrote to Dora Carrington that he had seen 'Dent, of course, in a corner' – slightly removed, observing, waiting to make his intervention.[73] Strachey's 'of course' reveals how much this self-placement was part of Dent's life. Yet, because he was the outsider on the inside, he had a particular potential – which he took up – of being transformative. From the corner, he also moved to a position of leadership where he was quietly revolutionary. He wanted to show that his work could change how culture was experienced, and thus how people might inhabit their lives better. This, too, is an art.

And then there was art itself. **Roger Fry** (1866–1934), whom we last saw not consummating a night's embracing with Goldsworthy Lowes Dickinson, came up to King's as an undergraduate in 1885, when he moved into G2 (the same room in which Percy Lubbock and Gerald Shove would live) and he became an honorary fellow in 1927.[74] He too, like Boris Ord, had been educated at Clifton College in Bristol. Fry was both a fine artist and a hugely influential critic – a surprisingly rare combination. He found his way into the Bloomsbury Group where he was looked up to by Virginia Woolf, who saw him as more mature and sophisticated than the rest of the gang, not without reason. She would write his biography after his death. As a critic, he introduced the British public to a group of French avant-garde painters whom he dubbed Post-Impressionists, a name that stuck, notably through a celebrated, controversial exhibition in London in 1910. In 1903 he co-founded the *Burlington Magazine* which he co-edited for ten years, and in 1906 became a curator in the Metropolitan Museum in New York: his reach was international. Kenneth Clarke, whose television show on 'Civilisation' (1969) itself influenced a generation of British public's appreciation of art, put him at the same level as John Ruskin in changing 'taste'. In this judgement he was echoing Virginia Woolf. Fry 'did more than anyone', she wrote, to make ordinary people (or at least her idea of ordinary people, people 'like us') 'enjoy looking at pictures'. After Fry, she recalled, the work of Cézanne, Gauguin, Matisse and Picasso became 'things we live with, and laugh at, love and discuss … It was

Roger Fry more than anybody who brought about this change.'[75] Like Forster in literature, Fry reached out to a large audience with his vision of art. Fry was 'the Victorian who remade himself as a Modern', and brought many along with him.[76]

Fry had been at a prep school where he was horrified by the beatings boys received for trivial offences – his descriptions of being required, as the captain of school, to hold down boys who were beaten into bloody pain are intensely vivid, and the memories are clearly traumatic and produced a horror of violence between men in him for the rest of his life. The headmaster, Fry recalled in his fragment of an autobiography, had 'an intense sadistic pleasure in these floggings' and was 'at least an unconscious Sodomite'.[77] Going to Clifton was a release from this horror, but it was only when he went to King's that Fry, according to his own account, discovered a social environment he could revel in, and the interests that would dominate his life. He met Carpenter and Ashbee and Oscar Browning, and with Goldsworthy Lowes Dickinson '[a]ll one hot moonlit night they sat and talked "while a great dome of pale light travelled round from West to East and the cuckoo and nightingale sang" and for a few hours "we cared only for the now which is the same thing as being eternal".'[78] That's Virginia Woolf channelling Fry's autobiographical memories in their shared creation, through the melancholia of loss, of the youthful pre-war days of self-discovery. 'It was a society of this kind then – the society of equals, enjoying each other's foibles, criticizing each other's characters, and questioning everything with complete freedom, that became the centre of Roger Fry's life at Cambridge.'

Fry actually read Natural Sciences at King's, before going to Paris to study art. He married Helen Coombe in 1896, and they had two children. She was hospitalised with mental disease in 1910 and stayed there for the rest of her life. A year later he started an affair with Vanessa Bell, Virginia Woolf's sister; when she fell in love with Duncan Grant, with whom she lived for the rest of her life, he was devastated. The three worked together in the Omega Studios that Fry founded. After a series of short affairs, he settled into a relationship with Helen Anrep. His relationship with Vanessa is not mentioned in Virginia's biography. Suggestions that Fry's relationships with men at King's were a 'phase' are inadequate accounts of the complexities of desire in the contingencies of self-discovery and self-expression over time. It is more salient – more telling of character – to compare Forster's insistence on the necessity of violence in his desire for men with Fry's horror of any form of violence, or to compare Forster's fascination with working-class men with Fry's passion for writers and painters.

The paintings of Fry, Grant and Bell surround the public life of King's today, a constant visual reminder of a specific time in the college's history, and a specific group of people in that history. The Audit Room, one of the nicest rooms for public meetings or seminars, is decorated across one of its huge walls with nine larger-than-life-size nude figures representing the arts and sciences that Maynard Keynes commissioned from Duncan Grant and Vanessa Bell, which had once been in Keynes' rooms (P3). The Saltmarsh Rooms, used primarily as dining rooms, are decorated with pictures by Roger Fry, though these are now being rehung. Other pictures are dotted around. I have three small paintings by Duncan Grant in my rooms, lent to me by the Student Art Collection, which owns them. Maynard Keynes collected art voraciously and with considerable success. Many of his paintings are in the Fitzwilliam Museum, but many too have come back into the public rooms of the college.

If you walk into the Senior Combination Room, the space where fellows meet as a community to have coffee, read the papers, take a light lunch, chat or have public meetings, you are faced by a self-portrait of Fry. It's an intense representation with a focus and brightness to the eyes that distract your gaze so that it is easy to miss that he is bizarrely wearing a collar and tie, under a jacket, but no shirt – a hint of the Bohemian, matched by the slightly crumpled clothes and hair, and the paintbrush in his hand. As you move round to the left, there is a sunnier portrait of Provost Sheppard, sitting back in his chair, in middle age, smiling with his characteristic hooded eyes, inviting you towards his space in the picture (see Plate 2).

In contrast with Fry, he is formally dressed with his stiff collar and suit, and academic gown, but he is leaning back, with his pipe in hand, as if a conversation is about to start. Unlike the familiar Victorian grand portraits of grand men, this is clearly a character study that rejects dignity – or pomposity – in the name of style. Opposite Sheppard, on the other side of the windows, there is a menacing picture of J. K. Stephen (see Plate 3).

He is swarthy, and the picture is dark: he is wearing a dark green suit of heavy cloth with a splash of a blood-red flower in his button-hole. He is leaning forward, his body bent over the back of a chair, his hands to the fore, intently pushing towards the viewer, staring with a light smile and very blue eyes. It is an uncomfortable picture, which captures both the charisma and danger of Stephen. Next to Stephen, over the mantlepiece, is a large, garish portrait of Noel Annan, painted by the modern Italian artist and fierce anti-fascist Renato Guttuso (see Plate 4).

Annan was said to hate this portrait, and for years the picture languished in a corner in the administrative part of the Provost's Lodge: it is now a real centre-piece, and its modernity, dominated by its grey and lurid fleshly pink palette and broad, slashing brush-work, stands out against the dark red wall of the room and the more traditional style of portraiture that surround it. Indeed, next to him on the left, framing the modern Annan with another Victorian man, is a portrait of Whitting, so dark that his beard, dark clothes and dark background almost completely swamp the figure itself: his face is three-quarters in shadow and barely emerges. The only flash of white is the white of his shirt, cut off by his waistcoat and beard, and the edge of his cuff. This brooding concealment of a picture is the portrait which the choirboys thank at Christmas for funding their entertainment. On a pillar to the left of Whitting is – finally – a small picture of a woman, Lydia Lopokova, Keynes' wife, painted by Walter Sickert: a deeply impressionist sketch, quite unlike the sexual and violent paintings for which Sickert is now notorious. Over the door, through which one enters, is a version of the famous portrait of Rupert Brooke, painted by Frau Dr Clare Ewald (who herself, with her son Paul, came to live in Cambridge in 1938) – see Plate 5.

Brooke is smiling with joy, blue-eyed and fresh-faced, his blond hair not quite covered by a large black floppy hat. This rare artist's impression has become part of the image of Brooke. The portrait – there is another copy in the National Gallery in London – was painted in Munich, where Brooke had gone to recover and where he forced himself on Ka Cox. The painting was brought back to Cambridge by Edward Dent, who presented it to the college – Dent was friends with the Ewalds, as he was with so many in the artistic and musical circles of Munich. To the right of the door is one of Duncan Grant's largest and best portraits, a picture of the elegant figure of Arthur Cole (see Plate 6). Cole was an undergraduate and honorary fellow at King's (as was Fry), and a benefactor who was responsible for the Rowe Music Library as well as various other gifts coming to the college.

Cole was somewhat eccentric, though a hugely successful barrister on whom Keynes relied for many contractual matters. He was self-consciously old-fashioned, refusing to use a typewriter and other modern technical contraptions, and he always dressed in thick old clothing and always wore a large blanket-like cape rather than an overcoat. Tall and thin and moustachioed, he is pictured by Grant in this cape, seated, with a cane, and somewhat distanced from the viewer. Intriguingly, the six-page college obituary of Cole refers to his daughter, but makes no mention of a wife, a generic oddity at the very least. His closest friend in King's was Jack Sheppard, whom he visited regularly, to stay in college. On the other side of the newspapers and the mirror is a rather undistinguished and traditional portrait of Edward Dent, in his professorial dignity. Finally, to the right of the Roger Fry self-portrait is the other image of a woman in the room, recently hung: a tiny picture of an anonymous sleeping girl by André Derain. The hang was originally designed

by Michael Jaffé, the Director of the Fitzwilliam Museum
and celebrated expert on Rubens – we will encounter Jaffé
in the next chapter – but the portraits of Annan and the
two women are recent additions (made by a woman,
Nicky Zeeman, Professor of Medieval English, slowly
and deliberately changing the feel of the place, still as
I write). Nonetheless, when you walk into the Senior
Combination Room, seven of the ten pictures are of
characters who have appeared in this book as men who
slept with men; of the other three, one is painted by a man
who slept with men; two, the most recent, are of women,
one of whom was married to a man who slept with men.
In the room that is designed for the expression of community, a very particular sense of community is represented on its walls.

When you leave the Senior Combination Room and
process towards the hall where dinner and other meals are
served, the corridor has a couple of larger pictures,
including a beautiful self-portrait by the red-haired
Phyllis Gardner, a lover of Rupert Brooke (whom she
first saw at a café in King's Cross Station and pursued
from that moment). When her painful, eloquent and
conflicted letters and memoir were released from
embargo by the British Library in 1998, they provided a
fresh image of Brooke's manipulative narcissism, even, in
the eyes of some, his cruelty.[79] They bathed together, and
she dried his wet body with her hair – the echo of Mary
Magdalen drying Jesus with her hair is no doubt deliberate and retrospectively all too bitterly ironic, granted his
attempt to have casual sex with her and her refusal
because she wanted a serious relationship and a child.
It is poignant that his portrait is in pride of place in the

SCR and she is in the corridor, still separated. There is, too, a portrait of Tess Adkins, the first Senior Tutor when the college went mixed in 1972, a picture matched by a remarkable image of Caroline Humphrey, Professor of Anthropology, which has a small figure of the scholar dwarfed by a slightly surreal Tibetan landscape inhabited by a line of Buddhist monks – the only picture here to challenge the expected model of the portrait. But the majority of the corridor's pictures are pencil sketches, or cartoons of fellows. My favourite is an image of Roger Fry as an arbiter of taste: Fry is depicted in cartoonish distortion, his body bent almost double in an anguish of appreciation with his finger and thumb pinched together, reaching out in performed discrimination and judgement – of a large toy soldier with a fat belly (see Plate 7). The picture nicely mocks Fry's reputation as the maker of British taste for new art.

There are several cartoons of Oscar Browning (inevitably: he attracted such loving mockery), one in particular with his short and comically fat body surrounded by hugely taller, thin royalty. Some of these may be destined for the storeroom soon. There are more careful and attentive pencil drawings of Boris Ord, Goldsworthy Lowes Dickinson and Frank Adcock, and a lovingly exaggerated sketch of E. M. Forster. The corridor is not a place where people stop and stare: it is for passing through. It echoes with the visual ephemera of a public community, snatches of stares turned into images through attentiveness or mockery.

When you come into the Great Hall, one side of its faux Gothic grandeur is lined with bewigged grandees of the seventeenth and eighteenth centuries, massive pictures designed for display in public halls of splendour. But along the facing wall, the usual route through hall from the Senior Combination Room, is another gallery of King's figures, all designedly more modern and the result of Nicky Zeeman's recent rehang. As you move along, you pass first, in the lower, eye-level row, Montague Rhodes James in ecclesiastical academic garb, pious and calm; then, Goldsworthy Lowes Dickinson, painted by Duncan Grant, an elderly Dickinson, a figure of a wise old man; then Milner-White, the Dean who brought the Festival of Nine Lessons and Carols to King's, pictured here in a smoking cap – like a Turkish hat – which Goldsworthy Lowes Dickinson also often wears. Milner-White came up as an undergraduate to King's in 1903, and, after a distinguished time as an army chaplain during the war, spent most of his life at King's, despite his appointment at York Minster. He never married. Next to Milner-White is the one woman, Lydia Lopokova, Keynes' wife, again, painted not very well by Duncan Grant, in a fancy gown with a wrap over her shoulders and a supercilious expression. (There's another Fry self-portrait above her.) Next to her, Julian Bell and Duncan Grant are playing chess, painted by Vanessa Bell, Duncan Grant's lover and Julian Bell's mother, an affectionate domestic picture of a quiet, softly lit evening at home, made melancholic by Julian's young death. Next to them is Keynes himself (another Grant), carefully kept apart from his wife; next to Keynes, Dadie Rylands, in old age, head rakishly at an angle, the brightest, lightest colours, and most modern of any picture in the hall – painted by Romi Behrens, the other female artist in this line-up. Finally there is a demure painting of E. M. Forster, writing, and, next to the door leading out of hall, a life-size formal portrait of Pigou, in his professorial pomp, rather than in his casual bad clothes – like Lydia, kept symbolically apart from Keynes. It is another line-up that sums up the history of the college: another nine portraits where seven are images of men who desired men, and where the two exceptions are the woman who married Keynes (again), and the celibate or at least unmarried Dean – and several are painted by artists in the same circle. The contrast between the line of large, gilt-framed bewigged excellencies on one wall and the smaller, more intimate pictures of modern men who struggled with their sexuality on the other, is a poignant and pointed exhib-ition of a question of value and representation – an invi-tation to find yourself in the parade of images, to locate yourself in a history of public self-representation and private self-understanding. These pictures designedly frame the everyday life of the college.

To walk as a fellow around the public rooms of King's College is to move through a spectacle of portraits of men who desired men and women who married them, painted by men who desired men and women who desired them. If all institutions work to represent themselves to them-selves and to the outside world, King's has its own history laid out as a community where heteronormativity is side-lined with a certain flaunting. The community remakes itself in the images it inherits and changes – and in the stories that make the images speak as more than a gallery of worthies. Of course, if you do not know what the pictures show, you see no more than decoration, a blanched idea of institutional memory – as when books do no more than furnish a room with a patina of colour and shape, a parody of culture, a simulacrum of history. Sheppard and his friends may have revelled in a certain style – an art of living, if you will; but the college now surrounds itself with the visual representation of those men, an invitation to see yourself in what can be called the art of homosexuality.

These artists, musicians, poets, actors and playwrights wanted to change the world of the imagination and the imagination of the world. Roger Fry was 'the greatest single influence of [the twentieth] century on both the practice and the appreciation of the visual arts in the English-speaking world'.[80] Dent was instrumental – institutionally, in and through performance, writing and planning – in bringing English music to Europe, European music to Britain, and modern music to modernity. Dadie Rylands helped change theatre and the spoken word for more than one generation. They all believed passionately in culture as a means of making humans better: they had inherited Matthew Arnold's commitment to 'the best that has been thought and known' – with all its worrying political exclusivities – and sought to create a contribution to that definition of culture and to pass on its masterpieces to the students they taught and to a broader public. This was how they explained their work – their mission – to themselves and to the outside world. Art was not for art's sake but always within the educational and personal frame in which their artistic aims were first tempered – which is also why Ashbee the architect could easily be in this chapter on art, and Dent could easily have been in the chapter on the politics of homosexuality. This mission took some forms that look rather dodgy to today's policemen and policewomen of cultural value, but it is impossible to fight for cultural change without imagining a better world, and finding a form for that imaginative projection. In this project it is inevitable to see an overlap between homosexual longing for a better world to live in, and the art that these gay men produced.

There is an extraordinary picture in the Wine Room over the long, dark table where the fellows drink wine after dinner. It is called *Pouring Tea* – as if that explained the scene – and it was painted in 1932 by Vanessa Bell, Virginia Woolf's sister and the lover of both Roger Fry and Duncan Grant. It was owned by Maynard Keynes. It is not by chance that it is the work of a woman (nor that it has been hung where it is by a woman). It is, I think, one of Bell's masterpieces (see Plate 8).

It shows one woman leaning towards a table in a richly coloured room, her head turned in focus as she reaches out towards the table, to pour tea. Behind her, a naked woman sits on a chair looking out of the canvas, a sadly reflective odalisque. The scene appears deeply social but equally unsettling in its apparent and unexplained sexuality and the disengagement of the pair of women. The planes of the surfaces, along with the fruit-bowl, show the influence of Cézanne, whom Fry taught Virginia Woolf to admire. The picture captures something crucial about the artistic drives of this community. It is figurative because it is profoundly concerned with human interaction – human interaction that does not deny its eroticism but also recognises its strangeness, an art that opens a conversation with the viewer by representing an exchange that needs interpretation. It knowingly plays off images like *Déjeuner sur l'herbe* with its asymmetry of nakedness, by having both figures as women, and by the shock of the juxtaposition of tea and nudity. There is nothing that immediately or adequately motivates the nudity, no bath, no discarded clothes, and, above all, no man to ground the gaze. The question it poses comes from within a smart conversation about art as well as about society. At the centre of the frame, between the women, a fire burns intensely – as the domestic is never less than charged, symbolic. In the broken gazes between the two women, the image also asks about how sexuality can be divisive as well as profoundly connective. Only connect … It is a remarkable and beautifully ironic picture to overlook the fellows as they gather to drink, eat fruit and talk.

Theatre, music and art have all been fields where the connections between performance and masking, self-representation and self-concealment, emotion and truth, have made them particularly charged homes for queer men and women. But perhaps in the work of the figures of this chapter we can see also the influence of the peculiar embrace of the community of King's in which these artists and performers were each formed – and the impact of this community therefore on the broader culture towards which they reached out.

4

The Burial of Homosexuality

~

If you have read Jane Austen's *Pride and Prejudice*, or seen any of the films or television series made of it, you will understand the full social weight of the word 'condescension' (especially through the character of Lady Catherine de Bourgh in the eyes of the odious Mr Collins). Condescension, explained John Dunn to me, was the primary mode of **Michael Jaffé** – 'he was *incredibly* condescending' – though, added John, it was unclear actually what he had to be condescending about, unless it was his wealth. ('Immense wealth', Martin Bernal called it, which, along with his 'shyness and more or less hidden bisexuality', caused, in Bernal's judgement, Jaffé's 'stiff and pompous' manner, which he found, bizarrely if generously, 'somewhat touching'.)[1] Michael Jaffé was the man who arranged the hang of the pictures in the Senior Combination Room and Hall, which Nicky Zeeman is gradually reorganising. He had attended Eton and came to King's as an undergraduate immediately after the Second World War and was elected a fellow in 1952. He stayed at King's until his death in 1997. He was a great expert on the paintings of Rubens, and was appointed the Director of the Fitzwilliam Museum in 1973, where he ruled the museum in a manner which even his laudatory obituary described (with a certain restraint) as follows: 'There was much to admire in Michael Jaffé as well as some things to mock, and a few things to be appalled by. Though he offended many people by his manner, he was infinitely kind to some.' A poised judgement.

Jaffé was also responsible for Rubens' painting, *The Adoration of the Magi*, being donated to King's. It was then the most expensive painting in the world, and the college agreed – in a highly contentious decision, still despaired of by many – to lower the steps of the sanctuary at the east end of the chapel, part of its unaltered fifteenth-century design, so that the picture could fit beneath the glorious stained glass of the east window where, for many viewers, the splendour of the picture and the spendour of the window clash garishly. Jaffé also redecorated the Hall and the Senior Combination Room, as well as arranging the portraits, and he returned the Gibbs Building to its eighteenth-century austere lines (no more window boxes with geraniums). He enjoyed the God-like business of creating the world he wished to see around him. He lived first in H4, as a young man, and then moved to the top floor of G staircase in the grandest rooms over the arch (Lowes Dickinson's old rooms), where he built a bath on a mezzanine level, from which he notoriously conducted his supervisions. The painting on the stairs up to it, appropriately enough, was 'Silenus and His Rout'. The echoes of Oscar Browning and his *levée* in the style of a Roman emperor are not by chance. Like Browning, Jaffé was a snob, and not afraid of appearing ridiculous in the grandiose way he expressed himself – his style bullied many into agreement. Stories about Jaffé, like stories about Browning, circulated enthusiastically. Jaffé insisted on testing both academics and others on their taste, of which he was the arbiter, the connoisseur. One alumnus who came back to college told me of his entrance interview. Jaffé gave him the small statue of a naked youth, and asked the then seventeen-year-old schoolboy, hoping to come to King's, whether the statue was an original Renaissance piece or a later copy. The boy was nonplussed, hummed and hawed, and finally confessed he had no idea how to tell. 'Ah,', said Jaffé with happy authority, 'the crispness of the genitals.' The interview obviously satisfied, as the applicant came up as a student the following autumn.

John Dunn, currently the Emeritus Professor of Political Thought and life fellow of King's, recalled his encounters with Jaffé to me one evening in the Senior Combination Room, over a bottle of wine, surrounded by those chosen portraits. He filled in the background, both his own and the historical moment. John had attended Winchester, the leading boarding school in the west of England. His parents lived on the other side of the world in India. He described Winchester as a sort of 'retouched Dotheboys Hall' – the horrific institution in Dickens' *Nicholas Nickleby*. There were no girls. And amid his other yearnings, he had a reasonable yearning to be somewhere else. Even though there was one boy who he could see was remarkably fetching, he felt absolutely nothing that could be regarded as physical desire towards him. 'I wanted love', he summarised years of dismay, 'but *that* was not the right thing at all.' John left Winchester, after the social revolt of refusing confirmation, and after a period of depression (a reasonable response to the conditions, thought his empathetic psychiatrist in the end), and eventually came up to King's where, in those days, there were also no girls.

He met Jaffé in the social circle of the Apostles. To set the scene, he remembered one evening in Forster's rooms. They were considering, as the Apostles seemed to have spent a great deal of time over the decades doing, who might be future members of the society. John suggested Joanna Ryan, Herbert Hart's daughter, who had, in his view, the right intellectual qualities (she would indeed become one of the very first female fellows of King's, which turned out to be another less than happy story, and an influential feminist writer on psychotherapy and politics). She was also a young woman. In the silence that followed his suggestion, Morgan Forster, who rarely spoke out with any aggression, stated, 'You are right but you can't possibly meet here again.' There was real shock that Forster had been so direct and final about the impossibility of female attendance in his rooms, the regular haunt of the Apostles. 'It was as if The Saint had spoken', recalled John, 'and said something *appalling*.' Although there were plenty of younger men there who would have agreed with John's proposal, nothing more was said. 'Everyone in the room winced.' I asked if his suggestion had been self-consciously provocative. 'I was not outrageous deliberately', John insisted. 'If I were to pick someone in the universe to be outrageous to, Morgan would be close to the bottom of the list.' It was, he reflected, 'a violent moment' and 'very upsetting'.

In fact, Bernard Shaw, on 3 March 1894, had proposed that the Apostles accept women (he was in love with a woman at the time), and the society had voted – with the exception of Goldsworthy Lowes Dickinson – in favour of the motion.[2] The first woman was not accepted until 1970, the year of Forster's death. When it comes to women at Cambridge, change in institutional power structures has its own pace (still).

It was in this social circle of acquaintance, a resolutely male environment, that John met Jaffé once or twice. Jaffé in such a setting was 'in his seignorial mode' and invited John to his rooms on G staircase for a drink. There was nothing untoward about such an invitation. For decades King's had prided itself on the lack of distance between students and fellows, especially when they shared the institutional encouragement of a club or society. They sat quite close together, as the seating space was quite confined, and talked, and had a drink, though neither drank very much. 'Then Michael leant forward emphatically and put his tongue in my ear. And I thought in the parlance of today *"fucking hell"*.' John anatomised his feelings with a slight lapse of his normally brilliant articulacy, even after all these years. 'I felt a combination of ... revulsion and panic, and just unclarity how to ... When I got over the revulsion and panic ... I braced myself for both ... I got out of earshot [laughter] ... I tried to compose myself. I said, hoping not to ruffle feelings ... This was a long time before me-too; not ruffling feelings would get not much social support ... I tried to convey the idea that although it filled me with revulsion it was not in *general* but because of this *particular* case.' And as a postscript: 'The idea that Michael had feelings you could readily hurt ...!' Panic, revulsion, but unwillingness to hurt feelings – and above all embarrassment and 'just unclarity' about the scene in which you find yourself, are all-too-familiar responses from the me-too archive. But here, at least, with minimal consequences, and a turn to reflective and even wry memory, formulated as anecdote.

A few months later – after minimal communication between them – Michael Jaffé invited John to lunch at his club in London, the Turf Club. 'What do I do *now*?' wondered John, and concluded that 'the Turf Club can't actually be a social hazard. I thought: it's *lunch*.' The invitation felt like 'a relatively fluent social next step'. After what was a very good lunch, Jaffé asked John what he was going to do in the afternoon. John said he very much wanted to see the exhibition of Keith Vaughan's paintings currently on at the Whitechapel Gallery, but feared it was closed. Michael Jaffé said 'You are on' – and they went to the gallery, which was indeed closed, but Jaffé pressured the staff to open just for him and John (the seignorial mode). He then 'chased me round Whitechapel Gallery while I tried to cast a fleeting glance at Keith Vaughan'. John was quite angry at this point, but 'I didn't feel physically in danger. But I felt socially in acute danger.' Looking back, John was baffled. 'How on earth did I get into the second of the settings?' And he concluded, not without some embarrassment for his younger self, that it stemmed from trying to minimise embarrassment.

The lack of consequence arising from such an old story allows it to be an anecdote told with laughter over wine, and to be an occasion to muse on the self's past. But it is telling nonetheless. It is salient at one level simply because it lets us see one reaction to a predatory academic, from a resolutely 'un homo' student, recollected now in tranquillity. The tale expresses the ingenuousness of the student vividly, along with the intense reflection on the 'how' and 'why' that such a scene prompts, both at the moment and later. Such a story – where its nastiness is partially deflected only by the untraumatic response of the pursued – is in stark contrast to the narrated encounters of Dadie Rylands, Jack Sheppard, Cecil Beaton and their pals, even if Arthur Benson would have embraced the combination of revulsion and embarrassment wholeheartedly. This very sense of embarrassment is also the glue of community, the glue that prevents transgressions from not merely ruffling feelings but actively fracturing the bonds of community. This sense of community – this social embarrassment – has probably repressed other such stories from the archives of earlier decades. But it also framed the conversation between John and me, the shared recognition that Michael Jaffé was part of the community, and that the story was part of a repertoire which could be shared and explored as part of a community, even and especially as the story's salience and narratability changes over time. To live in a community over time is to rehearse the stories that keep the community in awareness of itself as a community – and to be complicit with them.

The story is set in the early 1960s, however, probably the year before 'sexual intercourse began in 1963', as Philip Larkin would have it; that is, in a transitional moment of British society. The tale is very much of its time. Within a decade King's would be a mixed community, proudly the first previously all-male college in Cambridge to admit women; sex between men, at least men over twenty-one, would be legalised; the 1960s – as an idea as much as a date – would revolutionise attitudes to sexuality and social form. But not yet. In 1964 Michael Jaffé married, and he went on to have four children, and the happiness of his marriage is much lauded in all accounts of his life. The obituary in King's, the place that knew him especially well, listed 'impatient and abrasive …

arrogant, dismissive, and patronising' as Michael's defects, though quickly added that, set against 'his imagination, his flair, his loyalty and generosity to friends, and above all his love of his wife Patricia and their four talented children ... the defects crumble'.[3] Jaffé was typical of many men who desired men in the first decades in the post-war era in getting married (his future wife was pregnant already, which helped). Whatever the law stated, the denigration of homosexual men – which would tar all men who had sex with men – was particularly insistent in the public discourse of the period. The police were increasingly zealous in their pursuit of such sexual miscreants, and particularly violent in their treatment of them. As several historians of sexuality have explored, the 1950s across Europe, and especially in England, was a markedly conservative time, as the return of men from the war, and the consequent return of women into a more domestic role after the war's requirements, were matched by a particularly strident public projection of the nuclear family as a necessary and proper social formation.[4] Even sexology shifted perspective. Where Ulrichs, Krafft-Ebing, Havelock Ellis and Hirschfeld, writing before and after the First World War, were each fascinated by the abnormal, and explored homosexuality as a paradigm of such difference, Kinsey, the emblematic sexologist of this later period, insisted he was exploring the normal and set homosexuality as a norm (defined by the percentage of its occurrence within a range of normal). While his calculation of the number of men who were homosexual or who had had homosexual experiences proved scandalously high, his studies, however scandalous, were also characteristic of the period's desire for conformity, precisely because they placed homosexuality within the frame of the normal. The bland phrase of Martin Bernal, 'more or less hidden bisexuality', conceals a complex and painful transitional dynamic of public denial, concealment, private rapaciousness and transformation, set against a slowly changing public expectation, which managed to enact hostility despite or because of the increasing legal liberalism.[5] The tension between the inherited tolerance and flamboyance of the society of King's from the 1920s, say, and the new austerity of family life promoted in British society was powerfully felt.

Like Michael Jaffé, Noel Annan also married. Forster, according to Bernal, was not impressed by such a move: 'Forster ... told me that he saw Noel as having, by his pomposity, betrayed his youth. By that, I assume, he meant that Noel had ceased to be a homosexual and had married and had children. The old Noel, however, never completely disappeared.' This last phrase seems to refer to the repeated gossip that when Noel was drunk, even as Provost, he would make passes at young men, which, to the gossipers, explained why his wife moved to London, while Noel stayed in Cambridge. 'Excitement', explained Sir Geoffrey Lloyd, 'Noel loved excitement. He boasted of picking up boys in the loos in Leicester Square – when it was illegal. Excitement.' Noel was certainly very close with Dadie Rylands and with Steven Runciman, one of the more licentious gay fellows of Trinity, and a fine scholar of Byzantium. Noel and Michael Jaffé, too, went shooting duck together at Grantchester, two grandees with their guns. What is relevant here, however, is not 'the higher gossip' of which Noel Annan was himself the master, but the fact that Annan, who went on to be the

Chancellor of London University and to write the *Annan Report on the Future of Broadcasting*, had a public persona which had not a hint of any such life in King's. For his role in public life it would not be acceptable in the 1950s and 1960s to be evidently or openly other than a hetero-sexual man. It is a paradox of the time that the sexual freedom gradually brought by the 1960s and by the legalisation of homosexuality also made it easier than in previous times to make open accusations of homosexuality, accusations which remained extremely dangerous to a man's reputation and to his very ability to work in the public eye, especially in the political sphere – as demon-strated most dramatically by the case of Jeremy Thorpe (Eton and Oxford), the Liberal Member of Parliament who was prosecuted in the 1970s for plotting to arrange the murder of his former lover, Norman Scott, who had threatened to expose him. Thorpe had already been inves-tigated by the police, had an MI5 file opened on him and undergone a party enquiry because of his sexuality. He had good reason to fear a full-scale public exposure (not that murder is a calm or acceptable response to such a fear).

This tension between the generations found expression in the untimeliness of the older dons as it appeared to the eyes of the new students. Philip Brett came to King's as a choral scholar in 1955, where he studied music under Boris Ord, as well as Philip Radcliffe, Dent's student, and Thurston Dart, before returning as a fellow in 1963. He recalled the cliques around his teachers in these years of transition and tension: 'in my Cambridge days, most queer dons at the centre of such circles appeared complacent; their full access to male and class privilege enabled them to become inured, at least as far as one could see, to the social disadvantages of their homosexuality and cushioned them from fear of public exposure'.[6]

Philip Brett went to California in 1966 – like the poet Thom Gunn before him[7] – and became a leading scholar in queer musicology. He wrote a seminal paper linking Benjamin Britten's sexuality to his opera *Peter Grimes*, and was instrumental in setting up the American Musicological Society's Gay and Lesbian Study Group in the late 1980s. It is a striking sign of the changing times that, to Brett, the fellows of King's appeared not as examples or models of a tradition he felt able to join, but rather as unattractively smug and unworried in their established homosexuality, and unaware or unacknowledging of the more frightening world beyond the college walls. Much as Fred Benson saw a gulf between the 1920s and the Victorian times of his father, for Brett, after the Second World War, the 1920s seemed a long way away. What's more, Brett refers to the older generation as 'queer dons', a term it is hard to imagine Forster or Lowes Dickinson recognising. The language of male desire for males, a fugitive discourse, has kept moving through the twentieth century and beyond, despite the dominance in medical discourse of the pathology of homosexuality. One way that homosexuality has been buried is by the insistence on a new language of desire that privileges the once negative term 'queer', and has added LBGT (and more letters) as signs of multiplying positions. The simple definitional power of homosexuality may have had its day.

The difference between the generations is captured painfully by the different experiences of **Frank Adcock** and **Alan Turing**, two cryptologists. Frank Adcock

(1886–1968) was rare among the fellows I have been discussing in that he went to a grammar school in Leicester before he came as an undergraduate to King's, where he was appointed a fellow in 1911. He stayed at King's the rest of his life (he died in college), apart from the period of the two world wars when he was a cryptographer, for the Royal Navy at the Admiralty, and then, in the Second World War, at Bletchley Park. He held the Chair in Ancient History from 1925 to 1951. He was awarded the OBE after the First World War and knighted in 1954. It was a glittering career in both education and public service. Frank Adcock was small and round; his lectures were renowned for their wit, carefully prepared and rather too lovingly presented. His successor as Professor of Ancient History monumentalised his performance with careful distaste:

He was perhaps the last of the studied wits: his sallies were strategically prepared, and part of the fun of his famous lectures in the flat-accented, high-pitched, maiden-auntish voice was to detect the build-up of forces, feel the imminence of the punchline, observe the dawning of the tiny smirk on the bland face, and savour the release of tension when the *bon mot* came.[8]

This quotation comes from the *Oxford Dictionary of National Biography*, and is also quoted in the British Academy obituary of its author by another professor of history from the next generation: the circulation of witticisms about witticisms, enshrined in the monuments of official, national memory, show us also the institutional community forming itself through the complicit repetition of such lines, such stories: how (not) to be one of the guys. Adcock lived on G staircase, in the rooms that

Lowes Dickinson had inhabited and Jaffé would later have, and Keith Hopkins, who also became the Professor of Ancient History some decades after Adcock, recalls how as a student he was chased around the table by him: it cannot have been hard for the young Hopkins to escape the rotund Adcock, but, again, social embarrassment rather than anger or pain was the response to the older man's sexual advances. To be invited to play golf with Adcock was the usual sign of special attention. Adcock lived out his time in King's amid the older generation. There is a fine picture of him and Pigou processing along the back path towards Bodleys, under Dadie Rylands' rooms, the tall, thin Pigou and the short, plump Adcock making an unlikely couple of single men (see Figure 34).

Adcock was sixty years in King's and in the 1950s was very much a figure from another time. John Dunn remembered that when as a student he went up to say the grace for the college at dinner, Adcock stared at him with 'an intense and focused misanthropy'. Adcock did not know Dunn personally at all, so the feeling must have been a general antipathy. But, Dunn said with deep distaste, the man 'radiated unpleasantness'. It is easy to imagine that Philip Brett would not have found Adcock *simpatico*.

Alan Turing (1912–1954) was also an undergraduate at King's (1931–4), and was elected a fellow only a year after finishing his BA. Turing is famous for his contribution to the invention of the computer and for his work on the Enigma machine at Bletchley Park, where Adcock, twenty-six years older, also worked, during the Second World War. Unlike Adcock, however, Turing's life has

FIGURE 34 Adcock, looking malevolent, and Pigou, shabbily dressed – the odd couple.

become the stuff of movies, partly because of his brilliance in the secret world of cryptography, and partly as an iconic victim of the hostile turn towards homosexuality in the 1950s. (It is another one of the signs of the network that P. N. Furbank, the friend, holiday companion and biographer of E. M. Forster, appointed a fellow at King's while he researched what is still the standard biography, was also the literary executor of Alan Turing.) In 1941 Turing had proposed marriage to Joan Clarke, a colleague at Bletchley, who was unworried, it seems, by his confession of homosexuality to her; but he could not go through with it, and broke off the agreement very quickly. In 1951, while working at Manchester University, he had started living with a man he had met casually on the street, when his house was burgled. Manchester had neither the domesticity nor the walls of King's. He reported the burglary to the police and, in the course of the investigation, admitted that he was having a sexual relationship with the man living in his house, who actually knew the burglar. The police prosecuted Turing for 'gross indecency' and he was found guilty. The consequences were horrific. He was offered the choice of imprisonment or 'chemical castration': the injection of drugs, a synthetic oestrogen, that would feminise his body – he would grow breasts – and render him impotent. He chose the drugs and the treatment lasted a year. At the same time, he lost his security clearance and could no longer work as a consultant for the government in cryptography, and he was denied entry to the United States. At the end of the year, he was found dead from cyanide poisoning and the inquest determined it was death by suicide. It was not until 2014, and then only with a royal pardon granted by Queen Elizabeth, that the conviction for 'gross indecency' was wiped out.

Adcock stayed in college, avoided any publicity and was awarded a knighthood in 1954, when he had retired, and was still living in King's at the age of sixty-eight. Turing moved to Manchester – he had also lived in the United States – and because he had contact with the police and allowed the truth of his sexuality to be recognised, he was severely punished in sufficiently brutal a way to prompt his suicide at the age of forty-two. It is hard to credit that Keynes or Sheppard in the 1920s or 1930s would have faced such treatment. The history of sexuality is not linear or teleological, from darkness to light, from the benighted past to the truthful and righteous present, whatever the most recent revolution claims, and however much the not-yet-sufficient advances of feminism and queer liberation need further nourishing against the all-too-evident forces of retrenchment. It is not a surprise that many men chose to conceal their sexual desire for men, to bury their homosexuality.

Yet not everyone did. **Peter Avery** (1923–2008) came to King's thanks to the intervention of Noel Annan. He was an expert in Persian studies and had lived in Iran for some years before coming back to Cambridge as a fellow in 1964. He lived on H staircase in H2 for more than thirty years, and his rooms, as had been the case for Browning and others, became a lavishly decorated centre of brazen enjoyment of homosexual desire.

When Peter Avery was first a fellow he used to help Morgan Forster to bed, to save the nurse coming in, in the final years of Forster's life. Avery loved King's for its 'tremendous camaraderie', for the 'love and friendship' he found in the community, 'the almost cosy King's' he had first known (though it had 'high aesthetic values as well as scholarly').[9] To demonstrate his point, he also told the story himself of when the news broke that Anthony Blunt was the fourth of the Cambridge spies. Avery knew that Dadie Rylands had been a good friend of Blunt – Dadie also holidayed with Guy Burgess – and would be devastated by the revelation: 'I knew what a disappointment and dismay he was going through because of the revelation about Anthony Blunt.' In an interview, in 2008 when he was eighty-five years old, Avery recalled the story in his characteristic full, plummy voice, from which it would be hard to tell that he came from Derby and had attended a grammar school in Birkenhead near Liverpool, and then Liverpool University. Leaning back in his maroon waistcoat and red tie, he explained how he invited Dadie for a consolatory drink:

When Anthony was exposed, I happened to be going across to the pantry to get some drink, some *booze*, and I met Dadie coming along the path from where his rooms are in the Old Lodge, he had aged ten years in a matter of days. And so I waited for him at the door of the Combination Room complex, and I said when he came up to me, I said 'Come and have a drink'. He said 'yes, a little mi whisky'. So he came. I got the whisky, of course ... Crawfords was his favourite whisky, his favourite tipple. He came a few minutes later and we sat there in the outer room; and we drank and we talked; we talked about all sorts of things. And as he told Stephen Runciman, who was also a great friend of mine and of his, he told Stephen Runciman because Stephen then told me, 'It was extraordinarily tactful of Peter and rather typical of him. He had me for drinks. I knew why. And he never mentioned it.'

This floridly told anecdote is typical of the exchanges of community, not just because it is a tale about how exchanges work, and explicitly about the construction of the feelings of community, but also specifically because it turns on silence. Silence can be the violence of *damnatio*

memoriae, the desire to remove knowledge from the archive of memory, to bury it, which can turn to horror when
the ghosts do return to speak, as we saw even with the
gentle will of Monty James to silence Brocklebank's name
and misery. But silence can also be social tact and mutual
understanding. When the news of Rupert Brooke's death
reached Cambridge, Dent and Keynes walked together
around the back court of King's in silence: 'Nothing was
said of Rupert ... M[aynard] & I walked round the court
together for a little time afterwards – and came much
nearer to each other than in the last 12 years.'[10] Silence
can be a special, careful bond, as much as a concealment.
What is not said, and saying what is not to be said – the
dynamics of tacit knowledge integral to any community –
has a heightened charge when the love that dare not speak
its name is at stake. In such a case, the difference between
violent repression and social sensitivity is much harder to
calibrate. And how much more so when the immediate
anxiety is dismay at the hidden life of a treacherous
homosexual spy, at what has not been said to friends over
the years. Avery's story is self-promoting, for sure, but his
engagement with Dadie was motivated by care. Shortly
before Peter Avery's death, Daniel Boyarin, the great
Talmudist from Berkeley, was a visiting fellow at King's
and saw Peter being helped from H staircase towards the
Senior Combination Room and the Hall for dinner by
two younger fellows. Peter found it hard then to walk that
short distance unaided. To Boyarin this was a wonderful
sight. In Berkeley, he explained, when you retired, you
became a non-person, removed from the sight and concern of institutional attention, and the idea that a man in
his late eighties, retired for more than twenty years, would

still be living in college and helped by his younger colleagues to a High Table dinner, was an extraordinary and thoroughly unexpected gesture of personal and institutional care. Boyarin was moved by the sight of Avery's slow procession. The temporal trajectory of a life lived in college – Peter was there for forty-four years – is also – and, to my mind too, movingly – a trajectory of care given and received, over time.

It is as perverse to begin an account of Peter Avery with a story of tactful silence as it would be in the case of Oscar Browning (though Browning would have appreciated that Avery's story is a moment of self-praise). When I described H2 as a centre of brazen homosexual desire, the word 'brazen' was intended to cue Avery's notorious willingness to speak out, flamboyantly, outrageously. He was a Catholic, but had asked permission from the University's resident Catholic chaplain to attend chapel at King's, next to his rooms. But he declared at one party, 'Between my vice and my religion, I find myself constantly on my knees.' When he entered the chapel for a wedding of two former students, he was asked by the usher whether he was to sit on the bride's side or the groom's side. 'I don't know', he boomed, 'I have slept with both.' Chapel was both a serious business for him and a serious opportunity for transgressive performance. So too for academia. When a conversation about bedtime reading was burgeoning among scholars and budding scholars, he announced with slow insouciant pride, 'the only thing I read in bed is tattooos'.

There are many other such stories, which will undoubtedly be read differently in different regimes of sexual propriety, as outrageousness always is. His behaviour was equally extreme. Later in his life, there was a string of rent boys who came to H staircase – 'when you reach my age, you have to keep the cheque-book by the bedside', he declared. His bedder, Monica – the woman who cleaned his rooms and looked after the staircase – would regularly – and calmly – hear him ordering the services of a young man on the phone and trying to negotiate the price down ('I am a poor old man …'). In earlier days, he was having an affair with a student at Trinity, and when the Master of Trinity approached the Provost of King's to complain, they got short shrift (and long-lasting enmity) from Avery, though eventually even Avery was compelled, bad-temperedly, to concede. The alternative to burying homosexuality was flaunting it. It was one response to social expectation, made possible partly by the change in British law in 1967 to make homosexual sex between men over the age of twenty-one legal, and partly – mainly – by the privilege and care provided by the college environment. Avery was neither rich nor came from an upper-class background; his privilege came from where he lived and worked, a place he had earned through his research and scholarship. His style was an act of self-formation, a performance that demanded attention and demanded to belong, while knowingly crossing the usual boundaries of fitting in. His behaviour was outrageous, but enacted in an attentively boundaried community, which could carefully turn its gaze when it suited or was needed. H staircase provided the space for Avery to live the life he chose, and to express his wilful transgressiveness.

There will be few people even tangentially connected to education who will not wince or feel a certain shock, looking back to stories like this from where we are now are. Even retelling these stories as anecdotes enacts some complicity, as the amusing anecdote, like a joke, is designed, it will always seem, to avoid a more pointed scrutiny of what underlies it. Sleeping with students, even from another college or department, not to mention bringing sex workers into the college's residence, would be sackable offences in pretty well any Western university these days. And his open flamboyance or brazenness would not defend him, as it did Oscar Browning. Nor is 'of his time' an adequate framing for Avery. The change in law in 1967 did not change social expectations, at least not enough and not quickly enough. Indeed, in 1966 there were 420 men convicted of 'gross indecency', the crime for which gay men were prosecuted, but in 1974 there were 1,700 convictions. The increased aggression with which police pursued homosexuals, after the Sexual Offences Act changed the status of homosexual sex, has been repeatedly recorded. The decades following the change in law were scarred by virulence towards homosexuality in the press, culminating in the Conservative Government's notorious 'Clause 28' in 1986, which made it illegal to 'promote homosexuality' in any local government institution including schools (it is a model followed now by Vladimir Putin in Russia). This ban included teaching about homosexuality: it had to be buried in silence. The privilege Peter Avery made such use of was not afforded to many others (that is the nature of privilege), the others who struggled against the aggressive and often isolating social pressures that surrounded them. His use of sex workers had none of the carapace of social care with which Browning surrounded his engagements with young men. The violence of privilege was vividly

embodied in such financial arrangements. A story like
Peter Avery's – and this could apply to many of the men
I have been discussing – can be told as a story of community, care, self-expression and the challenge to repressive
social attitudes: a lived challenge to heteronormativity;
but it cannot be told without a recognition of the privilege
that defended him; and this privilege helps keep in place
the systemic violence of social hierarchies that underpin
the repressive social attitudes against which the outrageousness of his behaviour was self-consciously performed. This double and duplicitous narrative is integral
to the history of H staircase. Whatever the openness and
liberal values lauded in King's, and the tolerance thereby
allowed and cherished, this all comes with certain blinkers
too. For many in the 1980s, outrageousness became a
response to being out and the rage felt against society's
continuing distaste for gay lives: gay pride marches
enacted this dynamic publicly. The tension between outrageousness and the responsibilities of the institutional
life of a college is harder to manage. Peter Avery became
a figure of college imagination precisely because he put
such pressure on this tension. How you looked at such a
figure, then and now, says a great deal about how you
think the world should look.

The Vice-Provost for some of those latter years recollected that he knew well that Peter Avery ('at the end of
his life a rather unpleasant old man') regularly paid to
have men come to his rooms – 'truck drivers mainly,
making extra money … large men with tattoos carrying
crates of brown ale' – but, the Vice-Provost confessed, he,
along with the rest of the college, averted their eyes – as
they did for fellows who were alcoholics or just plain

difficult. The Vice-Provost, who is the person who officially oversees the fellows' relationship to the college and their use of rooms, reflected that the college at that time countenanced behaviour that would in any other sort of institution be stigmatised and result in dismissal. 'We just looked away, as long as there was no trouble.' A very British principle of no fuss. It was a strange sort of standard: he also recalled a notorious scandal of the day, when a fellow from Jesus College who wrote evaluative reports on the internet about female sex workers he had brought to his rooms, was sacked for 'bringing the college into disrepute'. The case appeared to turn on the publicity rather than the activity. By contrast, Avery's behaviour was buried in institutional silence. The more loudly Peter Avery dared to speak its name, the more intently his sexuality was publicly veiled in decent obscurity.

I also spoke to the Senior Tutor from those years, Tess Adkins, a wise and much beloved Scots woman of impeccable feminist credentials, and one of the earliest women to join King's as a fellow, more than fifty years ago now. She too had known about Peter Avery, who regularly 'summoned' her 'to his rooms to discuss the state of the college' (she averted her eyes from the videos he had on occasion left out). But like the Vice-Provost, she saw no reason to interfere. 'It didn't affect the students.' (One student, actually, was invited by Peter to join a rent boy to perform in front of him: both the younger men thought it ridiculous and went off for a drink together.) But Tess also considered the whole business now as a sign of the changing times. There was *now* much *more* of 'a judgemental, puritan' attitude among the young. By way of contrast, I asked her about one professor, a large and imposing man, who had had a very open affair – and then married – one of his female undergraduates. 'People tut-tutted', she recalled, but 'nothing formal' was said: she herself was just 'embarrassed'. Again the great British anxiety about social embarrassment ... She had not thought about it all in terms of power then, she replied to my obvious follow-up questions, because that was really not on the agenda at that time ('perhaps I was naïve...'). But, she also said with a certain sadness, there were many times that she had let the rules be bent in those days – a woman who gave birth in college, students living together – that would now be shut down by 'health and safety', the bane of gentle tolerance. The watch-word of her memories was just that: tolerance.

She did imagine that it was initially because she was from Scotland that she had more leeway as an outsider arriving in King's, not from one of the grand Bloomsbury families or grand schools. The contrast with Joanna Ryan's unhappy experience is striking. (Joanna Ryan was the woman, it will be recalled, whose proposed election to the Apostles caused Forster's outburst.) Looking back in 2015, in a discussion with Martin Richards, on how the Unit for Research on Medical Applications of Psychology started at Cambridge, she recalled how difficult she found her time as one of the very first women fellows at King's. Here's a brief extract of that conversation:[11]

MARTIN: But yeah, and don't forget, you made history because you were the first female fellow at King's. And all the hoo-hah about that.

JOANNA: As Quentin Skinner said at the time, 'you will be a footnote in history'... as written by him!

MARTIN: I suspect there is that footnote already somewhere
in King's.

JOANNA: But that was the kind of atmosphere and actually
it was a nightmare being at King's as far as I am
concerned …

She added that it was the sociality and the performativity
of college life that she liked least:

JOANNA: Well, and there was all the ridiculous rituals.
I mean I never went in to high table, but they
were very offended that I didn't. I never went into
the senior common room, I couldn't bear it.

The comfort and conviviality that so many of the gay
fellows found in King's could also produce an atmosphere
that felt alienating and rebarbative to others, maybe especially to young women making a career in resistant institutions. But unlike Joanna Ryan's response, for Tess
Adkins, looking back over a long career in King's,
although she recalled Joanna Ryan's feelings with recognition, it was tolerance that raised her smile of recollection. Or, as she concluded with amused contemporary
wonder as we discussed the exuberant transgressions of
the earlier generations, 'How did they get away with it?!'

The last figure in this history lived in H5 when
I arrived in King's as an undergraduate, and moved a
couple of decades later into G6. **Jim Trevithick** is an
economist and is the last retired fellow to be given permission to reside in college. With him a way of life will
pass. In many ways, although it seems strange to say this,
Trevithick, despite the shifts and changes in experience
across the decades I have been discussing, sums up many

of the aspects of gay experience that I have been tracing, at least in form. That is, much of the way he describes his life picks up on specific elements that we have seen in the past. But modernity – the modernity of today, that is – inevitably frames his story in a different light.

Jim was born in 1948, and went to school at Downside, a Catholic boarding school near Bath in the west of England. He refers, like Goldsworthy Lowes Dickinson, to 'it' or '"the" subject' when he talks about homosexuality. 'You want to talk about "it"?' he asked me – and talk he did. As with so many characters in the book, he first experienced sex at school with one particular boy. 'It was hard to find a place to do it', he recalled, but, as he discovered talking to other pupils later, apparently there was a lot of 'it' going on, though young Trevithick was totally unaware of all this activity at the time, not sure even where these other boys might have found for their privacy. Jim was straightforwardly direct: 'I liked being sucked off; I liked being jerked off. But there was no penetration and I never did anything to him.' The familiar Edwardian schoolboy narratives, which mix anxiety and casualness, denial and ignorance, become here with twenty-first century retrospect almost dispassionate in his clinical detail. Then, however, it still did not speak its name: 'It was very well disguised. No one talked about it at all.' However, he did not masturbate, he revealed, again quite straightforwardly, until he was in his late twenties. It's hard not to see a rather clichéd version of what Catholic schools can achieve in terms of transgression and guilt.

His undergraduate days were spent at the London School of Economics, where he lived in South

Kensington (one of the poshest bits of London) apart from a few months in Earls Court, his 'gay centre', though the attraction seems to have been not much more than sitting quietly in an ambience 'where there were people of the same persuasion'. The briefest of affairs with a Greek Cypriot (who went on to be a minister in the government there) started a new phase in his life, which shut down almost immediately when he went for a lectureship in Dublin, and three years of necessary celibacy – Dublin then being a city dominated by the internalised and practised moral authority of the Catholic church: homosexual sex was not legal in Ireland till 1993. Glasgow, a second lectureship, was not much more liberating, though he did share a flat with a German friend from the LSE, who became his most constant and closest friend, despite another very brief and rather drunken fling with him. 'We got on like a house on fire', he explained. Arriving as an economics teacher in King's in 1977 changed everything.

The college was 'crawling with gays', he said. 'I started consorting with gays.' Chapel was one route into this social world (several of the chaplains in this era were openly gay, but they have not had a place yet in this history). He recalled standing by the notice board outside the Porters' Lodge where chapel services were announced. 'Tomorrow's Parry should be good', a young man offered, commenting on the choice of service music. 'Are you going tomorrow?' Church music was the lure to attend and a cue between like-minded men. 'I discovered myself in a strange culture', he recalled (queer?). And he described a world of extremely camp undergraduates who actively sought out older men; the student who was sleeping with the chaplain; the young man who pursued the elderly Geoffrey Keynes, preserver of the flame of Rupert Brooke; the men of the choir, all of whom used girls' names when they talked about each other. He met Peter Avery downstairs who had an open house, and he met many of Peter's friends. 'There was', he concluded with a certain surprise, still 'a very strong gay ethos' in the college. As with Dennis Robertson or Charlie Ashbee, walking through the gates of King's opened a new world. 'You never feel under threat here.' Like so many of the characters in this book, the immediate comparison remained Trinity College: he told me that he went to dinner at Trinity and his host told him 'not to mention anything about homosexuality ... not to mention anything that might incriminate me or him'. 'It' was taboo at Trinity. Jim snorted with derision and, still, a little anger. Whether this reported anxiety reflected any reality or not, it was a story of self-definition. In King's, you could be open.

His lasting relationships, however, were not those with whom he had anything like an intense sexual link. His longest sexual affair, he confessed, lasted just a month, with a very good-looking young Neapolitan man, Carlo, who spoke no English. Trevithick went out to Naples to stay with him. Jim speaks quite good Italian and overheard Carlo make an assignation with an even better-looking young man, Marco (Carlo was surprised to know that Jim knew ...). It was too much: 'I packed my bags and took the train home.' This was before AIDS, but, he explained, he never liked promiscuity. 'I didn't *approve*.' Fidelity mattered. It is striking how often the trip abroad, especially to Italy, especially to Naples and Capri, has continued to play a part in these narratives of coming out. It is not just that coming out is easier when the restrictions and alienation of home are transformed into another place, with its different sets of watching eyes; it is also that a sense of otherness – which could be described more critically as exoticism – enters the dynamics of same-sex desire.

Jim was close to several undergraduates and graduates, but always knew that any erotic encounter with them was out of bounds (though he did recall with aged impishness the very occasional drunken grope with a mutual friend, a very good-looking anthropologist). It suited him. He went to gay bars and clubs, where he enjoyed watching the dancing: the best club was on the edge of town, where university men mingled with American Airforce staff from the bases and local young men. As with Keynes or Browning, crossing the class barrier was a positive attraction still. Yet, Jim declared, he was sentimental at heart, and would have liked 'to marry, to settle down, and find *lurve*', but had 'never met the right man'. He 'came to "it" too late', he reflected. 'If I had outed myself earlier, I would have had a better chance of a permanent relationship.' He did have a civil partnership with a man whom he saw from time to time, but this was a financially motivated relationship, to do with pensions, though based on an old if gentle friendship. But while many people were terrified of living alone, he said with feeling, living alone in college was different. He was 'so heavily institutionalised' – which he glossed by listing the benefits of having so many friends around and such a constant social interaction. He had taught so many, knew so many returning friends. Time was crucial: you had the time to meet new fellows and get to know them. It was a community, which lasted over time: he was alone but not in solitude.

A certain melancholia lingered, not just in the story of the ever unattainable satisfaction of love. Jim nearly drank himself to death in middle age and had surgery for cancer in his seventies. He has moved to a ground-floor apartment designed for those with mobility issues. He is pleased that his new motorised wheelchair will let him get to the pub more often. Although he has spent most of his life in a country where homosexual sex has been legal and most of his life in the supportive environment of H staircase and its environs, the scars and difficulties of his internal tensions are evident behind his openness and bravado. Even in openness there is something deeply buried.

This particular conversation took place in the Senior Combination Room, under the portrait of Dent, over-looked by Rupert Brooke, glowered at by Noel Annan. As we left, Jim tried to count the current gay fellows. He got, sadly, to just four, including himself. He shuffled out holding onto his Zimmer frame, shaking his head at the passing of things. He was off to the pub to meet an old friend, a former Member of the European Parliament, 'gay of course', to discuss ailments and fear of the end.

Conclusion

Place, Community, Temporality

~

H Staircase is not a metaphor, nor an allegory, nor a symbol. But place does matter, and does become charged with a heightened significance, layered with memory, a lure for stories. Topography, from atmosphere to institutional form, has proved crucial to the construction of the experience of men who desired men. The college has always been a privileged space. I do not mean simply that it has educated the rich and entitled, though it has certainly done that over the nineteenth and twentieth centuries, as, correspondingly, it has spent a lot of time and effort from the 1960s onwards trying to broaden access. (From an all-male institution it is now roughly equal in male and female students; the undergraduate student body over the last twenty-five years has been made up of between 75 per cent and 80 per cent pupils from state schools rather than the almost exclusively private school entrance of a hundred years ago; at undergraduate level and very noticeably at graduate level it is now also a thoroughly international intake.) Rather, I mean that the college has its own boundaries, both physical and conceptual, which have usually worked to create a space of safety, experimentation and licence for its included members. That is a real privilege. A licensed giddiness. It allows most of its members to feel not just safe but that they belong – though there will always be outsiders in any

246

community: it is not a real paradox that liberal societies also exclude, and no surprise that some students or academics (adolescents and obsessives) feel alienated from their surroundings. Nor is it a surprise that the formality – which often feels like performance – or exclusivity of college life makes some members deeply uncomfortable and even angry. The college, as a college, however, is proud of its history of inclusivity and open-mindedness. It could not be as open and embracing as it tries to be, if it did not also have this privilege of being able to shut its doors. It is a public-facing institution that protects its own privacy, and tries to set its own standards of acceptability, for all that everyone's behaviour is inevitably embedded in broader social frameworks. Many of the figures in this history made a real difference to national and even international culture, and they did so not only because of the education they received within the college, but also because the college provided them with a base that enabled, supported and *grounded* them.

Scale is integral to this space. The college had very few members at the end of the nineteenth century and is still only a medium-sized college by the standards of the university, and tiny in comparison to the huge universities of the United States, say. The size of the college – in numbers and in physical location – allows for intimacy, demands it even. The placement of accommodation in the centre of the college, and the use of such accommodation also for research and teaching, encourages an integrated life: integrated for the academics and students who live and work in the same space, integrated between academics and students who share the same work and living space. The fewer the number of fellows who live in college – and the numbers are shrinking – the less such integration holds. That fellows eat together and drink together at lunch and of an evening, as was the pervasive expectation of fifty or a hundred years ago, a practice now also on the wane, also produced over time long-term friendships as well as the regular serendipity of new or repeated casual acquaintance.

But it is hard to explain even so why over so many years King's also had so many gay fellows and students – a quite disproportionate percentage, it seems, in comparison to other colleges or other national institutions – or to explain its strikingly self-aware and proud self-representation as a haven for gay acceptability. 'The King's ethos was a queer ethos', as one Senior Tutor summarised, decades after holding office. As the novelist J. G. Ballard recalled, 'The ethos of the college was homosexual, and a heterosexual like myself … was viewed as letting the side down, as well as having made an odd choice in the first place.'[1] Odd to go to King's; or odd to be heterosexual …? Each year the college publishes an annual report which has obituaries of its members. One hilarious but exemplary sentence read: 'he was distinctive among his peers not only for his great height but also for his pronounced heterosexuality'. It is hard to imagine many educational institutions phrasing an obituary with such precise and knowing sexual irony.

But, as Thucydides puts it, 'the city is its men'. While space creates the topography, it is the men who create the community. And community is one evident reason why King's has had such a tradition of gay men in its walls. On the one hand, there is the social network which linked schools to college in both directions: pupils coming to college, graduates returning to teach at school, and the process of directed selection that formed a tradition of certain types going to certain places. Rooms were passed on and so was insider knowledge. Teachers recommended their own former teachers to future pupils, and recommended colleges or universities where their pupils would best fit in and be happy. This is another way that privilege works, and excludes, as it enables. On the other hand, many fellows stayed many years in King's, and taught generations of students, and formed long-term relationships based on place and affect. The college functioned as a community of men who supported and cared for each other, and fought and hated like a family, too – though how it is precisely *not* like a family is an equally fascinating commentary on what a community *can* look like. The community's glue was the stories it told of itself, to itself and to the outside world. How any institution represents itself to itself is crucial to its functioning, and King's was replete with conversation and repeated anecdotes, both about itself as an institution and about its men, and especially its more flashy or famous gay men. As the institution changed over time, and as the comprehension and versions of desire changed over time, the repeated stories and conversations about the college and about desire mapped these transformations, performed them, articulated them. What is taught in a college is much more than a subject, a discipline or a set of techniques. It is also a way of making a community, of living an embedded life, and King's prided itself on transmitting a set of values to do with tolerance, acceptance, generosity and serious critique. The stories told – how they are told and what they tell – are instrumental in the construction of these values of the community. The community of men who desired men was at times more or less boldly visible, more or less porous, more or less numerous, and it certainly does not track a path from the hidden to the open – the 1920s were far more brazenly performative than the 1950s – but the community continued to know itself and express itself within the college. This sense of community is rare in homosexual history. In the film *Cabaret*, based on Christopher Isherwood's autobiographical Berlin fictions, the homosexual hero comes from King's ('my college'), although Isherwood attended Corpus Christi College; the same little white lie appears in *Down There on a Visit*. The change is small but telling: a gay hero *should* come from King's. The judgemental moralist F. R. Leavis summed up his distaste for King's College in his imagined and impossible image of Lytton Strachey strutting by the college, arm in arm with Dadie Rylands and Rupert Brooke. From the outside, what horrified and fascinated was not just that King's was known for its gay life, but that it was apparently at ease with it. The liberal tolerance of King's was summed up by its gay politics – unimaginable without it.

I have used the word 'tolerance' in this chapter because it is the term that the people I am writing about use with real intent. Tolerance here, I think, is not what Goethe brilliantly diagnosed when he wrote, 'Tolerance should really only be a passing attitude: it should lead to recognition. To tolerate is to offend.'[2] So often, as Goethe knew, to talk of tolerance is a sign and symptom of the failure to integrate – and a hierarchical, patronising attitude towards others. We will tolerate you if you fit in with us: an attempt to keep power relations in place, while disavowing their force. But tolerance towards queerness is a much more unstable dynamic, which requires a different, more radical form of hospitality to otherness, and an acknowledgement of the impact of queerness on one's own sense of self, and a consequent loss of bearings. Tolerance in this sense is an exploratory value, and not just a gesture of political self-congratulation.

Community may be rare in homosexual history, but it is especially rare to have a community lasting so long. The institutional, educational frame provided stability. Through one lens, we can see someone like Dadie Rylands transforming from flirty young actor, kissing his way through a cast party, to the inspirational teacher of John Gielgud and Ian McKellen, to the spry old man lamenting that he had not known the depths of the secret life of his shamed friend, Anthony Blunt. Through another lens, we can see intricate social networks of friends and lovers and acquaintances growing and shifting over time, revolving around the same rooms and pathways, looked on by the portraits of the past. Experience was shared in part because careers were modelled by the similar academic routines and expectations of a career path: the academic year, with its influx of new students every autumn and the departure of a generation every summer, provides a calendar that over time comes to structure a life with familiar, embodied repetitions. In part, the community's sense of itself is produced because role models were endemic to the teaching environment. Generations of teachers taught generations of students: 'Like the generations of leaves, the lives of mortal men. Now the wind scatters the old leaves across the earth, now the living timber bursts with the new buds and spring comes round again. And so with men: as one generation comes to life, another dies away.' The current University of Cambridge Alumni magazine has a regular feature of taking a distinguished alumnus back to their room in college to meet the current inhabitant. The construction of tradition requires such imagining of passing on. To live on H staircase was to find oneself in a story of continuity.

As I write, Western society feels fractured, transforming, ill at ease with itself: recovering from a global pandemic, uncertain about the values of its governance, struggling with the consequences of its own technological inventiveness, horrified at the recurrence of war fuelled by nationalism, torn apart by the continuing impact of racial violence, and struggling with what the norms of social and sexual interaction should be. Imagining a better society is a necessity for making a better society. For all their narcissism, triumphs, foolishness, brilliance, arrogance, privilege, love, despair, the men whose lives I have put together here in the name of H staircase shared a will to imagine the world otherwise. Such a will is still much needed. Universities, too, embedded as they are in these aggressive and polarising social and cultural forces, are finding it harder and harder to maintain the open-minded, explorative, critical space that the college provided to the figures of this history. To maintain such a space is a fight worth the effort. It is not a question of a 'safe space' (although the gay men of King's felt safer in the college than in the society outside for good reason) but of a community that recognises the value of coming into contact with people and ideas who do not simply concur and support your own perspective. Such communities are where education takes place. Messier places, more discomforting places, even, but such openness to uncertainty, serendipity, risk and exploration is crucial for education, or at least for the transformational education that has the power to transform people and, through them, society into a better place.

That's what a staircase can mean to me, and why this story is worth the telling.

NOTES

A Brief Introduction to a Large Topic

1 On the language of male 'homosexuality', see: Halperin, D. *One Hundred Years of Homosexuality, and Other Essays on Greek Love* (London and New York, 1990); with the background of Bauer, H. *English Literary Sexology: Translations of Inversion 1860–1930* (Basingstoke, 2009); Oosterhuis, H. *Stepchildren of Nature: Krafft-Ebing, Psychiatry, and the Making of Sexual Identity* (Chicago, 2000); Bland, L. and Doan, L. eds. *Sexology in Culture: Labelling Bodies and Desire* (Cambridge, 1998); Cocks, H. *Nameless Offences: Homosexual Desire in the Nineteenth Century* (London, 2003); Cook, M. *London and the Culture of Homosexuality, 1885–1914* (Cambridge, 2003); Foucault, M. *History of Sexuality, Vol. 1*, trans R. Hurley (New York, 1978); Katz, J. *The Invention of Heterosexuality* (Chicago, 2005); Robb, G. *Strangers: Homosexual Love in the Nineteenth Century* (New York, 2003); Terry, J. *An American Obsession: Science, Medicine and Homosexuality in Modern Society* (Chicago, 1999); Weeks, J. *Sex, Politics and Society: The Regulation of Sexuality Since 1800* (London, 1989).

For the Uranian poets, see D'Arch Smith, T. *Love in Earnest: Some Notes on the Lives and Writings of English 'Uranian' Poets 1889–1930* (London, 1970); and for a more recent, detailed case study, Wilper, J. 'Translation and the Construction of a "Uranian" Identity: Edward Prime-Stevenson's [Xavier Mayne's] *The Intersexes* (1908)' in H. Bauer, ed. *Sexology and Translation: Cultural and Scientific Encounters across the Modern World* (Philadelphia,

2015) 216–32. Corey and Sayle who were part of this loose group will appear in the book later.

2 '**Fugitive discourse**': a gloss on Hartman, S. *Wayward Lives, Beautiful Experiments* (New York, 2019).

3 Davidson, J. *The Greeks and Greek Love: A Radical Reappraisal of Homosexuality in Ancient Greece* (London, 2008); Boswell, J. *Christianity, Social Tolerance and Homosexuality: Gay People in Western Europe from the Christian Era to the Fourteenth Century* (New Haven, 1980).

On molly houses, see Norton, R. *Mother Clap's Molly House: The Gay Subculture in England 1700–1830* (London, 1992).

4 '**Queer unhistoricism**': see Dinshaw, C. *How Soon Is Now? Medieval Texts, Amateur Readers and the Queerness of Time* (Durham, NC, 2012); Freccero, C. *Queer/Early/Modern* (Durham, NC, 2006); Freeman, E. *Time Binds: Queer Temporalities, Queer Histories* (Durham, NC, 2010); Halperin, D. *How to Do the History of Homosexuality* (Chicago, 2002).

'**we are doing battle here, *per amore*, with history**': Butler, S. *The Passions of John Addington Symonds* (Oxford, 2022) 121.

5 '**thriving subculture of sodomy**': MacCarthy, F. *Byron: Life and Legend* (New York, 2002) 58, who adds that Byron was inducted here by William Bankes, 'the father of all mischiefs'.

6 On Edward Carpenter, see Rowbotham, S. *Edward Carpenter: A Life of Liberty and Love* (London, 2008); Gandhi, L. *Affective Communities: Anti-colonial Thought, Fin-de-Siècle Radicalism and the Politics of Friendship* (Durham, NC, 2006) 34–66.

7 On Symonds, see Butler, S. *The Passions of John Addington Symonds* (Oxford, 2022), building beyond Grosskurth, P. *John Addington Symonds: A Biography* (London, 1964); Pemble, J. ed. *John Addington Symonds: Culture and the*

Demon Desire (Cambridge, 2000); Brady, S. *Masculinity and Male Homosexuality in Britain, 1861–1913* (Houndmills, 2005) 157–209.

'**He has read Havelock Ellis**': Noel Annan writing to Dadie Rylands, 1941, KCMA, in Noel Annan's papers, undated.

8 On working-class homosex, see Houlbrook, M. *Queer London: Perils and Pleasures in the Sexual Metropolis 1918–1957* (Chicago, 2005) 168: 'Engaging in homosex or an intimate relationship with another man was not incompatible with definitions of masculine "normality".' Also Katz, J. *Love Stories: Sex between Men before Homosexuality* (Chicago, 2001); Kaplan, M. *Sodom on the Thames: Sex, Love and Scandal in Wilde Times* (Ithaca, NY, 2005); McLaren, A. *The Trials of Masculinity: Policing Sexual Boundaries, 1870–1930* (Chicago, 1997); Dellamora, R. *Victorian Sexual Dissidence* (Chicago, 1999); Thomas, K. *Postal Pleasures: Sex, Scandal and Victorian Letters* (Oxford, 2012).

On Krafft-Ebing, see Oosterhuis, H. *Stepchildren of Nature: Krafft-Ebing, Psychiatry, and the Making of Sexual Identity* (Chicago, 2000).

9 '**feasting with panthers**': quoted in Parker, P. *Ackerley: A Life of J. R. Ackerley* (London, 1989) 91. See also Koven, S. *Slumming: Sexual and Social Politics in Victorian London* (Princeton, 2004).

10 '**conspiration of silence about homosexuality in England**': cited in Bauer, H. *English Literary Sexology: Translations of Inversion 1860–1930* (Basingstoke, 2009) 49. See also Janes, D. *Picturing the Closet: Male Secrecy and Homosexual Visibility in Britain* (Oxford, 2015).

11 On Berlin and Paris see Cook, M. and Evans, J. *Queer Cities, Queer Cultures: Europe Since 1945* (London, 2014), with Formby, E. *Exploring LGBT Spaces: Contrasting Identities,*

Belonging and Well-Being (New York and Abingdon, 2017), and Bell, D. and Valentine, G. eds. *Mapping Desire: Geographies of Sexuality* (London, 1995) (already rather dated). Homfray, M. *Provincial Queens: The Gay and Lesbian Community in the North-West of England* (Bern, 2007) glumly reminds us that for many places the question is whether there is anything recognisable as a community.

Modern socialists: see Formby, E. *Exploring LGBT Spaces: Contrasting Identities, Belonging and Well-Being* (New York and Abingdon, 2017) and Cook, M. and Evans, J. *Queer Cities, Queer Cultures: Europe Since 1945* (London, 2014) – both with extensive further bibliographies.

12 'There is no queer urban theory', writes Natalie Oswin trenchantly in 'Social Junk' in *Grammars of the Urban Ground*, ed. A. Amin and M. Lancione (Durham, NC, 2022) 27–40 at 27, before writing about urbanists' discussion of homosexuality from the Chicago school onwards (a view of 'social junk' which could go back to Mayhew in the nineteenth century).

13 **'friendship networks ...'**: Nardi, P. *Gay Men's Friendships* (Chicago, 1999) 13; see also Weston, K. *Families We Choose: Lesbians, Gays, Kinship* (New York, 1991). Edward Carpenter published the tellingly entitled *Ioläus: An Anthology of Friendship* in 1902; Whitman in *Leaves of Grass* extols the 'high-towering love' of an 'invincible ... new city of friends': the term 'friend' has a history of charged significance in gay discourse which is slightly different from, for example, Hannah Arendt's 'the political relevance of friendship' [*Men in Dark Times* (New York, 1968)], a line of political thought leading from Aristotle to Jacques Derrida's *The Politics of Friendship*, trans. G. Collins (London, 1997).

On community's recognition, see Waters, C. 'The Homosexual as a Social Being in Britain, 1945–1968', *Journal of British Studies* 51.3 (July 2012) 685–710;

Woolwine, D. 'Community in Gay Male Experience and Moral Discourse', *Journal of Homosexuality* 38.4 (2000) 5–37; Lauria, M. and Knopp, L. 'Toward an Analysis of the Role of Gay Communities in the Urban Renaissance', *Urban Geography* 6 (1985) 152–69; Ghaziani, A. *There Goes the Gayberhood?* (Princeton, 2014) who notes (58) that even in San Francisco in 2007 only 36 per cent of gay men said there was a gay community they identified with!

On ghettos, see Levine, M. 'Gay Ghetto', *Journal of Homosexuality* 4.4 (1979) 363–77. On 'gayberhoods', see Ghaziani, A. *There Goes the Gayberhood?* (Princeton, 2014); Brown, M. 'Gender and Sexuality II: There Goes the Gayberhood', *Progress in Human Geography* 38.3 (2014) 457–65.

'a spatial response …': Lauria, M. and Knopp, L. 'Toward an Analysis of the Role of Gay Communities in the Urban Renaissance', *Urban Geography* 6 (1985) 152–69 at 152.

On Brighton and lesbian life, see Browne, K. and Bakshi, L. *Ordinary in Brighton: LGBT, Activisms and the City* (Aldershot, 2013).

14 'construct a gay city …': Ghaziani, A. *There Goes the Gayberhood?* (Princeton, 2014) 14.

'inseparable from the development …': Castells, M. *The City and the Grassroots: A Cross-Cultural Theory of Urban Social Movements* (Berkeley, 1983) 157.

15 'more a concentration …', 'several networks …': Rothenberg, T. '"And She Told Two Friends": Lesbians Creating Urban Social Space' in D. Bell and G. Valentine, eds. *Mapping Desire: Geographies of Sexuality* (London, 1995) 165–81 at 172.

'There goes the gayberhood': Ghaziani, A. *There Goes the Gayberhood?* (Princeton, 2014); Brown, M. 'Gender and Sexuality II: There Goes the Gayberhood', *Progress in Human Geography* 38.3 (2014) 457–65.

Many cities: see Cook, M. and Evans, J. *Queer Cities, Queer Cultures: Europe Since 1945* (London, 2014) for twelve

European cities, along with Bell, D. and Valentine, G. eds. *Mapping Desire: Geographies of Sexuality* (London, 1995). Life-cycle: Simpson, P. (2015) *Middle-Aged Gay Men, Ageing and Ageism: Over the Rainbow?* (Basingstoke, 2015); Ghaziani, A. *There Goes the Gayberhood?* (Princeton, 2014) 51–3, 103–8.

16 On the 1950s see Bauer, H. and Cook, M. eds. *Queer 1950s: Rethinking Sexuality in the Postwar Years* (Basingstoke, 2012), especially 133–49; Bauer, H. (2012) 'Sexology Backward: Hirschfeld, Kinsey and the Reshaping of Sex Research in the 1950s'.

On the legal history, see Upchurch, C. *'Beyond the Law': The Politics of Ending the Death Penalty for Sodomy in Britain* (Philadelphia, 2021); Cocks, H. *Nameless Offences: Homosexual Desire in the Nineteenth Century* (London, 2003); both following Weeks, J. *Sex, Politics and Society: The Regulation of Sexuality Since 1800* (London, 1989).

17 'My real life ...': quoted in Stille, A. *The Sullivanians: Sex, Psychotherapy and the Wild Life of an American Commune* (New York, 2023) 154.

18 Some activist critics: see Edelman, L. *No Future: Queer Theory and the Death Drive* (Durham, NC, 2004); Muñoz, J. E. *Cruising Utopia: The Then and There of Queer Futurity* (New York, 2009); Halberstam, J. *In a Queer Time and Place: Transgender Bodies, Subcultural Lives* (New York, 2005).

19 'giddy places': Ahmed, S. *Queer Phenomenology: Orientations, Objects, Others* (Durham, NC, 2006) 9.

20 The information on Wedd comes from L. P. Wilkinson, 'Six Characters', KCMA GBR/0272/LPW 9.

21 On Jane Harrison see Beard, M. *The Invention of Jane Harrison* (Cambridge, MA, 2002), more sophisticated than Peacock, S. *Jane Ellen Harrison: The Mask and the Self* (Hanover, 1988). See also Robinson, A. *The Life and Work of Jane Ellen Harrison* (Oxford, 2002).

22 **'we need to articulate an ethics ...'**: Angel, K. *Tomorrow Sex Will Be Good Again: Women and Desire in the Age of Consent* (London, 2021) 40.

23 **'The longing for community...'**: Love, H. *Feeling Backward: Loss and the Politics of Queer History* (Cambridge, MA, 2007) 37; see also on shame Sedgwick, E. *Touching Feeling: Affect, Pedagogy, Performativity* (Durham, NC, 2003) 35–65; Warner, M. *The Trouble with Normal: Sex, Politics and the Ethics of Queer Life* (Cambridge, MA, 2000) 35–6.

24 **'nothing but wounded attachments'**: Love, H. *Feeling Backward: Loss and the Politics of Queer History* (Cambridge, MA, 2007) 42.

25 **'Stylistics of living'** refers to the late work of Foucault: see *The Birth of Biopolitics: Lectures at the Collège de France 1978–9*, ed. M. Senellart, trans. G. Burchell (London, 2008); *On the Government of the Living: Lectures at the Collège de France 1979–80*, ed. M. Senellart, trans. G. Burchell (London, 2008) with Elden, S. *Foucault's Last Decade* (Cambridge, 2016) and Elden, S. *The Archaeology of Foucault* (Cambridge, 2022).

26 **'Queerness'**: see Edelman, L. *No Future: Queer Theory and the Death Drive* (Durham, NC, 2004), discussed by Doan, L. *Disturbing Practices: History, Sexuality and Women's Experience of the Great War* (Chicago, 2013) 1–96; and Huffer, L. *Mad for Foucault: Rethinking the Foundations of Queer Theory* (New York, 2010); Herring, S. *Queering the Underworld: Slumming Literature and the Undoing of Lesbian and Gay History* (Chicago, 2007); Amin, K. *Disturbing Attachments: Genet, Modern Pederasty and Queer History* (Durham, NC, 2017).

Chapter 1

1 On Dennis Robertson, see Fletcher, G. *Dennis Robertson* (London, 2008)7: 'He was a fellow of Trinity, but looked ever towards King's.'

2 'Epistemology of the closet': see Sedgwick, E. *Epistemology of the Closet* (Berkeley, 1990), building on *Between Men: English Literature and Homosocial Desire* (New York, 1985).

3 On J. K. Stephen, see Leighton, D. J. *Privileges and Pitfalls: The Life of J. K. Stephen* (London, 2009); Kopley, E. 'Virginia Woolf's Cousin, J. K. Stephen: Forgotten but Not Gone', *ELT* 59.2 (2016) 191–209; Benson, A. C. 'J. K. Stephen', in *The Leaves of the Tree: Studies in Biography* (New York, 1911) 78–107; Browning, O. 'J. K. Stephen', *Bookman*, 1.6 (March 1892) 204–5; McDonald, D. *The Prince, His Tutor and the Ripper: The Evidence Linking James Kenneth Stephen to the Whitechapel Murders* (Jefferson, NC, 2007); and the unsatisfactory Newman, H. *James Kenneth Stephen: Virginia Woolf's Tragic Cousin* (London, 2008).

4 'J. K. Stephen was a young man ...': Benson, A. C. *Memories and Friends* (London 1924) 300.

5 'This great mad figure ...': Woolf, V. 'A Sketch of the Past,' in *Moments of Being: Unpublished Autobiographical Writings of Virginia Woolf*, ed. J. Schulkind (Sussex, 1976), 99. On their relationship, see Kopley, E. *Virginia Woolf and Poetry* (Oxford, 2020) 54–5.

6 'of an emotional nature ...': Benson, A. C. *The Leaves of the Tree: Studies in Biography* (New York, 1911) 87.

7 Cory, D. W. *The Homosexual in America: A Subjective Approach* (New York, 1951).

8 On Oscar Browning, see Anstruther, I. *Oscar Browning: A Biography* (London, 1984) – and further bibliography below.

On William Johnson/Cory, see Compton Mackenzie, F. *William Cory: A Biography* (London, 1950).

On anxiety about pupil–teacher relations, see Funke, J. '"We cannot be Greek now": Age Difference, Corruption of Youth, and the Making of *Sexual Inversion*', *English Studies* 94.2 (2013) 139–54; Hall, L. 'Forbidden by

God, Despised by Men: Masturbation, Medical Warnings, Moral Panic, and Manhood in Great Britain 1850–1950', *Journal of History of Sexuality* 2.3 (1992) 365–87; McBeth, M. 'The Pleasure of Learning and the Tightrope of Desire: Teacher–Student Relationships and Victorian Pedagogy', in J. Goodman and J. Martin, eds. *Gender, Colonialism and Education: An International Perspective* (London, 2002) 46–72; more generally, Holt, J. *Public School Literature, Civic Education and the Politics of Male Adolescence* (Farnham, 2008). Connolly, C. *Enemies of Promise* (London, 1938) 271, Etonian, characteristically sums up one line of self-recognition: 'the greater part of the ruling class remains adolescent, school-minded, self-conscious, cowardly, sentimental and in the last analysis homosexual'.

9 On Curzon, see Rose, K. *Superior Person: A Portrait of Curzon and His Circle in Late Victorian Britain* (London, 1969) who outlines Curzon's brutal childhood vividly.

10 **'O. B. used to talk to me about everything …'**: Wortham, H. *Victorian Eton and Cambridge, Being the Life and Times of Oscar Browning* (London, 1927) 66–7: the student was Vassall-Phillips whom we shall meet later.

11 **'the most brilliant young man …'**: Browning, O. *Memories of Sixty Years at Eton, Cambridge and Elsewhere* (London, 1910) 225.

12 On Prince Eddy: Aronson, T. *Prince Eddy and the Homosexual Underworld* (London, 1994); and for the over-heated discussion of evidence, see McDonald, D. *The Prince, His Tutor and the Ripper: The Evidence Linking James Kenneth Stephen to the Whitechapel Murders* (Jefferson, NC, 2007). On Cleveland Street, see Cook, M. *London and the Culture of Homosexuality, 1885–1914* (Cambridge, 2003); Kaplan, M. *Sodom on the Thames: Sex, Love and Scandal in Wilde Times* (Ithaca, NY, 2005); Thomas, K. *Postal Pleasures: Sex, Scandal and Victorian*

Letters (Oxford, 2012); with the background of Cocks, H. *Nameless Offences: Homosexual Desire in the Nineteenth Century* (London, 2003).

13 On A. C. Benson, see Newsome, D. *On the Edge of Paradise: A. C. Benson the Diarist* (London, 1980) and Goldhill, S. *A Very Queer Family Indeed: Sex, Religion, and the Bensons in Victorian Britain* (Chicago, 2016).

14 'It was in these rooms ...': ACB xxxviii 65.

15 'weak but singularly attractive ...': Benson, A. C. *Memoirs of Arthur Hamilton* (London, 1886) 24. 'What passed I cannot say ...': ibid.

16 'Then there was the Arthur Mason adoration ...': ACB xxxiv 131.

17 'Can one trust ...': ACB liii 11–12.

18 'I woke early ...': ACB xxix 73.

19 'open love letter': Regis, A. 'Late Style and Speaking Out: J. A. Symonds's *In the Key of Blue*', *English Studies* 94.2 (2013) 206–31, at 213, with Butler, S. *The Passions of John Addington Symonds* (Oxford, 2022).

20 'Are you blue?': Letter from F. W. Howlett to George Egerton, 22 September 1895. Princeton University Library. The writer, from New Zealand, also notes: 'Symonds is dead' (a past authority for 'blue') and goes on to quote Swinburne and Sappho, and to mention Sappho's homosexuality. Thanks to Stefano Evangelista who shared this letter with me.

21 'At a Safe Distance', mentioned with amusement by Benson: Lubbock, P. ed. *The Diary of Arthur Christopher Benson* (London, 1926) 147.

22 'The public fondling and caressing ...': ACB cviii 70.

23 'King's is damnable ...': Leo Maxse, letter to MRJ, 31 January 1886, Cambridge University Library MS Add. 7481 M197 (thanks to Darryl Jones for showing me this letter). Maxse also stated to A. C. Benson that 'King's is

reputed with suspicion of being unorthodox and immoral in theory so that parents hesitate to send their sons' (ACB cxxiii 33). It is not clear if the strange phrase 'in theory' is what Maxse said, or is Benson trying to temper Maxse's anger.

24 **'Yesterday evening will always mark ...'**: Keynes writing to Duncan Grant, quoted in Skidelsky, R. *John Maynard Keynes: Hopes Betrayed 1883–1920* (London, 1983) 235.

25 Goldhill, S. *A Very Queer Family Indeed: Sex, Religion, and the Bensons in Victorian Britain* (Chicago, 2016).

26 On Monty James, see Jones, D. *M. R. James: A Life* (Oxford, forthcoming), which improves greatly on Cox, M. *M. R. James: An Informal Portrait* (Oxford, 1983).

27 **'Do tell me whether you are staying ...'**: A. Cole, letter to Sheppard, 9 June 1902, KCMA.

28 **'in ghastly circumstances ...'**: O. R. Vassall-Phillips, letter to MRJ, 26 December 1926. Eton College Library M. R. James Miscellany vol. II/*Eton and King's* Inserts 2. Thanks to Darryl Jones for this reference.

29 **'a terrible and most pathetic letter ...'**: O. R. Vassall-Phillips, letter to MRJ, 26 December 1926. Eton College Library M. R. James Miscellany vol. II/*Eton and King's* Inserts 2. Thanks to Darryl Jones for this reference.

30 **'Altogether I miss you DREADFULLY ...'**: Anstruther, I., *Oscar Browning: A Biography* (London, 1984) 77. See Vassall-Phillips, O. *After Fifty Years* (London, 1928) 23–4, 92.

31 **'He loved & thought no shame ...'**: cited in Anstruther, I. *Oscar Browning: A Biography* (London, 1984) 90.

32 **'Poor Oscar Wilde ...'**: Vassall-Phillips, O. *After Fifty Years* (London, 1928) 58.

33 **'And so Father Vassall-Phillips ...'**: Jones, D. *M. R. James: A Life* (Oxford, forthcoming) ch. 4.

34 **'O. R. has a morbid predilection ...'**: ACB cxxxiv 43.

'I told O. R. he must drop these boys …': ACB cxxxiv 43.

'I told him today that it was a sexual perversion …': ACB cxxxiv 43.

35 'composing limericks …': Benson, quoted in Newsome, D. *On the Edge of Paradise: A. C. Benson the Diarist* (London, 1980) 333.

'I don't myself think …': ACB v 158.

'these things are mysterious': ACB v 54.

36 'a virtue because …': Havelock Ellis, H. *Studies in the Psychology of Sex*, 2nd ed. 6 vols. (Philadelphia, 1921 [1897–1910]) vi, 169; 'erotic chastity': vi, 155.

37 On 'productive sexual continence' see Green, S. *Sexual Restraint and Aesthetic Experience in Victorian Literary Decadence* (Cambridge, 2023).

38 'The Provost rapped sharply …': Nathaniel Wedd's unpublished memoir of Goldsworthy Lowes Dickinson, KCMA.

'James hates thought' recorded by J. Clapham, *Cambridge Review* (9 October 1936) 6. 'Unspeculative and exceedingly unpolitical' is Clapham's slightly kinder judgement.

39 On the ghost stories, see Murphy, P. *Medieval Studies and the Ghost Stories of M. R. James* (University Park, PA, 2017).

40 'genius flawed by abysmal fatuity': Benson, E. F. *As We Were: A Victorian Peep Show* (London, 1930) 129.

'Falstaff playing Hamlet …': Leslie, S. *The Cantab* (London, 1926) 80.

'The strangeness of the creation …': Lubbock, P. ed. *The Diary of Arthur Christopher Benson* (London, 1926) 119–20.

41 Browning's autobiographies: Browning, O. *Memories of Sixty Years at Eton, Cambridge and Elsewhere* (London, 1910); *Memoirs of Later Years* (London, 1923).

42 'He was the first tutor …': Marcus, J. 'Review: Ian Anstruther, *Oscar Browning: A Biography*', *Victorian Studies* 28.3 (1985) 556–8 at 556.

43 'corpulent person ...': Robinson, P. *Gay Lives: Homosexual Autobiography from John Addington Symonds to Paul Monette* (Chicago, 1999) 29.

44 'Browning held the unofficial Chair ...': Marcus, J. 'Review: Ian Anstruther, *Oscar Browning: A Biography*', *Victorian Studies* 28.3 (1985) 556–8 at 558.

45 'unpleasant homosexual appetite': Anstruther, I. *Oscar Browning: A Biography* (London, 1984) 189. Noel Annan, in *The Dons: Mentors, Eccentrics and Geniuses* (London, 1999) 103, is less sure: 'not a seducer but a jilt'.

46 'distinctly **urban** queer culture': Houlbrook, M. *Queer London: Perils and Pleasures in the Sexual Metropolis 1918–1957* (Chicago, 2005) 264.
   'Men neither understood themselves ...': ibid., 141.
   '[e]ngaging in homosex ...': ibid., 168.

47 'feasting with panthers ... a passion to civilise ...': quoted in Parker, P. *Ackerley: A Life of J. R. Ackerley* (London, 1989) 91.

48 'His ideal was higher than his practice ...': Sheppard, J., unpublished memoir of Goldsworthy Lowes Dickinson 20, KCMA.

49 'It is an awful picture ...': Benson in 1905, quoted in Anstruther, I. *Oscar Browning: A Biography* (London, 1984) 175.

50 'My beloved Browning ...': Jackson quoted in ibid. 139.

51 On Fred Benson, see Masters, B. *The Life of E. F. Benson* (London, 1991); Goldhill, S. *A Very Queer Family Indeed: Sex, Religion, and the Bensons in Victorian Britain* (Chicago, 2016).

52 'a cynical, aggressive, Mephistophelean ...': Holroyd, M. *Lytton Strachey* (London, 1994) 191, quoting Lionel Trilling quoting Forster.

53 'The dominant personality ...': Wedd, N. version 2, no page numbers, unpublished memoir of Goldsworthy Lowes Dickinson, KCMA.

54 'I feel perfectly mad about him ...': quoted in Masters, B. *The Life of E. F. Benson* (London, 1991) 86. Diary, Magdalene College Cambridge archives, 181 – followed by two blank pages, then 'better about Yorke'.

55 'There are some feelings ...': Benson, E. F., Diary, Magdalene College archives, Wednesday 26 January 1887, 105.

56 'They were quite without moral sense ...': Benson, E. F. *Colin* (London, 1923) 213–15. See for background, Pemble, J. *The Mediterranean Passion: Victorians and Edwardians in the South* (Oxford, 1987).

57 'Hughes used to be a ripper ...': Benson, E. F. *David Blaize* (London, 1916) 148–9.

58 'But ... what the hell ...': Waugh, A. *The Loom of Youth* (London, 1916) 53.

59 'the later Victorian moral hysteria ...': Holt, J. *Public School Literature, Civic Education and the Politics of Male Adolescence* (Farnham, 2008) 71. See also Deslandes, P. *Oxbridge Men: British Masculinity and the Undergraduate Experience, 1850-1920* (Bloomington, IN, 2005), which does not always spot the satire. In general on schooldays, see Richards, J. *The Happiest Days: The Public School in English Fiction* (Manchester, 1988); Newsome, D. *Godliness and Good Learning: Four Studies on a Victorian Ideal* (London, 1961); Chandos, J. *Boys Together: English Public Schools 1800–1864* (London, 1985); Bristow, J. *Empire Boys: Adventures in a Man's World* (London, 1991) with the background of Roach, J. *A History of Secondary Education in England, 1870–1902* (London, 1991); Mangan, J. *Athleticism in the Victorian and Edwardian Public School: The Emergence and Consolidation of an Educational Ideology* (Cambridge, 1981); Rothblatt, S. *The Revolution of the Dons: Cambridge and Society in Victorian England* (Cambridge, 1968).

60 Lyttelton, E. *The Causes and Prevention of Immorality in Schools* (London, 1887); *Training of the Young in Laws of Sex* (London, 1900).

61 'Farrar's *St. Winifred's* ...': James, M. R. *Eton and King's: Recollections Mainly Trivial, 1875–1925* (London, 1926) 5.

62 'saying that they had been at Harrow ...': Waugh, A. *The Loom of Youth* (London, 1916) 136. 'What fools ...': ibid., 135.

63 'a cynical old gentleman ...': Benson, E. F. *The Babe, B.A.* (London, 1896) 1. It has been claimed that Herbert Charles Pollitt, the flamboyant friend of Aubrey Beardsley, was the model for the Babe.

64 'in order that the emotional and romantic ...': Havelock Ellis, H. *Studies in the Psychology of Sex*, 2nd ed. 6 vols. (Philadelphia, 1921 [1897–1910]) ii, 339.

65 'a long and lover-like kiss ...': quoted in Newsome, D. *On the Edge of Paradise: A. C. Benson the Diarist* (London, 1980) 261.

66 'I think it will do him good ...': ACB iii 279.

67 'confused, alarmed and obsessed': Parker, P. *Ackerley: A Life of J. R. Ackerley* (London, 1989) 15–16.

68 'Mittel-Urning ...': Symonds, J. A. *A Problem in Modern Ethics* (London, 1896) 87.

69 '[T]o love boys ...': Hall, G. S. *Adolescence* (London, 1925) I 519. 'Attachment ...': ibid., II 107.

70 'The boundaries between Uranian ...': Ingleheart, J. *Masculine Plural: Queer Classics, Sex, and Education* (Oxford, 2018) 68.

71 'the courage to bear up ...': ACB cxxii 38.

72 'I the man fulfilled ...': Sayle, C. *Bertha: A Story of Love* (London, 1885) xiv; 'What made you kiss ...': ibid., 45.

73 'an undercurrent of sadness ...': Benson, A. C. 'Charles Sayle', *The Library* 5.3 (1924) 271–3. See Oates, J. 'Charles Edward Sayle', *Transactions of the Cambridge Bibliographical*

Society 8 (1982) 236–69. 'We old folk ...': quoted in ibid., 264.

74 'it was rather romantic ...': Benson Family Papers, Bodleian Library, Oxford, 3/4–5, Mary Benson to Edward White Benson, 1 December 1852.

75 On Minnie Sidgwick, see Bolt, R. *As Good as God, as Clever as the Devil: The Impossible Life of Mary Benson* (London, 2011) and Goldhill, S. *A Very Queer Family Indeed: Sex, Religion, and the Bensons in Victorian Britain* (Chicago, 2016).

'How I cried ...': Benson Family Papers, Bodleian Library, Oxford: 1/71–80, 17 March 1898, discussed in Goldhill, S. *A Very Queer Family Indeed: Sex, Religion, and the Bensons in Victorian Britain* (Chicago, 2016) 26–8.

76 'But two men ...': Foucault, M. 'Friendship as a Way of Life', in *Ethics, Subjectivity, Truth*, ed. P. Rabinow, trans. R. Hurley et al. (New York, 1994) 156.

77 'a real gulf ...': Benson, E. F. *As We Were: A Victorian Peep Show* (London, 1930) 22.

Chapter 2

1 'Dickinson's debt ...': Wedd, N. unpublished memoir of Goldsworthy Lowes Dickinson, KCMA, 7.

2 Proctor, D. ed. *The Autobiography of G. Lowes Dickinson*, with preface by Noel Annan (London, 1973); Forster, E. M. *Goldsworthy Lowes Dickinson* (London, 1934).

3 'preached flamboyantly ...': Chesterton, G. K. *Heretics* (London, 1905) 153; 'are envied and admired ...': 154; 'too solid': 155.

4 'I say that Simeon Stylites ...': Chesterton, G. K. *Heretics* (London, 1905) 55.

5 On Carpenter, see Rowbotham, S. *Edward Carpenter: A Life of Liberty and Love* (London, 2008); Gandhi, L. *Affective*

Communities: Anti-colonial Thought, Fin-de-Siècle Radicalism and the Politics of Friendship (Durham, NC, 2006) 34–66.

6 'The curious, passionate ...': Proctor, D. ed. *The Autobiography of G. Lowes Dickinson* (London, 1973) 89.

'agony and gloom': Robinson, P. *Gay Lives: Homosexual Autobiography from John Addington Symonds to Paul Monette* (Chicago, 1999) 41; 'As I write ...': 29.

'Then, one evening ...': Proctor, D. ed. *The Autobiography of G. Lowes Dickinson* (London, 1973) 90.

7 'I commend it ...': Proctor, D. ed. *The Autobiography of G. Lowes Dickinson* (London, 1973) 91; 'How could you ...': 280 – in the autobiographical poem 'Body and Soul'.

8 'We slept in the same bed ...': Proctor, D. ed. *The Autobiography of G. Lowes Dickinson* (London, 1973) 92.

9 'Every night he kissed me ...': Proctor, D. ed. *The Autobiography of G. Lowes Dickinson* (London, 1973) 94; 'To kiss you ...': 111; 'each of us did our best ...': 7; 'Probably, if I had ever loved a man ...': 10; 'I am like a man ...': 11; 'a woman's soul ...': 10.

10 'There was nothing ...': Wingfield-Stratford, E. *Before the Lights Went Out* (London, 1945) 175. The description of Wingfield-Stratford is Wikipedia's lavish summary. Peter Quennell (quoted by Max Beloff in the *DNB*) wrote: 'he was all of a piece, his physical build which was wonderfully large and expansive, his high ambitions and boisterous enthusiasms which were on the same gargantuan scale, even his fierce prejudices which lay scattered like rolled-up hedgehogs along the paths of his conversation'.

11 'sometimes tragic ...', 'The homosexual temperament ...': Proctor, D. ed. *The Autobiography of G. Lowes Dickinson* (London, 1973) 11.

12 'goes almost too deep ...', 'Most people ...': Letter from A. C. Benson to Ackerley, 9 June 1920, cited in Parker, P. *Ackerley: A Life of J. R. Ackerley* (London, 1989) 42.

13 Parker, P. *Ackerley: A Life of J. R. Ackerley* (London, 1989) 86.

14 'the sort of hopeless muddle ...': Parker, P. *Ackerley: A Life of J. R. Ackerley* (London, 1989) 89. 'He managed to sublimate it ...': 88.

15 'There is a pernicious set ...': McKenzie, N. ed. *The Letters of Sidney and Beatrice Webb*, 3 vols. (Cambridge, 1975): II 372.

16 'sought to remedy ...': Leslie, S. *Long Shadows* (London, 1966) 103.

17 'the soul of us ...': Ashbee papers, KCMA, document 46. On Ashbee, see Crawford, A. *C. R. Ashbee: Architect, Designer and Romantic Socialist* (New Haven, 1985); Goldhill, S. *The Buried Life of Things: How Objects Made History in Nineteenth-Century Britain* (Cambridge, 2015) 109–37.

18 'creativeness ... buoyancy ...': Ashbee, C. R. *American Sheaves and English Seed Corn: Being a Series of Addresses Mainly Delivered in the United States* (London and New York, 1901) 108–9.

    'the gates of Paradise ...': Ashbee, F. *Janet Ashbee: Love, Marriage and the Arts and Crafts Movement* (Syracuse, NY, 2002) 16.

19 'a day to be written down ...': Ashbee, C. R. unpublished diary, KCMA (1886) 137; 'And what do you think ...': 137–8.

20 'Comradeship ...': Letter, 2 September 1897, cited by Crawford, A. *C. R. Ashbee: Architect, Designer and Romantic Socialist* (New Haven, 1985) 75.

21 'Neither of us ...': Ashbee, F. *Janet Ashbee: Love, Marriage and the Arts and Crafts Movement* (Syracuse, NY, 2002) 24.

22 'With all his affection ...': Ashbee, F. *Janet Ashbee: Love, Marriage and the Arts and Crafts Movement* (Syracuse, NY, 2002) 106; 'The sacrifice of the animal ...': 107.

23 'I confess ...': Ashbee, F. *Janet Ashbee: Love, Marriage and the Arts and Crafts Movement* (Syracuse, NY, 2002) 133–6.

24 Ashbee, F. *Janet Ashbee: Love, Marriage and the Arts and Crafts Movement* (Syracuse, NY, 2002) xxviii.

25 'honour for the man ...': Ashbee, C. R. unpublished diary, KCMA (1884–5) doc. 43.

26 'human society defined by ...': Buckton, O. *Secret Selves: Confession and Same-Sex Desire in Victorian Autobiography* (Chapel Hill, 1998) 169.

27 On Forster, see Beauman, N. *Morgan: A Biography of E. M. Forster* (London, 1994); Moffat, W. *E. M. Forster: A New Biography* (London, 2011); and especially Furbank, P. *E. M. Forster: A Life*, 2 vols. (London, 1978). On queer expressivity, see Martin, R. and Piggford, G. eds. *Queer Forster* (Chicago, 1997), especially Bredbeck, G. '"Queer Superstitions": Forster, Carpenter and the Illusion of (Sexual) Identity', 29-58. Martin, R. 'Edward Carpenter and the Double Structure of *Maurice*', *Journal of Homosexuality* 8 (1983) 35–46.

28 'couldn't relax ...': Isherwood, C. *Christopher and His Kind* (London, 1977) 10.

29 'If I had to choose ...': Forster, E. M. *Two Cheers for Democracy* (London, 1951) 66. 'a kind of motto ...': Gopnik, A. *New Yorker* (12 September 2022) 64.

30 For Forster's meeting with James, see Furbank, P. *E. M. Forster: A Life*, 2 vols. (London, 1978) I 163–4.

31 'Oh dear, oh dear ...': quoted in Bristow, J. 'Fratrum Societati: Forster's Apostolic Dedications' in R. Martin and G. Piggford, eds. *Queer Forster* (Chicago, 1997) 113–36 at 118.

32 'a curious spinsterish ...': Leavis, F. R. in a 1936 review of Macaulay, R. *Writings of E. M. Forster*, quoted in Martin, R. and Piggford, G. eds. *Queer Forster* (Chicago, 1997) 15.

33 'He never "came out" ...': Bernal, M. *Geography of a Life* (London, 2012) 231. 'Morgan ... never mentioned ...': 231.

34 Leggatt, T. *Connecting with E. M. Forster: A Memoir* (London, 2012).

35 'the King's ideal ...': Annan, N. *The Dons: Mentors, Eccentrics and Geniuses* (London, 1999) 189 summing up 98–118.

36 'This masturbational eroticism ...': locked diary, quoted by Leggatt, T. *Connecting with E. M. Forster: A Memoir* (London, 2012) 7; 'I want to love ...': 105, a comment written 1935, consulted 1958, committed to the diary 1963; 'In the best ...': 105.

37 'when I am nearly eighty-five ...': Leggatt, T. *Connecting with E. M. Forster: A Memoir* (London, 2012) 105.

38 On Keynes, see especially Skidelsky, R. *John Maynard Keynes: Hopes Betrayed 1883–1920* (London, 1983); *John Maynard Keynes: The Economist as Saviour 1920–1937* (London, 1992); *John Maynard Keynes: Fighting for Britain, 1937–1946* (London, 2000). See also Moggridge, D. *Maynard Keynes: An Economist's Biography* (London and New York, 1992); Davenport-Hines, R. *Universal Man: The Seven Lives of John Maynard Keynes* (London, 2015); Carter, Z. *The Price of Peace: Money, Democracy and the Life of John Maynard Keynes* (New York, 2020).

39 'a gorged seal ...': Davenport-Hines, R. *Universal Man: The Seven Lives of John Maynard Keynes* (London, 2015) 191. 'Unimaginative' is a surprisingly obtuse judgement.

40 'my memory ...': Sheppard, J. unpublished memoir of Keynes, KCMA, 11.

41 'He brings off his copulations ...': Letter, Lytton Strachey to James Strachey, 16 December 1913, quoted in Moggridge, D. *Maynard Keynes: An Economist's Biography* (London and New York, 1992) 219.

42 'sunk in the isolation ...': Davenport-Hines, R. *Universal Man: The Seven Lives of John Maynard Keynes* (London, 2015) 206.

43 'Looking back I see him ...': Strachey, L. Letter, 5 February 1909, in Levy, P. ed. *The Letters of Lytton Strachey* (London, 2005) 170.

44 'yellow hair was the brightest ...': Levy, D. *Moore: G. E. Moore and the Cambridge Apostles* (Cambridge, 1979) 239.

45 'It was obligatory ...': Levy, D. *Moore: G. E. Moore and the Cambridge Apostles* (Cambridge, 1979) 140.

46 'The word bugger ...': Woolf, V. 'Old Bloomsbury' in *Moments of Being: Unpublished Autobiographical Writings of Virginia Woolf*, ed. J. Schulkind (Sussex, 1976) 56.

47 'practically everyone in Cambridge ...': Davenport-Hines, R. *Universal Man: The Seven Lives of John Maynard Keynes* (London, 2015) 213.

48 'I simply can't bear it ...': quoted in Moggridge, D. *Maynard Keynes: An Economist's Biography* (London and New York, 1992) 139.

49 'a homosexual with bi-sexual ...': Garnett, A. *Deceived with Kindness* (London, 1995) 33.

50 On Pigou, see Aslanbeigui, N. and Oakes, G. *Arthur Cecil Pigou* (New York, 2015); Kumekawa, I. *The First Serious Optimist: A. C. Pigou and the Birth of Welfare Economics* (Princeton, 2017); Aslanbeigui, N. 'Rethinking Pigou's Misogyny', *Eastern Economic Journal* 23 (1997) 301–16; Johnson, H. G. 'Arthur Cecil Pigou, 1877–1959', *Canadian Journal of Economics and Political Science* 26 (1960): 150–5.

51 '[h]e was addicted ...': Saltmarsh, J. and Wilkinson, L. P. unpublished memoir of Pigou, KCMA, 18.

52 'P. always has a passion ...': ACB clxxii 20–1; 'very nice but ...': Keynes to Strachey, quoted in Moggridge, D. *Maynard Keynes: An Economist's Biography* (London and New York, 1992) 83.

53 'He reveled in misogyny': Saltmarsh, J. and Wilkinson, L. P. unpublished memoir of Pigou, KCMA, 18.

54 'the famous heconomist ...': Saltmarsh, J. and Wilkinson, L. P. unpublished memoir of Pigou, KCMA, 27.

55 'Pigou is a fool ...': ACB xcii 70–1.

56 'World War I ...': quoted in Johnson, H. G. 'Arthur Cecil Pigou, 1877–1959', *Canadian Journal of Economics and Political Science* 26 (1960): 150–5 at 153. 'what he saw ...': 153.

57 'Ethics and economics stand together': Kumekawa, I. *The First Serious Optimist: A. C. Pigou and the Birth of Welfare Economics* (Princeton, 2017) 96; cf. 34.

58 Kumekawa, I. *The First Serious Optimist: A. C. Pigou and the Birth of Welfare Economics* (Princeton, 2017). 'Pigou – Keynes's "love-lorn" bachelor ...': 55. '"the revival of Puritan ..."': 23.

59 'I have no public spirit ...': Saltmarsh, J. and Wilkinson, L. P. unpublished memoir of Pigou, KCMA, 20.

60 On Brooke, the hagiographic Marsh, E. *Rupert Brooke: A Memoir* (London, 1918) has been roundly challenged by Delaney, P. *The Neo-pagans: Friendship and Love in the Rupert Brooke Circle* (London, 1987); Jones, N. *Rupert Brooke: Life, Death and Myth* (London, 1999, 2nd ed. 2014). See also Hassall, C. *Rupert Brooke: A Biography* (London, 1964).

61 'the filthy romanticism ...': Letter Dent to Denis Browne, quoted in Arrandale, K. *Edward Dent: A Life in Words and Music* (London, 2024) 261. Deep thanks to Karen for sharing the proofs of her biography with me.

62 'scorn, prejudice ...': Jones, N. *Rupert Brooke: Life, Death and Myth* (London, 1999, 2nd ed. 2014) xiii.

63 'he was sought out ...': Jacques Raverat's observation concerning Noel Olivier quoted by Jones, N. *Rupert Brooke: Life, Death and Myth* (London, 1999, 2nd ed. 2014) 132.

'the handsomest ...': Yeats, quoted in Jones, N. *Rupert Brooke: Life, Death and Myth* (London, 1999, 2nd ed. 2014) 110 – and many other places.

'**Rupert is a pseudo-beauty** …': Strachey, L. Letter 6 February 1908, in Levy, P. ed. *The Letters of Lytton Strachey* (London, 2005) 139.

'**the recipient of so much** …': Delaney, P. *The Neopagans: Friendship and Love in the Rupert Brooke Circle* (London, 1987) 133.

64 '**took with him** …': Delaney, P. *The Neo-pagans: Friendship and Love in the Rupert Brooke Circle* (London, 1987) 9.

65 '**We kissed very little** …': Hale, K. ed. *Friends and Apostles: The Correspondence of Rupert Brooke and James Strachey* (New Haven, 1998) 251–2.

66 '**extraordinarily randy state** …': quoted in Jones, N. *Rupert Brooke: Life, Death and Myth* (London, 1999, 2nd ed. 2014) 280.

67 '**The important thing** …': Delaney, P. *The Neo-pagans: Friendship and Love in the Rupert Brooke Circle* (London, 1987) 161.

68 '**It feels curiously unnatural** …': Marsh, E. *Rupert Brooke: A Memoir* (London, 1918) 104.

69 '**he never tired** …': quoted by Marsh, E. *Rupert Brooke: A Memoir* (London, 1918) 24.

70 Marsh, E. *Rupert Brooke: A Memoir* (London, 1918) 24.

71 '**conceived a light lust** …': Delaney, P. *The Neo-pagans: Friendship and Love in the Rupert Brooke Circle* (London, 1987) 50.

72 '**I don't know** …': Marsh, E. *Rupert Brooke: A Memoir* (London, 1918) 53.

73 '**I'd still to "only connect"** …': Delaney, P. *The Neopagans: Friendship and Love in the Rupert Brooke Circle* (London, 1987) 159.

74 '**they are all Forster characters** …': Marsh, E. *Rupert Brooke: A Memoir* (London, 1918) 61; '**a speech** …': 61.

Chapter 3

1 *Basileion* was also the magazine where Brooke's famous poem 'Grantchester' was first printed. See Tennyson, Sir C., ed. *Basileion: A Magazine of King's College, Cambridge 1900–1914* (Cambridge, 1974).

2 'the evening ended ...': Skidelsky, R. *John Maynard Keynes: Hopes Betrayed 1883–1920* (London, 1983) 300.

3 Sheppard on screen in a British Council Film, 1945: https://film.britishcouncil.org/resources/film-archive/cambridge.

4 'the attraction of his personality': Wilkinson, L. P., unpublished memoir of John Sheppard, KCMA 1.

5 '*Enfant-terrible* ...': Wilkinson, L. P. 'Six Characters', KCMA GBR/0272/LPW, 3.

6 Edmonds, D. *Wittgenstein's Poker* (London, 2001).

7 'Sh[eppard] is a wretched spectacle ...': Letter, 2 December 1904, in Levy, P. ed. *The Letters of Lytton Strachey* (London, 2005) 39.

8 'I took down ...': Letter, 28 February 1905, in Levy, P. ed. *The Letters of Lytton Strachey* (London, 2005) 53.

9 'I suppose we all wanted ...': Letter, 20 June 1918, in Levy, P. ed. *The Letters of Lytton Strachey* (London, 2005) 399.

10 'The Sheppard-Doggart ...': Letter, 30 May 1920, in Levy, P. ed. *The Letters of Lytton Strachey* (London, 2005) 463.

11 'pretty surgeon ...': Skidelsky, R. *John Maynard Keynes: The Economist as Saviour 1920–1937* (London, 1992) 6.

12 'You are really awfully like God': Sikedelsky, R. *John Maynard Keynes: Hopes Betrayed 1883–1920* (London, 1983) 255.

13 'I feel a fraud ...': Undated letter, Taylor to Sheppard in Sheppard's papers, KCMA.

14 'married couple', 'Sheppard was edgy …': James Strachey to Lytton Strachey, 1 October 1909, quoted by Skidelsky, R. *John Maynard Keynes: Hopes Betrayed 1883–1920* (London, 1983) 238.

15 'Dearest tutor-to-be …': This and the following quotations come from Sheppard's papers in the King's Modern Archive. Rylands' papers are voluminous, which makes the thinness of the account in Raina, P. *George 'Dadie' Rylands: Shakespearean Scholar and Cambridge Legend* (Oxford, 2020) all the more surprising.

16 'but at heart he is uncorrupted …': Nicholson, N. ed. *The Letters of Virginia Woolf* (London, 1975) III 1923–8: 145.

17 'Don't try him too much …': Taylor to Sheppard, undated letter in the Sheppard Papers, KCMA.

18 'a most charming, handsome …': quoted in Newsome, D. *On the Edge of Paradise: A. C. Benson the Diarist* (London, 1980) 360; 'He has a fine, beautiful …': 361; 'He is not handsome exactly …': 361; 'We had a strange intimate …': 361; 'Am I foolish about this boy? …': 363.

19 'I cannot hope …': Letter, 14 July 1923, Winstanley to Rylands. Ironically – painfully – enough, Benson and Lubbock were due for dinner the next day.

20 'I told him very simply …': Newsome, D. *On the Edge of Paradise: A. C. Benson the Diarist* (London, 1980) 366.

21 'looked sternly …': Newsome, D. *On the Edge of Paradise: A. C. Benson the Diarist* (London, 1980) 363.

22 'books, music and beautiful young men' is A. C. Benson's memory looking back to Charles Sayle, recalled nicely by Gillman, P. and Gillman, L. *The Wildest Dream: A Biography of George Mallory* (Seattle, 2000), recalling Benson's infatuation (shared by many) with Mallory.

23 'Their opinion of me …': Gallop, J. *Feminist Accused of Sexual Harassment* (Durham, NC, and London, 1997) 41.

24 'I was bowled over ...': Gallop, J. *Feminist Accused of Sexual Harassment* (Durham, NC, and London, 1997) 41; '[s]educing them ...': 42.

25 'King's has an unconquerable faith ...'; 'We care for what we call ...'; 'I never was attached': speech by Sheppard to the Apostles, unpublished, in Sheppard's papers, KCMA.

26 'never tired ...': Marsh, E. *Rupert Brooke: A Memoir* (London, 1918) 24.

27 'If we go down ...': Skidelsky, R. *John Maynard Keynes: Fighting for Britain, 1937–1946* (London, 2000) 160.

28 'platonically devoted': Annan, N. *The Dons: Mentors, Eccentrics and Geniuses* (London, 1999) 170–92 at 181.

29 'vitality and stamina ...': Annan, N. *The Dons: Mentors, Eccentrics and Geniuses* (London, 1999) 188; 'As a moral influence ...': 185; 'His friends thought of him ...': 192.

30 'acquired a reputation ...': Annan, N. *The Dons: Mentors, Eccentrics and Geniuses* (London, 1999) 180; 'volatile temper ...': 180; 'possessed his soul': 181.

31 'Dark and hideous ...': Annan, N. *The Dons: Mentors, Eccentrics and Geniuses* (London, 1999) 182.

32 'did not believe ...': Annan, N. *The Dons: Mentors, Eccentrics and Geniuses* (London, 1999) 182–3; 'He identified ...': 183; 'used his tongue ...': 182; 'when nervous ...': 183.

33 'He was an exacting friend ...': Annan, N. *The Dons: Mentors, Eccentrics and Geniuses* (London, 1999) 190.

34 On Dennis Robertson, see Fletcher, G. *Dennis Robertson* (London, 2008).

35 'This is the third year ...': Letter, Robertson to Rylands, 11 December 1926, KCMA.

36 'These rows ...': Letter, Robertson to Rylands, 11 December 1926, KCMA.

37 'You felt ...': Letter, Robertson to Rylands, 11 December 1926, KCMA.

38 'Darling Dadie ...': Letter, Robertson to Rylands, 27 April 1927, KCMA.

39 'You see, with my ex-nonconformist ...': Letter, Robertson to Ryland, not dated, but a Monday in 1930, KCMA.

40 'I think you misjudge ...': Letter, Robertson to Ryland, 7 August 1930, KCMA.

41 'I send you two ...': Letter, Robertson to Ryland, 7 August 1930, KCMA.

42 'I realised ...': Letter, Robertson to Ryland, 18 September 1930, KCMA.

43 'I've thought ...': Letter, Robertson to Ryland, 18 September 1930, KCMA.

44 'I hadn't realised ...': Letter, Robertson to Ryland, 18 September 1930, KCMA.

45 'And make allowances ...': Letter, Robertson to Ryland, undated, KCMA.

46 'a most intimate letter ...': Quoted in Newsome, D. *On the Edge of Paradise: A. C. Benson the Diarist* (London, 1980) 250. In 1924, there was another petty drama of letters. Dadie, 'looking very young and radiant', came for dinner with Benson. 'He had said that he and Dennis R had been reconciled over brandy; and had invented an imaginary dialogue' – another squall between Robertson and Rylands overcome – but added that ACB's 'last silly letter' ... 'was found on his table by Dennis and read by him. This does seem to me quite unpardonable. D.^{die} is to destroy all my letters for the future. How can a man do such things?' ACB clxxiv 45. Benson, as ever, outraged by exposure.

47 'Webster saw the skull ...': Eliot, T. S. 'Whispers of Immortality' in *Collected Poems 1909–1962* (London, 1963).

48 'in a blue dressing gown ...': Beaton, C. Diary, vol. 22, 12 March 1924, Trinity College, Cambridge. 'I was very surprised ...': ibid. 'I do think its extraordinary ...': ibid.

49 On this picture, see Janes, D. 'The "Curious Effects" of Acting: Homosexuality, Theatre and Female Impersonation at the University of Cambridge, 1900–1939', *Twentieth-Century British History* 33 (2022) 169–202.

50 'dull mauve ...' and the further descriptions of the party: Beaton, C. Diary, vol. 22, 14 March 1924, Trinity College, Cambridge. Arthur Jeffress, who also acted in female dress, became a very well-known wealthy playboy, was the lover of the photographer of the Soho art scene, John Deakin, and later became a successful gallery owner in London – while maintaining a house in Venice. He remained friends with Beaton – and killed himself in 1961 perhaps because – it was speculated – he had been denounced as a homosexual to the Venetian authorities: see Hedley, G. *Arthur Jeffress: A Life in Art* (London, 2020).

51 'I have seen ...': *Daily Sketch*, 5 October 1925.

52 'All musicians ...': Brett, P. 'Musicality, Essentialism, and the Closet' in *Queering the Pitch: The New Gay and Lesbian Musicology*, ed. P. Brett, E. Wood and G. C. Thomas (New York, 1994) 9–26.

53 Brett, P. 'Are You Musical?' *Musical Times* 135 (1994) 370–6 at 371.

54 'experience music ...': Hirschfeld, M. *Homosexualität des Mannes und des Weibes* (Berlin, 1914) quoted in Riddell, F. *Music and the Queer Body in English Literature at the Fin de Siècle* (Cambridge, 2022) 33. On Hirschfeld, see also Wolff, C. *Magnus Hirschfeld: A Portrait of a Pioneer in Sexology* (London, 1986) with the background of Bland, L. and Doan, L. eds. *Sexology in Culture: Labelling Bodies and Desire* (Cambridge, 1998).

55 'As to music …': Carpenter, E. *The Intermediate Sex* (London, 1908) 111, also quoted in Brett, P. 'Musicology and Sexuality: The Example of Edward J. Dent' in *Queer Episodes in Music and Modern Identity*, ed. S. Fuller and L. Whitesell (Urbana, IL, 2002) 177–88.

56 Cocks, H. *Classified: The Secret History of the Personal Column* (London, 2009) 4–15.

57 'symphonie incestueuse …': see Riddell, F. *Music and the Queer Body in English Literature at the Fin de Siècle* (Cambridge, 2022) 26. See also Fillion, M. *Difficult Rhythm: Music and the Word in E. M. Forster* (Urbana, IL, 2010).

58 'Some homosexual hearers …': Prime-Stevenson, E. [writing as Xavier Mayne] *The Intersexes: A History of Similisexualism as a Problem in Social Life* (Rome, 1908), 177. See Wilper, J. 'Translation and the Construction of a "Uranian" Identity: Edward Prime-Stevenson's [Xavier Mayne's] The Intersexes (1908)' in *Sexology and Translation: Cultural and Scientific Encounters across the Modern World*, ed. H. Bauer (Philadelphia, 2015) 216–32.

59 On Ord, see Day, T. *I Saw Eternity the Other Night: King's College, Cambridge, and an English Singing Style* (London, 2018) 150.

60 On Dent, see Arrandale, K. *Edward Dent: A Life in Words and Music* (London, 2024). 'It was a great waste of time …': 446.

61 'after lunch …': Arrandale, K. *Edward Dent: A Life in Words and Music* (London, 2024) 22; 'life only really …': 21.

62 'curious personality …': Arrandale, K. *Edward Dent: A Life in Words and Music* (London, 2024) 133.

63 'I always imagine …' Arrandale, K. *Edward Dent: A Life in Words and Music* (London, 2024) 1.

64 'suffered from residual …' Arrandale, K. *Edward Dent: A Life in Words and Music* (London, 2024) 13.

65 'became for years a regular uncomplicated companion ...': Arrandale, K. *Edward Dent: A Life in Words and Music* (London, 2024) 88.

66 'I consider my Bologna ...': Arrandale, K. *Edward Dent: A Life in Words and Music* (London, 2024) 91.

67 'But it is too bad ...': Arrandale, K. *Edward Dent: A Life in Words and Music* (London, 2024) 181.

68 '[i]n these years ...': Arrandale, K. *Edward Dent: A Life in Words and Music* (London, 2024) 180.

69 Forrester, J. and Cameron, L. *Freud in Cambridge* (Cambridge, 2017).

70 'Göring ordered a raid ...': Arrandale, K. *Edward Dent: A Life in Words and Music* (London, 2024) 479.

71 'I must be growing old ...': Arrandale, K. *Edward Dent: A Life in Words and Music* (London, 2024) 376.

72 'cared for poetry ...': Arrandale, K. *Edward Dent: A Life in Words and Music* (London, 2024) 20.

73 'Dent, of course, in a corner ...': Lytton Strachey to Dora Carrington, 1918, in Levy, P. ed. *The Letters of Lytton Strachey* (New York, 2005) 424.

74 On Roger Fry, see Woolf, V. *Roger Fry: A Biography* (London, 1940); Spalding, F. *Roger Fry: Art and Life* (Berkeley, 1980); Sutton, D. *Letters of Roger Fry*, 2 vols. (London, 1972).

75 'did more than anyone ...': Woolf, V. 'Roger Fry' in *The Moment and Other Essays* (London, 1947) 83; 'things we live with ...': 84. See Quick, J. 'Virginia Woolf, Roger Fry and Post-Impressionism', *Massachusetts Review* 26 (1985) 547–70.

76 'who remade himself ...': Elam, C. *Roger Fry's Journey: From the Primitives to the Post-Impressionists* (Edinburgh, 2006) 13.

77 'an intense sadistic pleasure ...': Woolf, V. *Roger Fry: A Biography* (London, 1940) 33.

78 '[a]ll one hot moonlit night ...': Woolf, V. *Roger Fry: A Biography* (London, 1940) 48. 'It was a society ...': 51.

79 Beckett, L. *The Second I Saw You: The True Love Story of Rupert Brooke and Phyllis Gardner* (London, 2015). To Gardner, Brooke defined his own attitude as 'to take what one wants where one finds it': 123.

80 'the greatest single influence ...': Levy, D. *Moore: G. E. Moore and the Cambridge Apostles* (Cambridge, 1979) 116.

Chapter 4

1 'Immense wealth ...': Bernal, M. *Geography of a Life* (London, 2012) 229.

2 See Shaw's paper on women: Levy, D. *Moore: G. E. Moore and the Cambridge Apostles* (Cambridge, 1979) 128.

3 'impatient and abrasive ...': Obituary, Michael Jaffé, unpublished, KCMA.

4 Sexology in the 1950s: see Bauer, H. and Cook, M. eds. *Queer 1950s: Rethinking Sexuality in the Postwar Years* (Basingstoke, 2012), especially 133–49; and Waters, C. 'The Homosexual as a Social Being in Britain, 1945–1968', *Journal of British Studies* 51.3 (July 2012) 685–710, reprinted in *British Queer History: New Approaches and Perspectives*, ed. B. Lewis (Manchester, 2013) 188–218.

5 'more or less hidden ...': Bernal, M. *Geography of a Life* (London, 2012) 229.

6 'in my Cambridge days ...': Brett, P. 'Musicology and Sexuality: The Example of Edward J. Dent' in *Queer Episodes in Music and Modern Identity*, ed. S. Fuller and L. Whitesell (Urbana, IL, 2002) 177–88 at 181–2.

7 Gunn maintained a close connection to King's College through his relationship with the great critic Tony

Tanner: see M. Nott, A. Kleinzahler and Clive Wilmer, *The Letters of Thom Gunn* (London, 2024). Tanner and Gunn seem to have had a road-trip fling back in the day.

8 **'He was perhaps the last ...'**: Crook, J. in the *Oxford Dictionary of National Biography* quoted by Garnsey, P. in Crook's obituary for the British Academy: 'John Anthony Crook 1921–2007' (12 June 2019) 116, available online: www.thebritishacademy.ac.uk/publishing/memoirs/8/crook-john-anthony-1921-2007/.

9 **'tremendous camaraderie ...'**: this and subsequent quotes from Avery are my transcription of the interview he gave to Alan Macfarlane; www.alanmacfarlane.com/ancestors/avery.htm.

10 **'Nothing was said ...'**: Arrandale, K. *Edward Dent: A Life in Words and Music* (London, 2024) 261.

11 The interview between Richards and Ryan can be accessed at www.cfr.cam.ac.uk/system/files/documents/joanna-ryan.pdf.

Conclusion

1 **'The ethos of the college ...'**: Ballard, J. G. *Miracles of Life: Shanghai to Shepperton, An Autobiography* (London, 2008) 146.

2 **'Tolerance ...'**: Goethe, J. W. *Maxims and Reflections* (London, 1999) no. 356.

WORKS CITED

Ahmed, S. *Queer Phenomenology: Orientations, Objects, Others* (Durham, NC, 2006).

Amin, K. *Disturbing Attachments: Genet, Modern Pederasty and Queer History* (Durham, NC, 2017).

Angel, K. *Tomorrow Sex Will Be Good Again: Women and Desire in the Age of Consent* (London, 2021).

Annan, N. *The Dons: Mentors, Eccentrics and Geniuses* (London, 1999).

Anstruther, I. *Oscar Browning: A Biography* (London, 1984).

Arendt, H. *Men in Dark Times* (New York, 1968).

Aronson, T. *Prince Eddy and the Homosexual Underworld* (London, 1994).

Arrandale, K. *Edward Dent: A Life in Words and Music* (London, 2024).

Ashbee, C. R. *American Sheaves and English Seed Corn: Being a Series of Addresses Mainly Delivered in the United States* (London and New York, 1901).

Ashbee, F. *Janet Ashbee: Love, Marriage and the Arts and Crafts Movement* (Syracuse, NY, 2002).

Aslanbeigui, N. 'Rethinking Pigou's Misogyny', *Eastern Economic Journal* 23 (1997) 301–16.

Aslanbeigui, N. and Oakes, G. *Arthur Cecil Pigou* (New York, 2015).

Ballard, J. G. *Miracles of Life: Shanghai to Shepperton, An Autobiography* (London, 2008).

Bauer, H. *English Literary Sexology: Translations of Inversion 1860–1930* (Basingstoke, 2009).

'Sexology Backward: Hirschfeld, Kinsey and the Reshaping of Sex Research in the 1950s' in H. Bauer and M. Cook, eds. *Queer 1950s: Rethinking Sexuality in the Postwar Years* (Basingstoke, 2012) 133–49.

Bauer, H. and Cook, M. eds. *Queer 1950s: Rethinking Sexuality in the Postwar Years* (Basingstoke, 2012).

Beard, M. *The Invention of Jane Harrison* (Cambridge, MA, 2002).

Beauman, N. *Morgan: A Biography of E. M. Forster* (London, 1994).

Beckett, L. *The Second I Saw You: The True Love Story of Rupert Brooke and Phyllis Gardner* (London, 2015).

Bell, D. and Valentine, G. eds. *Mapping Desire: Geographies of Sexuality* (London, 1995).

Benson, A. C. 'Charles Sayle', *The Library* 5.3 (1924) 271–3.

The Leaves of the Tree: Studies in Biography (New York, 1911).

Memoirs of Arthur Hamilton (London, 1886).

Memories and Friends (London, 1924).

Benson, E. F. *As We Were: A Victorian Peep Show* (London, 1930).

The Babe, B.A. (London, 1896).

Colin (London, 1923).

David Blaize (London, 1916).

Bernal, M. *Geography of a Life* (London, 2012).

Bland, L. and Doan, L. eds. *Sexology in Culture: Labelling Bodies and Desire* (Cambridge, 1998).

Bolt, R. *As Good as God, as Clever as the Devil: The Impossible Life of Mary Benson* (London, 2011).

Boswell, J. *Christianity, Social Tolerance and Homosexuality: Gay People in Western Europe from the Christian Era to the Fourteenth Century* (New Haven, 1980).

Brady, S. *Masculinity and Male Homosexuality in Britain, 1861–1913* (Houndmills, 2005).

Bredbeck, G. '"Queer Superstitions": Forster, Carpenter and the Illusion of (Sexual) Identity' in R. Martin and G. Piggford, eds. *Queer Forster* (Chicago, 1997) 29–58.

Brett, P. 'Are You Musical?' *Musical Times* 135 (1994) 370–6.

'Musicality, Essentialism, and the Closet' in *Queering the Pitch: The New Gay and Lesbian Musicology*, ed. P. Brett, E. Wood and G. C. Thomas (New York, 1994) 9–26.

'Musicology and Sexuality: The Example of Edward J. Dent' in *Queer Episodes in Music and Modern Identity*, ed. S. Fuller and L. Whitesell (Urbana, IL, 2002) 177–88.

Bristow, J. *Empire Boys: Adventures in a Man's World* (London, 1991).

'Fratrum Societati: Forster's Apostolic Dedications' in R. Martin and G. Piggford, eds. *Queer Forster* (Chicago, 1997) 113–36.

Brown, M. 'Gender and Sexuality II: There Goes the Gayberhood', *Progress in Human Geography* 38.3 (2014) 457–65.

Browne, K. and Bakshi, L. *Ordinary in Brighton: LGBT, Activisms and the City* (Aldershot, 2013).

Browning, O. 'J. K. Stephen,' *Bookman* 1.6 (March 1892), 204–5.

Memoirs of Later Years (London, 1923).

Memories of Sixty Years at Eton, Cambridge and Elsewhere (London, 1910).

Buckton, O. *Secret Selves: Confession and Same-Sex Desire in Victorian Autobiography* (Chapel Hill, 1998).

Butler, S. *The Passions of John Addington Symonds* (Oxford, 2022).

Carpenter, E. *The Intermediate Sex* (London, 1908).

Carter, Z. *The Price of Peace: Money, Democracy and the Life of John Maynard Keynes* (New York, 2020).

Castells, M. *The City and the Grassroots: A Cross-Cultural Theory of Urban Social Movements* (Berkeley, 1983).

Chandos, J. *Boys Together: English Public Schools 1800–1864* (London, 1985).

Chesterton, G. K. *Heretics* (London, 1905).

Cocks, H. *Classified: The Secret History of the Personal Column* (London, 2009).

Nameless Offences: Homosexual Desire in the Nineteenth Century (London, 2003).

Compton Mackenzie, F. *William Cory: A Biography* (London, 1950).

Connolly, C. *Enemies of Promise* (London, 1938).

Cook, M. *London and the Culture of Homosexuality, 1885–1914* (Cambridge, 2003).

Cook, M. and Evans, J. *Queer Cities, Queer Cultures: Europe Since 1945* (London, 2014).

Cory, D. W. *The Homosexual in America: A Subjective Approach* (New York, 1951).

Cox, M. *M. R. James: An Informal Portrait* (Oxford, 1983).

Crawford, A. *C. R. Ashbee: Architect, Designer and Romantic Socialist* (New Haven, 1985).

D'Arch Smith, T. *Love in Earnest: Some Notes on the Lives and Writings of English 'Uranian' Poets 1889–1930* (London, 1970).

Davenport-Hines, R. *Universal Man: The Seven Lives of John Maynard Keynes* (London, 2015).

Davidson, J. *The Greeks and Greek Love: A Radical Reappraisal of Homosexuality in Ancient Greece* (London, 2008).

Day, T. *I Saw Eternity the Other Night: King's College, Cambridge, and an English Singing Style* (London, 2018).

Delaney, P. *The Neo-pagans: Friendship and Love in the Rupert Brooke Circle* (London, 1987).

Dellamora, R. *Victorian Sexual Dissidence* (Chicago, 1999).

Derrida, J. *The Politics of Friendship*, trans. G. Collins (London, 1997).

Deslandes, P. *Oxbridge Men: British Masculinity and the Undergraduate Experience, 1850–1920* (Bloomington, IN, 2005).

Dinshaw, C. *How Soon Is Now? Medieval Texts, Amateur Readers and the Queerness of Time* (Durham, NC, 2012).

Doan, L. *Disturbing Practices: History, Sexuality and Women's Experience of the Great War* (Chicago, 2013).

Edelman, L. *No Future: Queer Theory and the Death Drive* (Durham, NC, 2004).

Edmonds, D. *Wittgenstein's Poker* (London, 2001).

Elam, C. *Roger Fry's Journey: From the Primitives to the Post-Impressionists* (Edinburgh, 2006).

Elden, S. *The Archaeology of Foucault* (Cambridge, 2022).
Foucault's Last Decade (Cambridge, 2016).

Eliot, T. S. *Collected Poems 1909–1962* (London, 1963).

Fillion, M. *Difficult Rhythm: Music and the Word in E. M. Forster* (Urbana, IL, 2010).

Fletcher, G. *Dennis Robertson* (London, 2008).

Formby, E. *Exploring LGBT Spaces: Contrasting Identities, Belonging and Well-Being* (New York and Abingdon, 2017).

Forrester, J. and Cameron, L. *Freud in Cambridge* (Cambridge, 2017).

Forster, E. M. *Goldsworthy Lowes Dickinson* (London, 1934).
Two Cheers for Democracy (London, 1951).

Foucault, M. *The Birth of Biopolitics: Lectures at the Collège de France 1978–9*, ed. M. Senellart, trans. G. Burchell (London, 2008).
Ethics, Subjectivity, Truth, ed. P. Rabinow, trans. R. Hurley et al. (New York, 1994).
History of Sexuality, Vol. 1, trans. R. Hurley (New York, 1978).
On the Government of the Living: Lectures at the Collège de France 1979–80, ed. M. Senellart, trans. G. Burchell (London, 2008).

Freccero, C. *Queer/Early/Modern* (Durham, NC, 2006).

Freeman, E. *Time Binds: Queer Temporalities, Queer Histories* (Durham, NC, 2010).

Funke, J. '"We cannot be Greek now": Age Difference, Corruption of Youth, and the Making of *Sexual Inversion*', *English Studies* 94.2 (2013) 139–54.

Furbank, P. *E.M. Forster: A Life*, 2 vols. (London, 1978).

Gallop, J. *Feminist Accused of Sexual Harassment* (Durham, NC, and London, 1997).

Gandhi, L. *Affective Communities: Anti-colonial Thought, Fin-de-Siècle Radicalism and the Politics of Friendship* (Durham, NC, 2006).

Garnett, A. *Deceived with Kindness* (London, 1995).

Ghaziani, A. *There Goes the Gayberhood?* (Princeton, 2014).

Gillman, P. and Gillman, L. *The Wildest Dream: A Biography of George Mallory* (Seattle, 2000).

Goethe, J. W. *Maxims and Reflections* (London, 1999).

Goldhill, S. *The Buried Life of Things: How Objects Made History in Nineteenth-Century Britain* (Cambridge, 2015).

A Very Queer Family Indeed: Sex, Religion, and the Bensons in Victorian Britain (Chicago, 2016).

Green, S. *Sexual Restraint and Aesthetic Experience in Victorian Literary Decadence* (Cambridge, 2023).

Grosskurth, P. *John Addington Symonds: A Biography* (London, 1964).

Halberstam, J. *In a Queer Time and Place: Transgender Bodies, Subcultural Lives* (New York, 2005).

Hale, K. ed. *Friends and Apostles: The Correspondence of Rupert Brooke and James Strachey* (New Haven, 1998).

Hall, G. S. *Adolescence* (London, 1925).

Hall, L. 'Forbidden by God, Despised by Men: Masturbation, Medical Warnings, Moral Panic, and Manhood in Great Britain 1850–1950', *Journal of History of Sexuality* 2.3 (1992) 365–87.

Halperin, D. *How to Do the History of Homosexuality* (Chicago, 2002).

One Hundred Years of Homosexuality, and Other Essays on Greek Love (London and New York, 1990).

Hartman, S. *Wayward Lives, Beautiful Experiments* (New York, 2019).

Hassall, C. *Rupert Brooke: A Biography* (London, 1964).

Havelock Ellis, H. *Studies in the Psychology of Sex*, 2nd ed. 6 vols. (Philadelphia, 1921 [1897–1910]).

Hedley, G. *Arthur Jeffress: A Life in Art* (London, 2020).

Herring, S. *Queering the Underworld: Slumming Literature and the Undoing of Lesbian and Gay History* (Chicago, 2007).

Hirschfeld, M. *Homosexualität des Mannes und des Weibes* (Berlin, 1914).

Holroyd, M. *Lytton Strachey* (London, 1994).

Holt, J. *Public School Literature, Civic Education and the Politics of Male Adolescence* (Farnham, 2008).

Homfray, M. *Provincial Queens: The Gay and Lesbian Community in the North-West of England* (Bern, 2007).

Houlbrook, M. *Queer London: Perils and Pleasures in the Sexual Metropolis 1918–1957* (Chicago, 2005).

Huffer, L. *Mad for Foucault: Rethinking the Foundations of Queer Theory* (New York, 2010).

Ingleheart, J. *Masculine Plural: Queer Classics, Sex, and Education* (Oxford, 2018).

Isherwood, C. *Christopher and His Kind* (London, 1977).

James, M. R. *Eton and King's: Recollections Mainly Trivial, 1875–1925* (London, 1926).

Janes, D. 'The "Curious Effects" of Acting: Homosexuality, Theatre and Female Impersonation at the University of Cambridge, 1900–1939', *Twentieth-Century British History* 33 (2022) 169–202.

Picturing the Closet: Male Secrecy and Homosexual Visibility in Britain (Oxford, 2015).

Johnson, H. G. 'Arthur Cecil Pigou, 1877–1959', *Canadian Journal of Economics and Political Science* 26 (1960) 150–5.

Jones, D. *M. R. James: A Life* (Oxford, forthcoming).

Jones, N. *Rupert Brooke: Life, Death and Myth* (London, 1999, 2nd ed. 2014).

Kaplan, M. *Sodom on the Thames: Sex, Love and Scandal in Wilde Times* (Ithaca, NY, 2005).

Katz, J. *The Invention of Heterosexuality* (Chicago, 2005).

Love Stories: Sex between Men before Homosexuality (Chicago, 2001).

Kopley, E. *Virginia Woolf and Poetry* (Oxford, 2020).

'Virginia Woolf's Cousin, J. K. Stephen: Forgotten but Not Gone', *ELT* 59.2 (2016) 191–209.

Koven, S. *Slumming: Sexual and Social Politics in Victorian London* (Princeton, 2004).

Kumekawa, I. *The First Serious Optimist: A. C. Pigou and the Birth of Welfare Economics* (Princeton, 2017).

Lauria, M. and Knopp, L. 'Toward an Analysis of the Role of Gay Communities in the Urban Renaissance', *Urban Geography* 6 (1985) 152–69.

Leggatt, T. *Connecting with E. M. Forster: A Memoir* (London, 2012).

Leighton, D. J. *Privileges and Pitfalls: The Life of J. K. Stephen* (London, 2009).

Leslie, S. *The Cantab* (London, 1926).

Long Shadows (London, 1966).

Levine, M. 'Gay Ghetto', *Journal of Homosexuality* 4.4 (1979) 363–77.

Levy, D. *Moore: G. E. Moore and the Cambridge Apostles* (Cambridge, 1979).

Levy, P. ed. *The Letters of Lytton Strachey* (London, 2005).

Love, H. *Feeling Backward: Loss and the Politics of Queer History* (Cambridge, MA, 2007).

Lubbock, P. ed. *The Diary of Arthur Christopher Benson* (London, 1926).

Lyttelton, E. *The Causes and Prevention of Immorality in Schools* (London, 1887).

Training of the Young in Laws of Sex (London, 1900).

MacCarthy, F. *Byron: Life and Legend* (New York, 2002).

Mangan, J. *Athleticism in the Victorian and Edwardian Public School: The Emergence and Consolidation of an Educational Ideology* (Cambridge, 1981).

Marcus, J. 'Review: Ian Anstruther, *Oscar Browning: A Biography*', *Victorian Studies* 28.3 (1985) 556–8.

Marsh, E. *Rupert Brooke: A Memoir* (London, 1918).

Martin, R. 'Edward Carpenter and the Double Structure of *Maurice*', *Journal of Homosexuality* 8 (1983) 35–46.

Martin, R. and Piggford, G. eds. *Queer Forster* (Chicago, 1997).

Masters, B. *The Life of E. F. Benson* (London, 1991).

McBeth, M. 'The Pleasure of Learning and the Tightrope of Desire: Teacher–Student Relationships and Victorian Pedagogy' in J. Goodman and J. Martin, eds. *Gender, Colonialism and Education: An International Perspective* (London, 2002) 46–72.

McDonald, D. *The Prince, His Tutor and the Ripper: The Evidence Linking James Kenneth Stephen to the Whitechapel Murders* (Jefferson, NC, 2007).

McKenzie, N. ed. *The Letters of Sidney and Beatrice Webb*, 3 vols. (Cambridge, 1975).

McLaren, A. *The Trials of Masculinity: Policing Sexual Boundaries, 1870–1930* (Chicago, 1997).

Moffat, W. *E. M. Forster: A New Biography* (London, 2011).

Moggridge, D. *Maynard Keynes: An Economist's Biography* (London and New York, 1992).

Muñoz, J. E. *Cruising Utopia: The Then and There of Queer Futurity* (New York, 2009).

Murphy, P. *Medieval Studies and the Ghost Stories of M. R. James* (University Park, PE, 2017).

Nardi, P. *Gay Men's Friendships* (Chicago, 1999).

Newman, H. *James Kenneth Stephen: Virginia Woolf's Tragic Cousin* (London, 2008).

Newsome, D. *Godliness and Good Learning: Four Studies on a Victorian Ideal* (London, 1961).

On the Edge of Paradise: A. C. Benson the Diarist (London, 1980).

Nicholson, N. ed. *The Letters of Virginia Woolf* (London, 1975).

Norton, R. *Mother Clap's Molly House: The Gay Subculture in England 1700–1830* (London, 1992).

Nott, M., Kleinzahler, A. and Wilmer, C. *The Letters of Thom Gunn* (London, 2024).

Oates, J. 'Charles Edward Sayle', *Transactions of the Cambridge Bibliographical Society* 8 (1982) 236–69.

Oosterhuis, H. *Stepchildren of Nature: Krafft-Ebing, Psychiatry, and the Making of Sexual Identity* (Chicago, 2000).

Oswin, N. 'Social Junk' in *Grammars of the Urban Ground*, ed. A. Amin and M. Lancione (Durham, NC, 2022) 27–40.

Parker, P. *Ackerley: A Life of J. R. Ackerley* (London, 1989).

Peacock, S. *Jane Ellen Harrison: The Mask and the Self* (Hanover, 1988).

Pemble, J. *The Mediterranean Passion: Victorians and Edwardians in the South* (Oxford, 1987).

ed. *John Addington Symonds: Culture and the Demon Desire* (Cambridge, 2000).

Prime-Stevenson, E. [writing as Xavier Mayne] *The Intersexes: A History of Similisexualism as a Problem in Social Life* (Rome, 1908).

Proctor, D. ed. *The Autobiography of G. Lowes Dickinson*, with preface by Noel Annan (London, 1973).

Quick, J. 'Virginia Woolf, Roger Fry and Post-Impressionism', *Massachusetts Review* 26 (1985) 547–70.

Raina, P. *George 'Dadie' Rylands: Shakespearean Scholar and Cambridge Legend* (Oxford, 2020).

Regis, A. 'Late Style and Speaking Out: J. A. Symonds's *In the Key of Blue*', *English Studies* 94.2 (2013) 206–31.

Richards, J. *The Happiest Days: The Public School in English Fiction* (Manchester, 1988).

Riddell, F. *Music and the Queer Body in English Literature at the Fin de Siècle* (Cambridge, 2022).

Roach, J. *A History of Secondary Education in England, 1870–1902* (London, 1991).

Robb, G. *Strangers: Homosexual Love in the Nineteenth Century* (New York, 2003).

Robinson, A. *The Life and Work of Jane Ellen Harrison* (Oxford, 2002).

Robinson, P. *Gay Lives: Homosexual Autobiography from John Addington Symonds to Paul Monette* (Chicago, 1999).

Rose, K. *Superior Person: A Portrait of Curzon and His Circle in Late Victorian Britain* (London, 1969).

Rothblatt, S. *The Revolution of the Dons: Cambridge and Society in Victorian England* (Cambridge, 1968).

Rothenberg, T. '"And She Told Two Friends": Lesbians Creating Urban Social Space' in D. Bell and G. Valentine, eds. *Mapping Desire: Geographies of Sexuality* (London, 1995) 165–81.

Rowbotham, S. *Edward Carpenter: A Life of Liberty and Love* (London, 2008).

Sayle, C. *Bertha: A Story of Love* (London, 1885).

Sedgwick, E. *Between Men: English Literature and Homosocial Desire* (New York, 1985).

Epistemology of the Closet (Berkeley, 1990).

Touching Feeling: Affect, Pedagogy, Performativity (Durham, NC, 2003).

Simpson, P. *Middle-Aged Gay Men, Ageing and Ageism: Over the Rainbow?* (Basingstoke, 2015).

Skidelsky, R. *John Maynard Keynes: The Economist as Saviour 1920–1937* (London, 1992).

John Maynard Keynes: Fighting for Britain, 1937–1946 (London, 2000).

John Maynard Keynes: Hopes Betrayed 1883–1920 (London, 1983).

Spalding, F. *Roger Fry: Art and Life* (Berkeley, 1980).

Stille, A. *The Sullivanians: Sex, Psychotherapy and the Wild Life of an American Commune* (New York, 2023).

Sutton, D. *Letters of Roger Fry*, 2 vols. (London, 1972).

Symonds, J. A. *A Problem in Modern Ethics* (London, 1896).

Tennyson, Sir C. ed. *Basileion: A Magazine of King's College, Cambridge 1900–1914* (Cambridge, 1974).

Terry, J. *An American Obsession: Science, Medicine and Homosexuality in Modern Society* (Chicago, 1999).

Thomas, K. *Postal Pleasures: Sex, Scandal and Victorian Letters* (Oxford, 2012).

Tyrrwhit, R. 'The Greek Spirit in Modern Literature', *Contemporary Review* 29 (March 1877) 552–66.

Upchurch, C. *'Beyond the Law': The Politics of Ending the Death Penalty for Sodomy in Britain* (Philadelphia, 2021).

Vassall-Phillips, O. *After Fifty Years* (London, 1928).

Warner, M. *The Trouble with Normal: Sex, Politics and the Ethics of Queer Life* (Cambridge, MA, 2000).

Waters, C. 'The Homosexual as a Social Being in Britain, 1945–1968', *Journal of British Studies* 51.3 (July 2012) 685–710; reprinted in *British Queer History: New Approaches and Perspectives*, ed. B. Lewis (Manchester, 2013) 188–218.

Waugh, A. *The Loom of Youth* (London, 1916).

Weeks, J. *Sex, Politics and Society: The Regulation of Sexuality Since 1800* (London, 1989).

Weston, K. *Families We Choose: Lesbians, Gays, Kinship* (New York, 1991).

Wilper, J. 'Translation and the Construction of a "Uranian" Identity: Edward Prime-Stevenson's [Xavier Mayne's] The Intersexes (1908)', in H. Bauer, ed. *Sexology and Translation: Cultural and Scientific Encounters across the Modern World* (Philadelphia, 2015) 216–32.

Wingfield-Stratford, E. *Before the Lights Went Out* (London, 1945).

Wolff, C. *Magnus Hirschfeld: A Pioneer in Sexology* (London, 1986).

Woolf, V. *The Moment and Other Essays* (London, 1947).

Moments of Being: Unpublished Autobiographical Writings of Virginia Woolf, ed. J. Schulkind (Sussex, 1976).

Roger Fry: A Biography (London, 1940).

Woolwine, D. 'Community in Gay Male Experience and Moral Discourse', *Journal of Homosexuality* 38.4 (2000) 5–37.

Wortham, H. *Victorian Eton and Cambridge, Being the Life and Times of Oscar Browning* (London, 1927).

INDEX